SUCCESSFUL
FUNERAL
SERVICE
PRACTICE

SUCCESSFUL
FUNERAL
SERVICE
PRACTICE

Edited by **HOWARD C. RAETHER**

Executive Secretary
National Funeral Directors Association

PRENTICE-HALL, INC.   Englewood Cliffs, N. J.

PRENTICE-HALL INTERNATIONAL, INC., *London*
PRENTICE-HALL OF AUSTRALIA, PTY. LTD., *Sydney*
PRENTICE-HALL OF CANADA, LTD., *Toronto*
PRENTICE-HALL OF INDIA PRIVATE LTD., *New Delhi*
PRENTICE-HALL OF JAPAN, INC., *Tokyo*

Library of Congress
Catalog Card Number: 73-141440

"This publication is designed to provide
accurate and authoritative information in regard to the subject matter covered. It is sold
with the understanding that the publisher is
not engaged in rendering legal, accounting or
other professional service. If legal advice or other
expert assistance is required, the services of a
competent professional person should
be sought.

*. . . From the Declaration of Principles jointly
adopted by a Committee of the American Bar
Associations.*"

PRINTED IN THE UNITED STATES OF AMERICA

ISBN-0-13-862656-1

B & P

Dedication

To those in the funeral profession whose service to mankind contributed to the philosophy and knowledge that made this book possible.

THE CONTRIBUTORS

Bollman, Paul E. Long-time expert on funeral home construction and lighting. President of a funeral supply and chemicals company with home offices in Dallas, Texas.

Bustard, William L. Executive Secretary, National Selected Morticians, whose headquarters office is in Evanston, Illinois. Practiced funeral service in Casper, Wyoming between 1937 and 1965 when he assumed his present position.

Clark, Thomas H. Member of the law firm of Clark, Robinson and Hellebush of Cincinnati, Ohio, which has been the General Counsel of NFDA for over forty years.

Foran, Eugene F. Management consultant to funeral service for well over a quarter of a century. Has conducted the annual NFDA statistical study since 1957.

Fulton, Robert. Professor of Sociology at the University of Minnesota and Director of the Center for Death Education and Research there. Editor of *Death and Identity* (Wiley, 1965).

Griffin, Glenn H. Practicing funeral director in Pontiac, Michigan since 1936. Past President of NFDA and a lecturer in funeral service management.

Jackson, Edgar N. Methodist minister, pastoral psychologist and counsellor. Author and lecturer on death, grief and bereavement. Former U.S. Air Force Chaplain.

Nichols, Charles H. Director and trustee of the National Foundation of Funeral Service at Evanston, Illinois. Dean of the Foundation's School of Management.

Slater, Robert C. Professor and Director of the Department of Mortuary Science at the University of Minnesota where he has been on the faculty since 1947.

ABOUT THE EDITOR

Howard C. Raether holds a Ph.B. and J.D. from Marquette University in Milwaukee, Wisconsin. He has been involved in funeral service for thirty years and Executive Secretary of the National Funeral Directors Association since 1948. He was consultant to the United States Government Department of Transportation, National Highway Safety Bureau, and is on a committee serving the Department of Health, Education and Welfare. He was given the highest honor the U.S. Army makes to a civilian—the Distinguished Civilian Service Award. He also is a member of the National Council on Tissue Transplantation and Utilization. He is editor of the NFDA monthly journal, *The Director*, and creator of the *Reference Manual* for funeral directors. In addition his recent writings include, as co-author, *A Compendium of Basic Information on Funeral Establishments and Funeral Establishment Employees and The Fair Labor Standards Act, as Amended* (1968); *Organ and Tissue Transplantation and Body Donation* (1970); and *Personnel Guidance Manual for Funeral Service Practice* (1970).

How This Book Will Help
You Manage More Successfully

Those in funeral service must be aware of the increasing importance of "care-giving" and "care-taking" in their practice. "Care-taking" following a death is necessary because splintering of the extended family unit is evident. In addition, a large number of young people have not experienced a death. That same youth culture tends to deny if not defy death as it tries to intellectualize its emotions when death comes.

The funeral director is asked an increasing number of pointed questions by families arranging services with him. He is queried at his service club. He is requested to talk to a group in his church. In all these instances, and more, there will be some person or persons who will probe the reason for a facet or facets of the funeral. Such persons won't accept the answer that what is done is because it has been done before.

This book offers answers to questions. It presents models of public information programs. It urges modifications in practices to make funeral service truly "people to people." What the book presents is based on sound evaluations of changing attitudes and the growing body of knowledge on death, grief and bereavement. It tells how to help fill human fulfillment wants and needs.

For most people the funeral is a religious rite and clergy and funeral directors provide a "united" service to the bereaved. Methods for smooth relations between the clergy and funeral director are clearly enumerated in the book. The contemporary service brought about by change, the new "white" Mass or "resurrection" Mass of the Catholic Church and children and the funeral are part of the text with long-term meaning and value.

The growing complexity of our society has resulted in laws which in some respect almost daily govern some part of the operation of a funeral home; minimum wage, truth in lending and prefinanced funeral payments are but some examples. Then too, there are laws dealing with probate, estates and taxes which are important to the funeral director in the operation of his funeral home and in the planning for his own estate.

9

This book covers these well at the federal level and makes worthwhile suggestions where state statutes are involved.

Competition has taken on new forms. Multi-unit operations, some of them public stock corporations, branch establishments and horizontal and vertical expansion are "facts of life." This book tells the funeral director how to approach new business structure intelligently and arms him with a working set of instructions.

The book also fulfills its purpose as to the business aspects of a funeral service practice in other ways. Proven and acceptable pricing methods are reviewed. There is an evaluation of the casket selection room. Multiple forms are illustrated to assist in recording the numerous details essential to every funeral.

Questions about re-locating an existing firm or opening an entirely new business or establishing a branch are answered in two ways. First there are the considerations in the decision to go ahead. Then there is advice and also illustrations in planning, designing and decorating the facilities.

Ten men contributed to this book. Close to 200 years of their collective professional lives have been devoted in whole or in part to funeral service. This is the greatest asset of this collection of material. The reader may not agree with everything written. But if he is helped, my collaborators and myself will have achieved our purpose.

Howard C. Raether

CONTENTS

Seeing the Body of the Deceased the Last Time. The Funeral Service.
The Funeral Procession. The Committal. When Less Than a Complete
Funeral Is Desired. Post Funeral Counselling and Services.

1

DETERMINATIONS AND CONDITIONS
IMPORTANT TO A
FUNERAL SERVICE PRACTICE

Howard C. Raether

Funeral service in the United States is unique. Most men of most cultures in most nations have viewed their dead and buried them with ceremony throughout recorded time. But in no other nation has a functionary developed to the extent that the American funeral director, mortician, or undertaker has—whatever you choose to call him.

The mid-twentieth century "total" funeral is predicated on Judaeo-Christian beliefs. It is made up of practices, burial merchandise and methods of memorialization which had beginnings in Egypt, Rome, Greece and in other ages and civilizations.

The present-day funeral director is a composite of his predecessors—the British underwriter, the colonial nurse, and the nineteenth century cemetery sexton, cabinet maker, liveryman and undertaker.

The present-day funeral director cares for the dead as he serves the living. As he does this he gives dignity to man. And to do this he invests much money in facilities and equipment and often in staff. He also dedicates his life to the service he provides.

Most times the funeral home or chapel or mortuary or undertaking establishment is a *one purpose* building. Likewise, much of the equipment used is *specially designed* and has little or no use except for funeral service.

With this preliminary statement we look at some of the determining factors, trends and conditions important to a funeral service practice.

A Limited Practice

With few exceptions there is only one funeral per person. In some instances death occurs at a place distant from where the burial or cremation will be. This results in two periods of the funeral, which could involve two funeral directors or funeral firms. But in the vast majority of cases there is one funeral period and one funeral directing firm per death.

Because the number of potential funerals is determined by the number of deaths, a need for funerals cannot be created or expanded as it is for most other services and for most goods.

The business can be shifted between funeral homes where there is more than one firm serving an area. But again such shift takes place within the funerals available determined by the number of deaths.

A limited practice and a unique service rule out many economic principles and advertising practices applicable in other fields. The funeral director must know this. He must realize that some "market place" activities would work against him.

Race and Religion

In 1961 the Supreme Court of Rhode Island had before it a case involving a funeral home and the exception made to an ordinance by the Zoning Board of Review of the City of Cranston. In its opinion the court said:

> We must also be realistic and recognize the obvious fact that generally ethnic and religious segments of our population, especially in time of stress and emotion resulting from the decease of dear ones, prefer the services of funeral directors of their own ethnic or religious background. This is not due to discrimination of an odious nature. On the contrary people generally have such preferences because it is a part of human nature for people in times of stress to seek the help of those they know best.

In many parts of the country there still are funeral homes whose clientele is made up primarily of people of one race and/or religion. And often those who call these places disregard newer and more commodious facilities in favor of the personalized service of those they know best and have called in the past when death has taken a member of their family.

But this is changing. In the main, the black community calls Negro funeral directors when available. But as to all others, with the exception of some funeral homes "dedicated to serving the Jewish community," a funeral home's clientele cuts across ethnic and religious backgrounds.

It is foolish to plan otherwise. These are times of ecumenicalism, of brotherhood of man, of separation of families by age, distance and beliefs, and of convenience. The family funeral director still is a predominant factor. But when death occurs where there is no funeral home which has served the family previously with some of the same personnel on hand, race and/or religion may be a factor in deciding whom to call, but often it will not be the determining one.

Growing and Shifting Population

There are communities that have had but one funeral home and this will not change. They are located in rural areas serving a population which is stable or declining both economically and in number.

There are funeral homes which for years served a town or village completely even though a neighboring community was only a few miles away. Business and church affiliations and transportation kept the funerals in the community for individuals who lived, died and were buried there. Now good transportation, widened interests, and the expanding of these villages and towns often result in funeral homes in separate communities serving overlapping areas.

There are towns and villages which previously were separately identifiable that have been annexed to large cities, or at least swallowed up into a metropolitan area. Many of the funeral homes in them benefit by the population expansion. Others, for the first time, are facing competition with the branch establishments of the firms in the city.

There are funeral homes in large cities that have been affected by some inner city decay, by urban redevelopment, by expressway projects, by the relocation of a church, and by "dying off" or the moving away of the families which had been a mainstay of support.

The same situations—good and bad—confront those in other professions and businesses. But many times the plight is not as great and the shift not nearly as "expensive" in financial terms or in the needs of those who might be left behind. Nor is the decision to expand or relocate as difficult in trying to ascertain what lies ahead.

Realizing the Potential

It is not a difficult task to determine the approximate number of funerals there will be in a community. The annual death rate averages out at about ten per thousand of population. This fluctuates according to the age of the inhabitants as follows:

- In areas in which the age groups run the gamut from young to old, the average will prevail.
- In older communities or neighborhoods where there are more middle-aged persons and senior citizens, the rate will be higher.
- In new suburbs or subdivisions where the younger set is settling, the rate will be much lower. Deaths for years will be limited to the unexpected—those of an accidental nature or heart seizures and the like.

Knowing the area is more important than it has ever been.

Smaller dwellings and differences in ways of life result in fewer instances of a parent who has survived the death of a spouse living with the family of a child. Furthermore, as parents or childless couples grow old together they often seek to live in a community of older persons because they want to, or because they feel they no longer fit into the family "picture" as our country shifts from a family to a generation culture.

In 1969 there were fewer than 23,000 funeral homes and just over 1,900,000 deaths. This is close to 85 deaths per funeral home.

In some communities the number of deaths per establishment is considerably less. In some of the larger cities it is much greater.

For many years 40 funerals provided an adequate living for a funeral director operating only with the occasional assistance of his wife.

For a long time funeral service was provided in many places in conjunction with a furniture store or another business, often from a building which housed both endeavors.

The so-called combination business is disappearing. There are still many funeral homes that have about 40 services annually. But inflation and higher living standards, plus the limited potential, have lessened the desirability of that volume business from the viewpoint of the buyer of an existing business and in the opinion of someone who is going to start a new business or establish a branch operation.

Other Factors in a Funeral Service Practice

There is funeral home income beyond the fees for the funeral. The amount of such income often depends upon the customs and practices of the area in which the funeral home is located.

Burial Vaults

In 1958 a burial vault was used in 52% of all funerals and in 68% of the regular adult services. The charge for the vault then made up 10% of the total funeral service charges. In 1969 the burial vault's use had increased to 61% of total services and 75% of adult funerals. The charges for vaults equalled 11% of total funeral service charges paid to the funeral director for his services and merchandise and as a reimbursement for monies he advanced as an accommodation to the family.

The increase is attributed to more vaults being used in the New England, East North Central, West North Central, South Atlantic, East South Central, West South Central and Mountain States.

Decreases in the percentage of vault sales are noted in the Middle Atlantic and in the Pacific Coast States.

Where funeral director vault sales are less, some of the decrease can be attributed to such sales by cemeteries, by an increase in the amount of above ground burial space being sold, and by a slight increase in the number of cremations. Such "competition" for the vault sale is bound to increase.

Clothing

Only about 1% of total funeral service charges has been for clothing for each year during the past ten years. This recently has become mostly a convenience item, generally for the funerals of elderly persons and for others who had limited wearing apparel during their life. There certainly will be no percentage expansion of this market.

Automobiles

A funeral director once said he thought there always would be a place for funeral directors to provide and/or to rent funeral cars, especially limousines. He believed this because many of his families told him the only time they rode in a Cadillac was when they went to a funeral.

That too has changed. There is a decreased need for limousines at a funeral as more people have their own cars and want the convenience of using them. Most times a funeral home owned or rented car is still available for the family and for the pallbearers. But they are being used less and less. About two thirds of the funeral homes own all of their motor equipment. The balance own part and rent part or they rent all the equipment they need. Also, there is some pooling of equipment.

There will be funerals where there will be income for extra cars. There also will be times when one funeral firm will rent cars from another firm. And there are some funeral homes which operate a livery service. But the opportunities for appreciable income from automobiles as part of a funeral practice are limited.

Ambulance Service

In 1958, 59% of the funeral homes in the country provided ambulance service. By 1969 that percentage was reduced to 26%.

The reasons for the reduction in funeral homes with ambulance service are increased costs in providing the service; inadequate fees in return; and, a growing dislike of ambulance duties on behalf of funeral service licensees. Then, too, there has been a shift in the primary purpose of an ambulance. Formerly it was a vehicle used to take the sick and injured to a medical facility. Now with more calls of an emergency nature it is viewed as a medical facility for transporting those in need of emergency medical services.

Very few funeral-home ambulance operations were self-supporting even when combination vehicles were used, i.e., vehicles used both as a hearse or casket coach and as an ambulance. Ambulance service was viewed as a community service and/or a means of advertising the funeral home. As to the former—funeral directors going out of the service are assisting in getting a replacement for the service they eliminated. Regarding the latter—the advertising or promotion value of an ambulance is now disproportionate to the cost of providing the service.

Ambulance service will continue to decrease in the funeral service practices of the future.

Miscellaneous Items

Folding chairs, hospital beds and wheel chairs used to be rented by some funeral homes. A few still do this, but the number is decreasing.

Some funeral homes sell urns for cremated remains. The income from such sale might increase in certain metropolitan areas. But the total income to any firm will be small.

There are still some areas in which funeral directors benefit by a discount they get for ordering and/or advancing money for livery, flowers and newspaper death notices. But here again the practice is not growing and the total amount involved is small.

The fee for the funeral in 1969 constituted 76% of all funeral service charges as to the funeral director.

The percentage of income from burial vaults was 11% and from clothing 1%.

The balance of 12% is for accommodation items for which cash is advanced such as cemetery charges, clergy and musicians' honorariums, newspaper notices and flowers. Few funeral homes realize any income on this exchange of cash as noted above.

This clearly points to the conclusion that the *funeral* is the greatest determinant and condition to a funeral service practice. Anyone considering purchasing an existing business, starting a new practice or establishing a branch operation must first look to the community and its people to ascertain what they will want "funeral wise" and what they will support in the way of a funeral practice.

2

THE WHOLE-MAN
TOTAL-FUNERAL CONCEPT

Howard C. Raether
and
Robert C. Slater

Example: John J. Jones dies of a disfiguring malignancy. He is survived by his widow, one son, two daughters, one daughter-in-law, one son-in-law and two grandchildren. At the time of his death his married daughter is less than a month from having her first child. His unmarried daughter is engaged. Her fiance is in the army on duty within the country.

During the first contact with the son who is handling arrangements tentatively awaiting final plans for the funeral, four areas of concern of the family become apparent. They are:

1. Will restoration of the father's face be such that viewing will be possible?
2. The pregnant daughter was her father's favorite. How will she hold up? To what extent should she participate in the arrangements and during the various periods of the funeral.
3. What about the son-in-law to be? Might he get an emergency leave to be at the funeral? He could be a real comfort to his future bride.
4. The two grandchildren are ages 7 years and 10 months. The boy, 7, the first grandchild of the deceased, loved his "Bompa" very much. Should he be allowed at the funeral home? Should he see the casketed body of his grandfather? Should he go to the service?

This hypothetical situation could well be a real one. It could be more complex or consist of only one or two "concern areas." It is spelled out not to present some problems and the solutions to them. Rather it is outlined to introduce what happens daily in funeral homes and two ways of considering what the funeral home owner(s) and other licensees should know and do in this situation.

Two Schools of Thought

There are two basic schools of thought regarding the serving of families and the role of funeral service licensees and the education necessary for them to fulfill their tasks. One is known as the whole-man–total-funeral concept. The other is the owner-manager-technician concept. A statement on how two funeral homes, one using the whole-man concept and the other the owner-manager-technician concept, might serve this family is essential to any present-day appraisal of funeral service practices.

Before spelling out this appraisal it should be made clear that this is not a discussion of the philosophies of funeral homes with a sizable number of funerals annually and those with a small volume. There are large firms with the whole-man–total-funeral concept. There are small firms with the owner-manager-technician philosophy, firms which use service companies to do some of the things involving personal contact even when the funeral-director–owner or an associate is available.

The Whole-Man–Total-Funeral Concept

In a funeral home where the whole-man–total-funeral concept prevails, after the receipt of the call on the death of John Jones the funeral-director–owner and/or manager or one of his staff would have the responsibility to follow through with the family. This licensee would provide the person-to-person professional service outlined in another chapter. He would tell of the advantages of viewing the deceased and if he did not do the restorative work to make the viewing possible, he would check on it periodically.

The person "waiting on" this family would alert the others on the staff to the condition of the pregnant daughter. Throughout the arrangements and period of the funeral he would watch for signs that would indicate the mother-to-be ought to be momentarily removed from the central scene. If need be, he might suggest calling her doctor.

This funeral director also could suggest contacting the Red Cross, or he might do it himself if the fiance asks for emergency leave and can't get it. He might also talk to the clergyman to see if he feels it important enough to call the chaplain for the fiance's army unit about the leave.

He undoubtedly would counsel with the family about the grandson's viewing the body and his part in the funeral, if any. There again he would talk to the clergyman and if the youngster knows the cleric well, he might be one of the two or three with the boy as he goes to see his "Bompa."

The whole-man–total-funeral concept makes one person licensed to practice funeral service responsible to a family to try to meet all their needs in relation to the total funeral. While there undoubtedly will be some delegation of duty and authority, the person "waiting on" the family is responsible for the funeral of the one they loved. And if the funeral home owner is not the one, he will at some time or times check with the licensee responsible and the family to see how things are coming.

The Owner-Manager-Technician Concept

When the original death call is received by a funeral home administered under the owner-manager-technician concept there are variations in what might happen depending on the size and practices of the firm. But unlike the previously described concept, the same licensee will not be involved in all facets of the funeral. Rather there will be one or more persons with specialized knowledges or skills who will perform their tasks and having done so their responsibility for that "service" ends. For instance, at the time of the removal a family may ask about several matters pertaining to funeral arrangements which the specialized technician may not be able to answer, necessitating a referral to another staff person.

In some funeral homes with this concept there are persons who do the arranging, there are others who are with the family for the casket selection, there are those who only embalm, and there might be some who just direct the actual funeral service.

Most times these individual functionaries report to a central office or person. Sometimes that person is not a funeral service licensee. What complicates the situation is that anyone of these individuals will find he must act alone sometimes without support from anyone else.

Following the death of John Jones the areas of concern might become apparent to those associated with the funeral home with the owner-manager-technician concept. But those who argue for the whole-man concept—as the authors of this chapter do—say that the chances are less that they will for two reasons. First, the departmentalized or specialized services of the funeral home bring no single staff member in constant communication with the family so as to allow them a total picture of what is happening and what is needed. Second, because the family sees and makes various arrangements with two or three people, they are less likely to get sufficiently close to one of them to make some requests they might have, or to "unload" some of their feelings.

Rabbi Dr. Earl A. Grollman, who is a well-known pastoral psychologist, paraphrased an article for clergymen in the following manner: "The word *cure* has its root in a word that originally meant *care*. The funeral director is someone who cares about, who takes care, and who takes care of. He is called upon to cure, to encourage as well as to console, to overcome soul-wounds. His is part of a meaningful care-taking profession."

This definition fits most funeral service licensees. But its ultimate more often than not is found in those practicing with the whole-man—total-funeral concept.

Licensing—Education—Recruitment

It is estimated that approximately 75% of all persons licensed in funeral service hold a funeral director's *and* an embalmer's license, or a combination of both. There are seven states which do not license funeral directors as such. There are eleven states where there is a single license law covering both funeral directors and embalmers, or where the requirements for funeral directors include embalmer prerequisites.

The whole-man—total-funeral idea is best served when the licensee is educated *and* licensed to do all that is done or might have to be done in a funeral service practice.

The reasoning for this is valid when looking outside of funeral service and when realistically confronting the facts within funeral service.

It is admitted that there are men and women who prefer the technical aspects of the profession. They like to embalm and do restorative work. It is also true that some licensees seldom prepare a remains because their personal contact and administrative duties keep them fully occupied.

There are physicians who specialize in surgery. There are lawyers who do nothing but tax work. There are dentists whose practice is limited to extracting teeth and pharmacists who are research chemists. But in each of these fields the *general* education and license is that which must first be obtained and the specialization follows.

In funeral service the reasons are as logical and compelling.

It is helpful in the serving of people for all licensees to be fully qualified. As an example, the owner or manager should have the basic knowledge if not the experience to understand an embalming problem and perhaps help solve it, or at least to be able to relate it to someone.

Likewise a licensee specializing in technical functions should be able to fill in in other capacities in the absence of those who do this normally. He should also be able to serve those who may want him as their funeral functionary.

The following chapter deals with personnel practices. But it is pertinent at this point to state that for the funeral to continue with care taking personalized service given by licensed personnel there must continue to be an influx of such personnel to replace those who die, retire, or leave the field.

As long ago as 1957 the Joint Commission on Mortuary Education said in its report that the concept of the person licensed to practice funeral service must reintegrate the embalming with the funeral directing function. Also the role of the licensee must be expanded to include services which have a therapeutic and mental health value performed for the living.

The Commission was formed in April 1956 "to examine the bundle of tasks that have been socially and legally assigned as the occupational province of present-day American funeral service personnel with a view to determining the educational experiences, both preparatory and in-service, needed for their efficient and satisfactory performance."

The conclusion previously stated was predicated on the finding that embalmers were faced with an occupational dilemma—with ambiguous status. The reasons for this were summarized in the following manner:

1. Embalming in the minds of funeral service personnel is associated with the "back room" of the funeral home.
2. Dealing with the clientele "out front" is valued by funeral service staffs.
3. While not all who are primarily embalmers are discontented, those who are are critical in a manner symptomatic of frustrated career aspirations.
4. Funeral directing only in the dual license sense (funeral director and embalmer) means management, personal contacts and funeral direction. Paradoxically in many states this requires the least formal education and training.
5. Embalmers and other technicians have had little success in organizing associations other than unions.

There is one other point that the Commission made more than a decade ago which might be viewed as prophetic. In its analysis the Commission used the phrases "house of management" and "house of labor." It is our opinion that the whole-man–total-funeral concept with the single license will discourage a division of personnel whereas the owner-manager-technician concept will encourage it to the point where there may be a separation of "management" and "labor" in a funeral home.

A funeral home owner must face up to the following facts:

"Back room" men can be obtained, but often they must be paid as much or more salary as are qualified personnel. Also, these men *do* represent the funeral home and the owner(s) for better or worse. However, it is rare that a man who will make a worthwhile staff member can be recruited to be a "back room" man, a "second class citizen." There are times when the owner is away and one or more staff members fill in for him. Or he may be busy. The funeral is just as important to the people served by these staff members as it is to those served by the owner or manager. Irreparable harm can be done by a mistake or mistakes. There is no doing it over. The greater the education of a survivor or survivors the greater the possibility of his expecting good service by an equally or better educated person associated with the funeral home. The more closely a man fits the requirements of the whole-man concept the greater his chances are of meeting the challenge and needs of those of the "new" generation.

Paul R. Keenan, now of the University of Missouri, put it well when he said in his "Education for Tomorrow" :

> If the funeral service practitioner of today and tomorrow is to be successful in his contacts with other members of his community, he will be expected to meet them on an equivalent academic basis. If he does not, not only will he be at some disadvantage, but many opportunities both personal and professional which he might otherwise enjoy will not be available to him.

> We must also be aware that the basic fund of knowledge is increasing in this day and age at a rate in which it is doubled every ten years. This has resulted in many changes in sociological and professional practices. In many fields it has resulted in computer storage of information—in others it has established specialties, and sub-specialties within professions and occupational groups. Employment opportunities unknown ten years ago are commonplace today, and this has contributed much to the complex situation in which today's citizen must function and which he hopes to understand.

> There is no doubt, unless some unforseen circumstance arises, that knowledge will continue to become available at a constantly accelerating rate, accompanied by a comparable complexity of life; and the person who finds himself unprepared for it will experience some difficulty in keeping abreast of new developments in everyday living. If this is true of citizens attempting to find a place in life which is satisfying to them, it will also be true of the professional who will find the many faces of society constantly changing, and who will have to cope with these changes if he is to survive. It should be remembered that he must operate both as a member of his society and also as a professional person to satisfy special needs of the community in which he elects to function.

> Funeral service has been comfortable in the knowledge that it has developed according to specific customs based on the needs of the people, but no one can adequately predict the lines on which it will develop further. It does not, however, require a soothsayer to

predict that funeral service will be subjected to changes because the needs and demands of the public are changing, and will continue to change.

In the almost 100 years of licensing the funeral functionary, there have been three basic steps of progression to meet the *needs and demands of change,* with a fourth now developing fast:

1. The embalmer–public-health concept.
2. The advent of the funeral director license to embrace more than embalming and to place responsibility for actions beyond preparation of the body.
3. The dual license law in most states with most licensees being both funeral directors and embalmers, or holding a combination license.
4. The single license to practice funeral service predicated on the whole-man–total-funeral concept to encompass services essential to the place of the licensee as a "care-taker," or "care-giver," or "gate-keeper" in America in the last third of the twentieth century.

3

FUNERAL HOME
PERSONNEL PRACTICES

Robert C. Slater
and
Eugene F. Foran

The largest single expense item that goes into the operation of a funeral home is that incurred for personnel, including compensation for both owners and staff. This fact alone would make the personnel practices in the funeral home an item of paramount importance. However, overshadowing even this factor is the need for trained, intelligent, perceptive, neat-appearing and well-adjusted individuals to meet and serve the public when their emotional reactions are hypersensitive. Every staff member and the owners or employees, licensed or non-licensed, must sense the needs and desires of the families being served by the funeral home.

Current statistics reveal that there are on the average two licensed staff and two non-licensed staff persons per funeral home. Often two or more of these persons are family related. A great number of funeral homes have five or six staff persons and a few funeral homes will have staffs of 15 to 25 persons.

Many funeral homes will have not only licensed and non-licensed help, but full- and part-time staff. Licensed personnel on the staff of the typical funeral home will be of the whole-man–total-funeral concept type as described in Chapter 2. In only a minority of funeral homes will you find personnel assigned only to one area of funeral service practice. Non-licensed staff will usually fill either the assignments of receptionist, bookkeeper, office staff, or lady assistants, or a combination thereof, in addition to those of maintenance.

The part-time staff of a funeral home will usually be non-licensed personnel in one of the categories mentioned in the preceding paragraph. Part-time staff may also be licensed and called in only when added licensed personnel is needed to perform certain tasks requiring licensed personnel.

It is to the obvious advantage of a funeral home to have a full-time permanent staff with as little turnover as possible. It is this kind of staff to which we will address our attention in this chapter. However, when licensed or non-licensed part-time staff is employed what is said regarding full-time personnel is equally applicable to part-time staff. The all-inclusive philosophy of a successful funeral practice is that each staff person *is* that funeral home as he meets and serves individuals who have chosen it to serve them. It is immaterial whether that person is the licensed man directing the funeral or the driver of the family car. Funeral service to the individuals being served *is the staff member* presently serving him.

The individual staff member who has chosen funeral service as a vocation expects and even demands from his job certain satisfactions and fulfillments. In order to understand more adequately the needs of personnel and to establish procedures to meet those needs it is well to understand what these incentives and gratifications might be.

Changing Times in its April 1969 issue reviewed a compilation of these job "motivators" as social researchers had identified them. The list in order of importance to the employee was as follows:

1. Security	7. Supervision
2. Interesting work	8. Social aspects of the job
3. Opportunity for advancement	9. Opportunity to learn or use ideas
4. Recognition	10. Hours
5. Working conditions	11. Ease of job
6. Wages	12. Fringe benefits

Late that year the National Funeral Directors Association did a study of non-owner full-time funeral service licensed personnel in which these twelve "motivators" were listed. The following is the rank order of the first choices of those who participated in the study:

1. Opportunity for advancement	7. Hours
2. Wages	8. Supervision
3. Interesting work	9. Recognition
4. Security	10. Social aspects
5. Working conditions	11. Fringe benefits
6. Opportunity to learn or use ideas	12. Ease of job

At first reading this list might surprise funeral-home owners and/or managers even as it does other personnel supervisors. Yet this list is typical of the satisfaction desired by young persons entering any profession or vocation today. Let us review these as they might be applied specifically to funeral service personnel policy and procedure.

Opportunity for Advancement. This perhaps is the most difficult "motivator" for an employer to develop except in those few funeral homes where the staff numbers six or more employees. It is true that in smaller staffs as vacancies due to resignation or retirement occur the staff may advance, but in the typical funeral home the need for advancement must be satisfied in other ways. These primarily are either more involvement in the total operation, or the varying of staff assignments and responsibilities. Ordinarily advancement by title or job description is limited and often the position to which a man is hired becomes his permanent position on the staff.

Wages. Once the fact that wages is not the number one item is fully accepted and appreciated it becomes rather obvious. The satisfied employee must receive a salary commensurate with his worth and sufficient to meet his personal needs. But the employee more fully appreciates an adequate salary when the preceding motivator also exists. Even a higher than average salary cannot fully compensate if the intangibles that go to make up total job satisfaction are not also present. Salary or real wages must be continually evaluated. The kind of person desired by most funeral homes today is also the person sought by other occupations. This becomes more and more evident as the demand for intelligent, neat-appearing, understanding, emotionally mature and stable young men and women increases. These credentials are the entree for many social services occupations and funeral service must become competitive for the services of the persons who possess them. The extent to which it does will determine the extent to which it will attract such persons. Salary as a tangible reward must be adequate and be in addition to the intangible motivators that comprise the rest of this list.

Interesting Work. The young man or woman who seeks out funeral service as his or her profession sees in it the challenge of serving others and contributing to the general welfare of the families and communities served. This for them means interesting work. The funeral home employer who varies the assignments of his staff so that they can meet a variety of needs will find the staff responding more readily than when assignments remain routine and therefore become dull and uninteresting.

Security. A funeral home made up of carefully chosen staff cultivated for stability and permanence will give much attention to this "motivator." A staff person wants to feel and to know that his job is not a day-to-day or even a year-to-year position. If it is, he will spend more effort searching out his next job than he will performing his present one. The employee wants to know that as long as he produces to the best of his ability his job is secure, that there will continue to be a place for him on the staff, and that he will be considered a part of the future of the firm.

Working Conditions. Pride and self-fulfillment play an important function under this heading. The staff member who wants good working conditions and is granted them will be proud to maintain and improve those conditions. If he is proud to have his peers and family see where he works and under what conditions, he will also seek to improve them further. A clean, attractive, well-maintained funeral home has many assets not the least of which is a good environment conducive to ultimate performance by the staff that serves in that funeral home. It is obvious that poor and undesirable working conditions usually produce less than acceptable performance and service by those working under them. The very environment in which a service is performed creates the attitude that will prevail in the performance of that service.

Opportunity to Learn and Use New Ideas. "How would you suggest we proceed?" is a welcome question if an employee knows he will be listened to and if his ideas will be tried and fairly evaluated. However, to be continually asked for ideas and then to have them ignored seems to deaden the enthusiasm for furnishing such ideas. A valuable procedure is to try to learn from each new experience. A staff evaluation that directs itself to the questions, "What did we do right?", "What did we do wrong?", "What could we have done better?", "How should we proceed next time?", will soon pay dividends in the form of ideas and training experiences that will continually upgrade the service offered by the funeral home.

Hours. The importance of "hours" falls more than halfway down the list. It becomes evident that employees are not as prone to "clock watching" when their work is filled with purpose and meaning and contributes to the fulfillment of the needs of both the family being served and the provider of the service. There is no comparison between the hours of productive and meaningful service and the hours that are merely "put in" to fulfill a specified duty schedule. An employee wants to know what is expected of him hour-wise and the good employee goes far beyond that expectation when the occasion demands if he knows he will be given compensating time off when it becomes available. A truly dedicated person counts not the hours but the results of those hours upon the lives of others when he knows that such service contributes not only to his own welfare, but to the overall success of the firm especially when he is made to feel a part of that firm.

Supervision. "He never tells me what to do or how to do it, but criticizes me when I don't do something, or if I do something wrong according to his way of doing things." This sums up this point quite well. Most employees appreciate a clear and concise list of duties and responsibilities and adequate supervision in performing them as long as it is necessary. They also appreciate being told of special non-recurring tasks and an opportunity to understand fully what is to be done and how. "Go ahead and use your own judgment" or "do it your own way" is devoid of meaning and even insulting if the employee is later criticized for the judgment or action he did employ.

Recognition. This "motivator" perhaps can be the most effective yet the least expensive one available to an employer. The failure to recognize and to commend for a job well done can often be very demoralizing to the employee. In funeral service especially, every commendation directed to a staff person whether in word or writing should be transmitted to the person responsible for creating that commendation. Whenever possible the staff person should be called in to receive the recognition personally from the person who is making the commendation. The employer should also be as quick to grant recognition for good performance as he is to give criticism for poor performance. This is not to say that "negative recognition" cannot also be a valuable "motivator." The competent staff person desires to be told when his performance is not adequate in order that he might change it in such a way as to gain the "positive recognition" that will become an incentive for him to increase his level of performance for even more recognition.

Social Aspects of the Job. Man is a social being. He thrives on social interaction with his fellowmen especially when he has chosen a profession based on such social relationships. Funeral service is devoted to meeting the needs of those who survive. Unless a person can come into contact with these persons and relate to them, his vocational challenge is unfulfilled. He wants to see the results of his actions serve the needs of others. If he is not exposed to these persons periodically at the time of removal, arrangements, visitation, during the funeral or the post-funeral period, he will find himself wondering if what he does or how he does it has any significance or social value.

Fringe Benefits. Frequently fringe benefits are referred to as "the frosting on the cake." It is interesting to note that funeral service licensed employees list them second to last on the list of the twelve "motivators" as if to say, "Give me the more important first and then you can consider fringe benefits." This is the key to satisfied personnel—fulfill the primary benefits of the job and the fringe benefits truly become benefits in recognition above and beyond the basic incentives and gratifications.

Ease of Job. The easiest job is difficult if it is not personally satisfying, and the most difficult of jobs becomes easier when desire and motivation to complete that job are of the highest level. Ease of job can be equated with job satisfaction. Doing that which is disliked is always more difficult. Therefore, it is only natural that a person seeks ease in a job consistent with his satisfaction in doing that which is required of him.

**   **   **

It behooves the successful funeral service owner as manager continually to reexamine how he can best meet these needs of the personnel he hires for his funeral-home staff. His ability to do so and his desire to provide these basic motivators forecasts not only the kind of staff he will have, but also its overall effectiveness.

Communications

Today the professions, business and industry seek professional advice on how best to communicate between employer and employee. Funeral service cannot prove an exception in this matter. A staff of two has as much need, if not more, to communicate well than a larger staff. The necessity of adequate communications is heightened when total responsibility rests on just two persons. Frequent scheduled and non-scheduled staff meetings are a necessity. As indicated earlier in this chapter, continual evaluation is always a consideration of inter-staff communication.

A sharing of the projections of the future of the funeral home, plans for changes or re-adjustments, and contemplated actions that will reflect directly on the staff will alleviate much concern and uncertainty which can affect the overall performance of the staff.

Talking over matters such as unsatisfactory performance, lack of responsibility, use of poor judgment and a lack of sensitivity as to needs of the family can often lead to an immediate correction of the detail and prevent a festering of the concern to a point where it can jeopardize the overall success of the firm.

Policy and Philosophy

Basic to any successful funeral-home operation is a clear concept of and an adherence to a basic philosophy and policy to be accepted by all personnel—owner and non-owner, licensed and non-licensed, full- and part-time staff alike. One person who either does not know or does not accept such a basic philosophy can easily act or speak in such a way as to counteract the effectiveness of the whole staff.

Unless each member of the staff understands and believes in the basic significance and value of that which the funeral home has to offer, such a lack of understanding or non-belief becomes a threat to the success of the funeral practice in meeting the needs of the families it serves. A person who cannot accept, or does not believe in what he is doing, does not perform to the level of his ability and therefore leaves something to be desired by those he is serving.

When *each* member of the staff sets forth the same goal or objective and believes in that which is done for the benefit of those in need, *the team* effort multiplies the overall effectiveness of each individual action.

Specific Recommended Practices

Application. It is recommended that each staff member submit a letter of application or complete an application form at the time of his original employment. Even though the funeral home staff might be small and the need for such a record might seem unnecessary, it has significant value. It will record a personal history of the employee, his record of previous employment, give personal and character references, and serve as a statement of desire to become a part of the staff. It should be basic to his personal file which will also contain social security and tax information that might be required by proper authorities.

Physical Examination. Funeral service is fast becoming a recognized part of the health sciences. As such the personal health of each individual staff member should be of concern to the employer. Such an examination is also a protective action for the employer in the event of later health problems. The physical condition of the staff member can also determine his effectiveness as a part of the staff. Another fine practice is to provide an annual physical during employment. This is not only prophylactic but provides opportunity for proper immunizations and periodic evaluation of exposure to communicable diseases such as tuberculosis. A concerned employer is interested in the total well-being of his staff, including their personal health. This concern is also the basis for many firms to provide psychological evaluation of their staff. The demand in funeral service for emotionally stable and mature personalities cannot be overlooked.

Individual Concerns. Each staff person is entitled to know in full the conditions of his employment, his work schedule, his compensations, other benefits (insurance, bonus, pension, profit sharing), probationary periods, vacation—sick leave, absentee policy, and the provisions for termination of employment. In these areas there is no room for speculation or lack of specificity. Good employer-employee relations are based on a complete and open understanding of these basic factors.

Staff Organization. The flow of authority and interrelationship of the staff needs concise and clear interpretation. Each staff person should know *to* whom he is responsible and *for* whom he is responsible. Indecision or the practice of disguising of authority can only lead to misunderstanding, hard feelings and a decrease in the effectiveness of the staff.

Individual Responsibility. Each staff person must know *before* he accepts employment the latitude of responsibility for his personal decisions and actions and to what extent they may affect his relationship to the firm. The meaning of "on duty" and "off duty" should be fully discussed and understood prior to accepting a job. Funeral service, being a *personal* service profession, cannot afford to offend the personal sensitivities of the families it might, has, or will serve. To do so would reflect unfavorably on the reputation of the funeral home. Each staff member must understand and accept such personal limitations as a professional obligation, including the confidentiality of information and procedures that are involved. Dress, appearance, communication, reputation and civic, community and religious involvement should also be discussed and agreed upon prior to employment. This should include an understanding as to responsibility for the expenses involved in clothing, memberships, dues and personal expenses incurred while representing the funeral home.

Professional Responsibilities. Each person should be fully informed as to his professional practice as a staff member. If his involvement is to be total and include all phases of funeral service, his qualifications and willingness to so practice should be clearly understood. If he is not to be permitted to practice in all phases, such limitations (i.e., not to make arrangements, etc.) should be clearly defined and acceptable to him. To be restricted in certain areas of practice by the employer when it is not convenient nor desirable for the employee to be so involved and then to suddenly have these restrictions removed when it is convenient to the employer is grossly unfair to the integrity of the employee. If the employee is fully qualified to practice in all areas of funeral service he should be permitted to do so, and if competent the result of such practice will not only accrue to the good of the funeral home, but give variety to the competence of the staff.

Additional Responsibilities. If an employee will be expected to perform non-funeral related duties (i.e., maintenance, housekeeping, etc.) this should be fully explained. Most competent employees can accept such additional duties as a part of funeral service if they are allowed to practice the profession for which they have trained as their primary function. Otherwise these duties should be relegated to non-professionals unless there are no professional functions for the staff to perform and these related duties become secondary only when professional functions are not available. It is difficult and potentially tension-producing for an employee to be allowed to practice that for which he is trained *only* when secondary functions have been completed.

Manual of Procedure and Practices

The contents of this chapter, together with a Preface and a History of the firm, become the basis for a Personnel Manual. Each firm no matter how small or how large should have such a Manual. It should be presented to each prospective employee for his information and guidance in deciding whether or not he wants to accept employment in the firm. It should be reviewed periodically in staff meetings. It should be evaluated and revised as necessary. It should serve as the basic reference manual for all procedures and practices of the firm. In the absence of expressed personal authority or supervision, it should be accepted as the guide to actions, decisions or practices. As such it will be able to serve as the "referee" in many disputed actions or procedures.

The following is an outline of a manual of procedures or practices for use by everyone within a funeral home:

I. INTRODUCTION
  a. An outline of the origin and subsequent history of the firm, its founders and successors.
  b. The basic principles of the practice as developed over the years, including civic achievements by the organization.
  c. The attitude of the firm on all matters concerning the release of policy statements or other data for publication.
  d. A career in funeral service, its advantages and demands.

II. THE FUNERAL HOME AND GROUNDS
  a. Description of the building and its environs.
  b. Purpose and use of each facility within the area including restrictions, if any.
  c. Care of all property, equipment and grounds.
  d. Air comfort control and proper lighting.

III. ADMINISTRATION
  a. Flow of authority.
  b. Assignment of duties.
  c. Access to records.
  d. Use of firm properties.
  e. Expense re-imbursement.
  f. Extension of credit.
  g. Collection procedure.
  h. Records and office forms and their use.

IV. PERSONNEL
  a. Employment policy, including basic qualifications and work-schedule probationary period.
  b. Compensation, opportunities for advancement.
  c. Vacation schedule, other absence from duties.
  d. Insurance benefits—life, health, hospitalization.
  e. Sickness and compensation during such absence.
  f. Personal appearance, grooming, smoking.
  g. Personal conduct, within premises, on duty at both visitations and funeral services, off-duty hours.
  h. Responsibilities; daily procedure as well as professional procedure.
  i. Dismissal, list of causes for discharge.
  j. Professional educational programs.
  k. Medical examinations, frequency.

V. PROFESSIONAL
  a. Manners, respect—personal contact and telephone.
  b. Professional terms and usage.
  c. Confidential and fiduciary capacity and responsibilities.
  d. First call, outline all details.
  e. Care and handling of the body of a deceased person.
  f. Courtesy—to the relatives, friends, clergy, others.
  g. Salutations: clergy, medical practitioners, town, city, state and federal office holders, university or school personnel, others.
  h. Ritualistic equipment (all occasions).
  i. Funeral service arrangement procedures and records required.
  j. Arrangements, including fees, for services on ship-in from another funeral director.

k. Explanation of items included in a standard service, (1) when the casket is furnished by the firm, (2) when the funeral service is a ship-in and the casket supplied by the funeral director at the place of death.

l. Basic fee for specific situations, i.e. preparation of deceased for another funeral director, first call, removal, permits, use of facilities on occasion by another firm.

Summary and Concluding Thoughts

As can be observed, no funeral home can function without a staff. The extent to which each member of that staff sees his ultimate potential as a funeral service practitioner, communicates with other staff members, accepts and subscribes to the philosophy of the funeral home which employs him and is treated as an individual with complete understanding of all of the specific conditions of his employment, the funeral practice will meet and serve the needs of the families that choose that funeral home to serve them. It is a truism that a funeral home is its staff and a staff is the funeral home. Each represents the other in an undeniable association. The degree to which this inter-representation is fulfilled is the degree to which the individual funeral home will fulfill its obligation to the public it serves and the profession to which it belongs.

There are two added factors regarding personnel which should be obvious to the reader. However, they were not spelled out previously so that their importance could be highlighted here as concluding thoughts. They are:

1. Most funeral service personnel are men and they are married. In most of the "motivators" reviewed, a happy or an unhappy wife can be pictured depending on what is or is not done by the employer. Also, the nature of funeral service is such that the attitude of the "woman in funeral service," including the wife, is of greater influence within and outside of the funeral field than in many other endeavors. This is especially true as to the "regular" or "established" clientele of a funeral firm. Decisions and practices affecting a staff member must consider his wife. Conversely, the staff must be reminded that what the wife of any funeral director does or says could reflect on funeral service as well as on the firm with which that funeral director is associated either in an owner or a non-owner capacity.

2. There is a growing interest among staff members to expand their knowledge in matters regarding death, grief and bereavement. Chapter 15 of this book goes into professional growth through recently acquired knowledge. It urges "total participation" and says that the owner who does not permit periodic staff participation in learning experiences such as seminars and conferences is self-defeating. Often the desire to learn is accompanied by a desire to belong to one of the associations made up of those in and representing funeral service. The authors of this chapter recommend membership in established associations be made available to employees as part of the whole man concept. This will tend to discourage the establishment of employee organizations and the polarization of owners and managers in one group and staff members in another.

4

FUNERAL SERVICE
INCOME AND EXPENSE

Eugene F. Foran
and
Howard C. Raether

When a person decides to try to establish a funeral practice, or to buy an existing business, he does so believing that the service he will provide and the merchandise he will have available will be useful to the community. From that he deduces that he should be reasonably compensated for his personal efforts and should be entitled to a fair return on his investment if he meets the needs and wants of his clientele and the competition of other funeral homes, if there be such, in his area.

The following are basic needs following the death of most persons. In most instances the needs are met in whole or in part by a funeral home or mortuary and its staff.

    a. Care of the body of the deceased.
    b. Arrangements for and fulfillment of family, religious and community needs through the medium of the funeral.
    c. Final disposition of the body of the deceased by earth burial, entombment, or cremation.

Social and economic considerations must be satisfied in light of the circumstances of each situation. One will differ from the other in many respects, making standardization impractical if not impossible.

The costs involved in a practice are directly related to needs and requirements. The largest single cost is for the personnel required to staff the practice. This is followed by expenses of the physical plant and its furnishings and equipment especially designed for the purpose. There is the continuing need for motor vehicle use by the funeral home with a lessening need for the funeral home to have automotive equipment to be used by others.

The similarity of characteristics of a funeral service effectively camouflage the distinct variation in requirements and needs between all services, thereby providing a little understood but definite economic factor. There is no presently accepted standard measure as to what will constitute a funeral service.

The variations which exist often compensate for each other in the matter of costs, time and/or expense. It is this multiplicity of conditions, circumstances and situations which are continuously changing which require full knowledge of the expenses of the practice so that the pricing method used or contemplated will be fair and acceptable to the community and will allow the funeral home to continue in business.

Expenses of the Practice

From time to time surveys of income and expenses involved in funeral service practice reflect a pattern of stability. Starting in 1958 the National Funeral Directors Association sponsored an independent survey to study income and expense patterns in funeral service practice. It now has an experience of 12 years of comparable data.

Expenses were grouped in eight categories as shown in the following tabulation which also reflects the ratio of each expense classification to total expense:

Chart No. 1

Expense Classification	1969	1958
I Occupancy	19%	18%
II Taxes	5	4
III Collection Costs	3	3
IV Funeral Service Supplies	5	4
V Personnel including Owner's Compensation	47	47
VI Promotion	5	6
VII Automobile	9	11
VIII General	7	7
Total Expense	100%	100%

In 1969 the average expense per funeral service (including infants, children, indigent and welfare services) was $652.00 as compared to an average of $421.00 for the year 1958. These expenses include only the items shown in the expense classifications and do not reflect the cost of caskets, vaults or burial clothing.

The dollar increase in expenses of the practice in this 12-year period was 55%, a ratio that reflects a stable condition and efficient administration when compared with increases in other types of services and/or material items.

The change most noticeable is in the costs of furnishing transportation which follows a trend away from the use of funeral limousines.

Unit of Measure

The economic surveys of the past decade support the use of the "funeral" as a basis for measuring or weighing the statistical data of the practice. This is reflected in the following tabulation which compares average funeral service expense for the classifications given with average investment for firms in four volume sizes (1969 data):

Chart No. 2

		AVERAGE ALL SERVICES		
	All Firms	*Less than 100*	*100–199*	*200–299*	*300 and Over*
Services per Firm	129	62	141	242	447
Funeral Service Expense	$652	$674	$642	$655	$629
Investment per Firm	$152,564	$97,069	$170,690	$268,664	$359,196

The above table reflects the basic economic fact in funeral service practice that with all facets about the same, as the number of services increase so does the requirement for personnel and investment in physical plant which entails automatic increases in taxes, insurance, maintenance and others to the degree that a large volume of services does not reflect an appreciable decrease in average operating expenses. A supporting element reflected in the survey is the requirements for expansion in personnel, physical plant and equipment for each 30–33 services conducted by the practice.

Many economic theories which apply to manufacturing and other measurable processes are not applicable to a funeral service practice due to innumerable variations therein.

There undoubtedly are some who will point to a funeral home or a number of establishments which are under the same ownership and say their cost of operation is less. This could be true if less was available in services and facilities on a per funeral basis.

But even under these conditions, as the volume of a firm with limited service and/or facilities grows, even those limited facilities and personnel must expand.

If a funeral home or mortuary is operating at peak or maximum with 250 funerals a year with the body present, it cannot expect *successfully* to handle 300 services with the same facilities and staff and provide the same service.

Changes in Values and Increases in Costs

Personnel expense is the largest of all expenses of a funeral service practice. This item includes both employees and owners in the firm. In 1958 the personnel costs were 47% of total expenses or $197 per funeral service, including all categories of services. In 1969 the dollar cost had increased to $307 per service but remains at 47% of total expenses. In this 12-year period promotion costs per service decreased 1% of total expenses, from 6% or $24 per service in 1958 to 5% or $31 per service in 1969.

In the future funeral service practices will doubtless undergo a measurable increase in personnel costs and a proportionate or greater decrease in non-essentials. This statement is predicated on the care-taking and care-giving aspects of a funeral practice essential in the survival of the funeral as a public event serving the living while caring for the dead.

In the following chart the eight classifications of expense compare the average dollar cost for the year 1969 with the comparable cost 12 years prior in 1958. While the percentages on Chart No. 1 appear to be the same from 1958 through 1969, the dollar values reflect the actual increases in expenses.

Chart No. 3

DOLLAR VALUES

Average Expenses—All Services

		1969	1958
I	Occupancy	$122	$ 74
II	Taxes	35	18
III	Collection	18	16
IV	Funeral Service Supplies	33	18
V	Personnel	307	197
VI	Promotion	31	24
VII	Automobile	59	46
VIII	General	47	28
	Total	$652	$421

These averages were determined by dividing the total expense in each classification by the total of all services. The term "all services" and its significance in funeral service practice must be understood and therefore explained.

The term "all services" means the total number of funerals conducted by a given firm. It includes infants, children, indigent and welfare services and also those services which are referred to as "forwarding" or as "receiving" services. These words "forwarding" and "receiving" describe the situation when a funeral firm provides less than a complete service and another firm provides the balance. As an example, John Jones dies while vacationing in Phoenix, Arizona. A funeral director will be engaged there by the family, or their hometown funeral director, to call for the remains, prepare them and put them in a shipping receptacle and send them to the place where the visitation, funeral and disposition of the body will take place.

Or the converse could be true. Peter Smith has lived in Los Angeles for 21 years since he moved away from Pontiac, Michigan. When he dies a complete funeral lacking just the interment is in Los Angeles. His wife and children want him buried on the family plot in Pontiac, Michigan. So the Los Angeles funeral director does everything but assist with arrangements for the committal. This is done by the firm in Pontiac whose personnel meet the plane at Metropolitan Airport in Detroit, take the remains to

Pontiac where the committal or even a brief graveside service may be conducted.

Years ago there were many more outright charity cases than there are today. That was before numerous social changes and before Social Security.

Today there are few outright charity funerals but there are more services in which an agency of government, religious groups, or some other organization pays in whole or in part for the funeral. And with people getting older and using much if not most of their own monies and then turning to government for financial assistance, their funeral could become an increasingly significant economic segment for the funeral director, especially if death occurs some distance from where the funeral and/or burial are going to take place.

Charges made in these funerals often are not sufficient to recover basic direct costs of merchandise and supplies, not to mention personnel or facility expenses, and for this reason these specific types of services have been separately classified in all economic surveys. In addition, special considerations and separate accounting for these services must be made when developing fees for the recovery of both expenses and merchandise costs, as well as to provide a margin of return on investment in the practice.

Therefore, a term has been used to define all services except infants, children, indigent, welfare, outgoing and receiving services. It is *"regular adult services."*

The following chart reflects the results of the total expenses in each of the general classifications divided by the total of the regular adult services only, to obtain an average for the practical matter of establishing funeral service fees:

Chart No. 4

Average Expenses
Regular Adult Services Only

		1969	*1958*
I	Occupancy	$150	$ 97
II	Taxes	43	24
III	Collection	22	21
IV	Funeral Service Supplies	41	24
V	Personnel	378	257
VI	Promotion	38	32
VII	Automobile	73	60
VIII	General	58	36
	Total	$803	$551

Chart No. 4 shows the condensed makeup of the average expense of a funeral home, recovery of which requires consideration of many other factors. In Chart No. 2 we found the average size of firm included in the 1969 survey was 129 total all services for those who participated. Of this number 19% or 25 services were in the category of infants, children, indigent, welfare and others, leaving 104 regular adult services.

As shown in Chart No. 4, the average expense per regular adult service was $803 in the year 1969. This would mean a direct expense budget of $83,512.00, not including funeral merchandise, nor does this include a provision for return on investment.

This is evidence of the economic principles which are unique to a funeral service practice.

Details of Expenses

Chart No. 5 outlines the various items included in the eight General Expense Classifications shown in Charts Nos. 1, 3, and 4.

Chart No. 5

I. OCCUPANCY
   Utilities
   Insurance
   Maintenance—Repairs
   Depreciation
      Building
      Furnishings
      Equipment
   Rent
II. TAXES
   Real Estate
   Personal Property
   Use—Sales
   Payroll Federal and State
   Other
III. COLLECTIONS
   Attorney Fees
   Agency Fees
   Discounts Allowed
   Loss on Bad Accounts
IV. FUNERAL EXPENSES
   Embalming Supplies
   Funeral Supplies
   Funeral Trip Expense
   Other Funeral Directors

V. PERSONNEL
   Salaries—Employees
   Medical—Hospital Ins.
   Pension Costs
   Owners, Partners, Officers'
      Compensation
VI. PROMOTION
   Advertising
      Newspaper
      Other
   Contributions
VII. AUTOMOBILE
   Gas, Oil, Grease
   Repairs, Parts
   License
   Outside Rental
   Insurance—Auto
   Depreciation—Auto
VIII. GENERAL
   Postage, Printing,
      Stationery
   Office Expense—Licenses
   Telephone—Telegraph
   Freight—Express
   Laundry—Cleaning
   Dues—Subscriptions
   Interest and Bank Charges
   Travel Expense—Business
   Legal and Accounting Fees

Income-pattern

The income-pattern (or income-mix) of funeral service fees furnishes some insight into the economics of a funeral service practice. A careful examination of the basic factors reflects the necessity of giving consideration to two elements simultaneously, i.e: (1) the number of services in each of the wide dollar-ranges of service fees, and (2) the total fees which are generated in each income classification and the total fees possible as a result.

Chart No. 6 shows 15 general income classifications in the left-hand column. The percentages of number of services and total fees for each income classification are recorded first for the calendar year 1969 and on the right-hand side of the page for the calendar year 1958. This shows the average experience in funeral service fee patterns in a 12-year interval. These data are taken from *Funeral Service Facts and Figures* published by the National Funeral Directors Association.

Chart No. 6

	1969 PERCENTAGE		1958 PERCENTAGE	
	Services	*Fees*	*Services*	*Fees*
Children	4.5%	0.7%	7.6%	1.1%
Indigent	4.2	1.3	5.8	1.8
Services	10.0	2.3	9.6	1.7
$200	0.8	0.2	3.4	1.6
300	2.2	1.0	7.3	4.9
400	3.2	1.9	10.7	9.2
500	5.1	3.6	12.2	12.8
600	6.9	5.8	13.3	16.5
700	10.8	10.5	11.9	16.9
800	13.6	14.9	8.4	13.6
900	12.6	15.4	4.6	8.3
1,000–1,100	14.2	19.8	2.8	5.8
1,200–1,400	8.5	14.3	1.2	3.0
1,500–1,900	2.7	5.9	1.0	1.7
2,000–Over	0.7	2.4	0.2	1.1
All Services	100.0%	100.0%	100.00%	100.0%
Regular Adult Only	81.3%	95.7%	77.0%	95.0%

The experiences reflected in the surveys for 1969 and 1958 show the following averages of casket value supplied in the various income classifications. Chart No. 7 reflects the average fee in each group and the average casket cost for each of the years.

Consideration must be given to additional income factors that are not reflected in Charts 6–7; they are (1) income from the sale of burial vaults or other types of outside receptacles, (2) burial clothing, and (3) charges for extra services not included in the standard service fee. These other items would be charges for extra cars, mileage and special services of various sorts which are in addition to the normal requirements.

Chart No. 7

	1969 AVERAGE		1958 AVERAGE	
	Fee	Cost	Fee	Cost
Children	$ 130	$ 32	$ 73	$ 21
Indigent	254	51	170	45
Service	177	0	92	0
$200	240	59	252	51
300	356	61	358	61
400	461	70	458	75
500	563	80	558	97
600	663	95	657	123
700	763	117	756	151
800	861	140	855	188
900	959	170	959	224
1,000–1,100	1,099	209	1,085	261
1,200–1,400	1,327	275	1,324	351
1,500–1,900	1,694	415	1,714	506
2,000–Over	2,619	751	2,858	929
All Services	$ 787	$141	$ 531	$107
Regular Adult Only	$ 926	$169	$ 661	$134

There are variations in practices in different communities. These variations and additional income factors are reflected in Chart No. 8 on page 42. The figures are averages—the total of all figures in a category divided by the individual entries. The statistics for vault and clothing and other charges represent the average spent for all funerals reported regardless of whether a vault and/or clothing were sold, or if there were other charges.

The Burial Receptacle

In just about every culture of every nation in the world man views his dead. In some places where death is commonplace insofar as family and friends are present when death occurs, the viewing is done immediately, sometimes with the body in a receptacle, sometimes not.

In most countries it is difficult to get a body embalmed. Then the cost of embalming is such that only the wealthy can afford it. Most times the funeral services are held as soon as possible. In many parts of the world there are no funeral functionaries or there are functionaries who do not know how to embalm. The preparation of the remains then is done by doctors when required or requested.

But whether embalming is or is not done, or the funeral rite is primitively simple or highly organized, most times there is some sort of container for the body for the funeral and to transport the remains to the place of final disposition.

Chart No. 8

1969 FUNERAL SERVICE SURVEY

ANALYSIS of FEES and CHARGES

By Population, Groups, By Region and By Size of Firm

		POPULATION				
AVERAGE CHARGES		*Under 20,000*	*20,000 to 49,999*	*50,000 to 99,999*	*100,000 to 399,999*	*Over 400,000*	*United States*

All Services

AVERAGE CHARGES *All Services*		*Under 20,000*	*20,000 to 49,999*	*50,000 to 99,999*	*100,000 to 399,999*	*Over 400,000*	*United States*
Funeral Service Fees		$ 778	$ 779	$ 773	$ 771	$ 870	$ 787
Vault Sales		136	112	100	101	75	114
Clothing Sales		7	6	7	6	7	7
Other Charges		111	138	136	118	137	124
	Total	$1,032	$1,035	$1,016	$ 996	$1,089	$1,032

Regular Adult Services

Funeral Service Fees		$ 908	$ 919	$ 917	$ 936	$ 998	$ 926
Vault Sales		151	126	114	121	85	130
Clothing Sales		8	8	9	7	8	8
Other Charges		124	157	156	141	153	140
	Total	$1,191	$1,210	$1,196	$1,205	$1,244	$1,204

Average Funeral Service Fees

Regular Adult Services Only by Region

		Under 20,000	*20,000 to 49,999*	*50,000 to 99,999*	*100,000 to 399,999*	*Over 400,000*	*United States*
A—New England		$ 772	$ 879	$ 986	$1,119	$ 931	$ 938
B—Middle Atlantic		942	980	876	954	1,114	947
C—East North Central		973	1,011	953	982	1,004	983
D—West North Central		888	880	1,104	966	1,038	902
E—South Atlantic		917	853	943	797	1,090	912
F—East South Central		867	914	953	1,024	950	915
G—West South Central		951	956	842	1,058	1,088	987
H—Mountain		796	783	809	755	871	800
I—Pacific		781	774	787	808	961	829
	United States	$ 908	$ 919	$ 917	$ 936	$ 998	$ 926

		SIZE OF THE FIRM				
AVERAGE CHARGES *All Services*		*Under 100 Funerals*	*100– 199*	*200– 299*	*300 and over*	*United States*
Funeral Service Fees		$ 805	$ 778	$ 793	$ 777	$ 787
Vault Sales		147	114	109	81	114
Clothing Sales		7	7	7	6	7
Other Charges		120	125	143	109	124
	Total	$1,079	$1,024	$1,052	$ 973	$1,032

The receptacles range from wooden boxes with nothing or just a cloth or sheet inside, to highly ornate coffins or caskets— proportionately much more expensive than those used in the United States today.

Some of the early American colonists wrapped their dead in a cerecloth shroud to preserve the body for a short period of time and placed it in a coffin before burial. As early as 1758 there were advertisements for coffin furniture in daily prints. And the custom, first a coffin and later a casket as a burial receptacle, became a part of the American funeral tradition.

As the funeral functionary evolved he became associated with burial merchandise. He still is, as the casketed body is an integral part of the funeral service.

A review of Charts 6, 7 and 8 gives a picture of income patterns. And only an understanding thereof in each individual funeral practice can lead to a determination of the casket value relative to each income classification he offers the public. This is especially true where the single unit or standard service pricing method is used where the charge is for the funeral service including the casket as selected—a method used by a large majority of funeral homes in the United States.

Regardless of the pricing method used, the casket in one way or another produces income for the funeral director. Therefore, the selection of casket merchandise must be based upon the requirements, demands, and desires as well as the economy of the community being served. The selection of caskets by the funeral director to be used in the various income classifications must be done with attention to the relative degree reflecting variations in values. The number of each group of caskets shown in a casket selection room must of necessity be sufficient to satisfy the needs based upon the experience of that community, including its customs. The use of the word community in this instance means the clientele of the practice because there can be several communities within one city or within one section of a large metropolitan area.

The number of each quality of caskets shown and the variation in materials and styles will be determined differently for each practice. The range should be great enough to give complete freedom of selection from the least expensive to the best quality available and within the scope of the economy of the community.

This statement on the "burial receptacle" as it relates to funeral service income and expense is followed by "Casket Selection Room Procedure" in the next chapter on "Business Aspects of a Funeral Service Practice." Also a part of the chapter "Person-to-Person Professional Service" goes into "The Selection of the Casket."

Summary

In this chapter we have reviewed and compared funeral service income and expense patterns both in percentages and in dollars. We have looked at sizes of firms, "all services" and "regular adult services" and the cost of caskets provided. We presented a comprehensive analysis of fees and charges by population, groups, region and size of firm. As to a comparison of net margin, the study of all of the income and expense data herein is rounded out with the 1958 net margin figure of 6.8% (before income taxes) of total charges and the 1969 net margin of 8.7% (before income taxes) of total charges. Such margin is in addition to the salaries of the owners.

5

BUSINESS ASPECTS OF A
FUNERAL SERVICE PRACTICE

Eugene F. Foran
and
Howard C. Raether

Funeral director–sociologist Vanderlyn Pine says that there are multi-professional dimensions of a funeral service practice. He maintains that a funeral director is a professional, an administrator, a coordinator and a businessman.

Funeral service is not exempt from the requirements of sound business practices. Conversely, there are some built-in limitations to it.

In the chapter on determinations and conditions important to its practice, the uniqueness of funeral service was made clear. There is only as much need for the service of a funeral director or funeral directors as there are deaths and funerals and burials or cremations. Facilities and services will be used only to the extent that there is need for them. Therefore an all-important consideration is whether there is or will be sufficient deaths to support the investment in and remuneration necessary for a funeral service practice.

Once a funeral home or mortuary is opened, income and expense patterns should be watched as an important yardstick or guideline. To do this effectively a proper system of accounts is necessary.

Classification of Accounts

(Taken from chapter on Funeral Directing by Foran in *Encyclopedia of Accounting Systems,* Volume 2, Williams and Doris, Eds., Prentice-Hall)

The account classifications and the books of accounts described herein provide a framework for any system. The general provisions of this system have been accepted and are used more extensively than any other system of accounts for funeral directing.

System Requirements. The system of accounts is basic and simple. In addition to the asset and liability accounts common to all businesses, an account is provided in which to record Advance Deposits on Contracts for Future Funeral Services, with a contra account showing Trust Funds for Advance Deposits on Contracts for Future Funeral Services. These accounts, while offsetting each other, should be shown on the balance sheet to disclose contingent liabilities and trust funds held. Income accounts are designed especially for the profession, and expense accounts are divided for convenience into general and automobile classifications. The costs of burial goods and supplies are determined by direct charges and credits to inventory and purchases accounts and the application of physical inventories of these items.

The Accommodation Account. In many areas funeral directors advance monies, as an accommodation to the family being served, for the payment of cemetery charges, clergy and musicians' honorariums, telephone and telegraph tolls, transportation charges, and any other items of expense incidental to the funeral. The Accommodation Account is debited when payment is made by the funeral director; and this account is credited with a like amount when a charge is made to the funeral account. Any balance indicates an incomplete record of the transactions. One ledger account may be used; however, many prefer to use two ledger accounts, one for Cash Advances (debit) and the other Cash Advances Recovered (credit), the credit posting coming from the Funeral Service Charge record.

Statement form preferred in this system. Funeral directing accounting requires only a combination journal and a funeral service charge (sales) journal. In a volume operation a cash receipts record and a check record might be preferred in place of the combination journal. Therefore, instead of presenting a list of accounts and their obvious posting source, we are presenting a suggested form for the balance sheet (Figure 2) and for the income and expense statement (Figure 3). Special attention is called to the presentation of income, costs and expenses, because funeral service income consists of a combination of charges for professional and personal services, together with charges for burial goods. The determination of "gross margins" is completely omitted. Data showing "gross margins" or "gross profit" distort the facts and do not provide the reader proper information.

STATEMENT OF ASSETS, LIABILITIES, AND NET WORTH (CAPITAL)

ASSETS:

Cash . . . .$		x
Bank		x
Accounts Receivable		x

Inventories:

Caskets . . . .$	x	
Vaults	x	
Clothing	x	
Embalming Supplies	x	
Funeral Supplies	x	
Prepaid Expenses		x
Total Current Assets . . . . $		x
Trust Fund for Future Services . . . . $	x	
Less, Contracts for Future Services	x	x

	Cost		Depreciation Allowed		Carrying Value	
Property Accounts:						
Land	$	x	$	x	$	x
Buildings		x		x		x
Funeral Service Equipment . . .		x		x		x
Furnishings		x		x		x
Motor Equipment		x		x		x
Total Cost and Depreciation	$	x	$	x		

Net Carrying Value . . . . $		x
TOTAL ASSETS . . . . $		x

LIABILITIES:

Accounts Payable . . . . $		x
Accrued Taxes (detailed)		x
Accrued Expenses		x
Total Current Liabilities . . . . $		x
Long-Term Indebtedness		x
TOTAL LIABILITIES . . . .$		x

NET WORTH (CAPITAL):

Owners' Equity (Capital) . . . .$		x
Net Gain for the Year		x
Total . . . . $		x
Less: Owners' Withdrawals		x
TOTAL LIABILITIES		x
TOTAL LIABILITIES AND NET WORTH. . . . . $		x

Fig. 2. Balance Sheet

STATEMENT OF INCOME, COSTS, AND EXPENSES

INCOME:

Funeral Service Fees	$	x
Burial Vault Sales		x
Clothing Sales		x
Other Service Fees		x
Sundry Income		x
Interest Income		x
TOTAL INCOME	$	x

COSTS AND EXPENSES:

Burial Goods and Supplies	$	x
Advertising		x
Collection Costs		x
Depreciation		x
Dues and Subscriptions		x
Employees—Salaries		x
Funeral Service Expense		x
Utilities		x
Insurance		x
Interest and Bank Service Charges		x
Laundry and Cleaning		x
Legal and Accounting Fees		x
Office Expense and Licenses		x
Repairs and Maintenance		x
Services—Other Funeral Directors		x
Taxes (detail)		x
Telephone—Telegraph		x
Travel		x
Automobile Expense		x
Gasoline—Oil—Supplies		x
Auto Repairs		x
Auto Insurance		x
Auto License		x
Rental of Equipment		x
TOTAL FUNERAL COSTS and EXPENSES	$	x
NET GAIN FOR PERIOD	$	x

Fig. 3. Statement of Income, Costs, and Expenses

Records peculiar to the system. The Division of Vital Statistics of the Department of Public Health in each of the states supplies death certificate forms. This record is completed and filed with the proper authorities, and in exchange the funeral director receives a burial permit, or a removal permit if disposition is to be at some other place. Statistical data required for the death certificate, together with information for the obituary, is retained by the funeral director. Usually these data are gathered on forms reflecting the custom of the community. Standard forms are available.

Funeral Service Agreement. A funeral service agreement is recommended. In addition to showing the funeral service fee, cash advances, and other items, the terms and manner of settlement should be stated and the persons responsible asked to authorize the service. These contracts are important when estates and other sources of settlement do not provide sufficient funds.

The accounts receivable record and all indexing should be in the name of the deceased. A chronological record as well as an alphabetical record is recommended. This is not a requirement for accounting, but it provides easy reference to each family group.

Record of funeral charges and direct costs. A record is maintained for entering funeral service charges and direct costs for each funeral. Figure 4 illustrates such a record. On this record funeral fees, vault sales, clothing sales, and cash advances

DIRECT COSTS							
	Casket Cost	Vault Cost	Clothing Cost	Cash Advances		Total Direct Costs	

(RIGHT SIDE)

FUNERAL SERVICES Month of ______ 19____									
Date	Name of Deceased	Acct. No.	Funeral Fee	Vault Sales	Clothing Sales	Cash Advances		Total Charge	

(LEFT SIDE)

Figure 4. Record of Funeral Charges and Direct Costs.

(accommodations) are shown in separate classifications. Direct costs are listed for caskets, vaults, clothing, and cash advances. This record is the source for establishing the income pattern and it is also the source for posting (1) the general ledger income accounts, (2) charges to accounts receivable, and (3) inventory control accounts for caskets, vaults, and clothing.

Cash, check and invoice record. In the average instance, a combination journal may be used to record cash receipts, bank deposits, checks issued, and invoices for merchandise purchased. The use of accounts payable is optional, because of the small number of transactions as compared with other types of businesses. There are no particular problems in connection with the use or form of these records. The handling of the payroll is by the ordinary method.

Frequency of reports to management. The frequency of reports to management varies with the volume of services. Quarterly interim reports are usually sufficient when the number of services is 750 or less; when the volume of service is larger, management would be better informed through the use of monthly reports.

Type of reports. The report to management should include the following statements, together with the necessary supporting schedules:

1. Statement of Assets, Liabilities and Net Worth (See Figure 2)
2. Statement of Income, Costs and Expense (See Figure 3)
3. Statement of Source and Application of Funds
4. Statement Showing Income Pattern and Overhead Allocations

The manner of accumulating detailed information will vary with the style of record keeping preferred. The use of monthly summary and recapitulation sheets for income and expense classifications is recommended to eliminate multiple postings to the general ledger and to provide a chart of the monthly progress in the operating section of the accounting system.

Data for Computation of Cost of Operation per Service

There is disagreement among those in funeral service as to the extent to which the average cost per funeral should be used, especially in making it the basis for a pricing method. There is little or no disagreement, however, as to the value of computing the average cost per service if for no other reason than to make those in a funeral firm aware of their costs.

The following breakdown or breakout of expense will be helpful. In introduction to its use it should be pointed out that there is a theory used by some to the effect that total expense should be reduced by a percentage of vault and clothing sales, and also reduced by the margin between fee and casket cost on children and indigent or publicly paid-for services, and dividing the balance by the total regular adult services. Also, if the purpose is to use the average as a method for helping to determine the fee or selling price of a funeral service, care should be exercised to provide for the recovery of costs in excess of fees on all services in which the average overhead plus the casket cost exceeds the fee or charge for such services.

DATA FOR COMPUTATION OF COST OF OPERATION PER SERVICE

Funeral Service Expense

Advertising, Promotion and Entertainment _____

Collection Costs _____

Dues and Subscriptions _____

Pension Costs _____

Freight and Express _____

Funeral Service Expense _____

Funeral Trip Expense _____

Heat, Light, Water _____

Insurance General _____

Insurance Health _____

Insurance Life (Partners—Officers) _____

Interest and Bank Charges _____

Income Tax (Local and State) _____

Laundry and Cleaning _____

Office Expense _____

Professional Services _____

Rent _____

Repairs—Maintenance _____

Taxes—General _____

Taxes—Other _____

Taxes—Payroll (State and Federal) _____

Taxes—Sales and Use Taxes _____

Telephone—Telegraph _____

Travel—Business _____

Motor Equipment Expense

Chauffeur's Salaries _____

Gasoline, Oil, Supplies _____

Insurance Premiums _____

Licenses _____

Outside Rental _____

Repairs—Maintenance _____

Other Costs

Employee's Compensation _____

Owner's Compensation _____

Loss on Uncollectible Accounts _____

Discounts Allowed _____

Depreciation Charges All Items _____

Contributions _____

Funeral Service Supplies _____

Embalming Supplies _____

Flower Costs Not Recovered _____

Accommodation Items Not Recovered _____

TOTAL _____

The total of these expenses divided by the TOTAL of ALL Services will give the cost of operation per service.

Collection Methods

Extension of Credit

Death causes a change in the legal status concerning the liabilities of, and on behalf of, an individual. Contracts, verbal or otherwise, made by an individual during *his* lifetime are his liabilities; however, the funeral and interment expenses for a deceased person are not *his* liabilities, but are liabilities of either (1) his estate, (2) persons legally responsible for them, or (3) those persons who may have assumed such responsibilities. Therefore, the extension of credit in a funeral service practice follows a different pattern from that followed elsewhere. This is basic; however, other factors may apply.

The rapid changes in social and economic conditions in recent years reflect a series of variations in the matter of payment for funeral and burial expenses. These include allowances available through governmental agencies such as Veterans Administration benefits for funeral and burial expenses for veterans who qualify; the various military funeral allowances, Army, Marines, Navy, Air Force, Coast Guard; Social Security benefits when not paid direct to a spouse; Public Aid assistance for recipients of public aid which are subject to regulation by each state government. There are also fraternal and union benefits available under certain circumstances.

Prearranged and Prepaid Funeral Contracts

Prearranged funeral service contracts (or pre-need as they are sometimes identified) may be in the form of a contract to be completed and paid for under various methods, or they may be prepaid contracts. In such situations the provisions of the contract may be such as to void payments by other agencies referred to in the preceding paragraph. (See chapter 12 on this subject.)

Estate Sources

Extending credit to the estate of an individual may pose some problems. The conditions existing at the time of death do not always present an opportunity to determine just who possesses the authority to bind the estate for funeral expenses and in some states funeral expenses are divided into more than one class of claim. Generally the expense of burial, being a liability of the estate and not of the decedent, is classified as a first class claim; however, some states limit the amount which will be considered as first class and any balance would be subject to treatment as a general creditor of the decedent.

Funeral Service Agreement

The first step in collection of accounts in any business or profession is a distinct understanding of all facets of the transaction, a determination of the source of funds from which payment is to be made, the manner of payment, and who is responsible for the payment.

To facilitate these areas in extending credit in a funeral service practice a *Funeral*

Service Agreement form should be employed as an aid to all concerned. This form should provide for all the requirements of both Federal and State laws concerning the extension of credit and the terms of payment including Truth in Lending. For instance, under the Federal Law offering a discount of more than 5% is considered as really two prices, i.e. the cash price or the time payment price. Such a circumstance requires the statement of annual percentage rate of interest and of "discount" if it is more than 5%. Care should be exercised in the printing and use of a form. Consult your attorney or proper governmental authority.

The type of form to be used will depend entirely on the method or pricing used by the funeral service practitioner. The following are forms suggested for adaptation by the National Funeral Directors Association. The "space for insert" has to do with the Truth in Lending Law. Data thereon is also in this chapter, starting on page 58.

Form 1. (Single Unit)

FUNERAL SERVICE FOR_____

Professional services including care and preparation of the body; consultation with family and clergyman; arrangement and direction of the visitation and funeral; preparation and filing of necessary notices, authorizations and consents; and, other services and attendance prior to, during and following the funeral. Local transportation of the body. Use of establishment facilities and equipment and casket (_____) as selected.

$ . . . .

Outside receptacle (_____) $ . . . .
Clothing (_____) $ . . . .
_____ $ . . . .
_____ $ . . . .
_____ $ . . . .

TOTAL OF OUR CHARGES $ _____

CASH ADVANCES FOR YOUR CONVENIENCE

Additional automotive equipment . . . . . . $ . . . .
Train, air or long distance funeral coach . . $ . . . .
Flowers . . . . $ . . . .
Cemetery or crematory charges . . . . $ . . . .
Newspaper notices . . . . $ . . . .
Clergy honorarium . . . . $ . . . .
Transcripts . . . . $ . . . .
Telegrams and long distance telephones . $ . . . .
_____ $ . . . .
_____ $ . . . .
_____ $ . . . .

TOTAL OF CASH ADVANCES $_____

Total for Our Services, Merchandise, and Cash Advanced for your Convenience . . . .$_____

(Space for insert)

The foregoing memorandum has been read by (to) me and I hereby acknowledge receipt of a copy of same and agree to pay the above funeral account and such additional services and materials as ordered by me, on or before _____ , 19 _____

The liability hereby assumed is in addition to the liability imposed by law upon the estate and others, and shall not constitute a release thereof.

Legal rate of interest will apply to past due accounts. Any charges incurred after this date will be billed later.

By . . . .
. . . . (L.S.)
. . . . (L.S.)
. . . . (L.S.)
Date . . . . , 19 . . . .

THIS IS AN AGREEMENT

Form 2. (Bi-Unit)

FUNERAL SERVICE FOR_____

Professional services including care and preparation of the body; consultation with family and clergyman; arrangement and direction of the visitation and funeral; preparation and filing of necessary notices, authorizations and consents; and, other services and attendance prior to, during and following the funeral. Local transportation of the body. Use of establishment facilities and equipment. $........

MERCHANDISE SELECTED

Casket (_____) $........
Outside receptacle (_____) $........
Clothing (_____) $........
_____ $........
_____ $........

TOTAL FOR MERCHANDISE $_____

CASH ADVANCES FOR YOUR CONVENIENCE

Additional automotive equipment ...... $ ....
Train, air or long distance funeral coach .. $ ....
Flowers .... $ ......
Cemetery or crematory charges .... $ ......
Newspaper notices .... $ ......
Clergy honorarium .... $ ......
Transcripts .... $ ......
Telegrams and long distance telephone .. $ ....
_____ $ ....
_____ $ ....
_____ $ ....

TOTAL OF CASH ADVANCES $_____

Total for Our Services and Use of Facilities; For Merchandise Selected; and For Cash Advanced For Your Convenience .... $_____

(Space for insert)

The foregoing memorandum has been read by (to) me and I hereby acknowledge receipt of a copy of same and agree to pay the above funeral account and such additional services and materials as ordered by me, on or before _____ , 19_____

The liability hereby assumed is in addition to the liability imposed by law upon the estate and others, and shall not constitute a release thereof.

Legal rates of interest will apply to past due accounts. Any charges incurred after this date will be billed later.

By ....
....(L.S.)
....(L.S.)
.... (L.S.)
Date ...., 19 ......

THIS IS AN AGREEMENT

Form 3. (Multi-Unit)

FUNERAL SERVICE FOR_____

SERVICES AND USE OF FACILITIES

Preparation of body . . . . $ . . . .
Other professional services . . . . $ . . . .
Use of funeral home and providing
of register book, acknowledgment
cards, etc. $ . . . .
Use of automotive equipment
  Removal . . . . $ . . . .
  Casket coach . . . . $ . . . .
  Passenger car . . . . $ . . . .
  Flower car . . . . $ . . . .
  Other . . . . $ . . . .
  Total automotive . . . . $ . . . .
TOTAL FOR SERVICES
AND FACILITIES $_____

MERCHANDISE SELECTED

Casket (_____) $ . . . .
Outside receptacle (_____) $ . . . .
Clothing (_____) $ . . . .
_____ $ . . . .
_____ $ . . . .
TOTAL FOR MERCHANDISE $_____

CASH ADVANCES FOR YOUR CONVENIENCE

Train or air transportation . . . . $ . . . .
Flowers . . . . $ . . . .
Cemetery or crematory charges . . . . $ . . . .
Newspaper notices . . . . $ . . . .
Clergy honorarium . . . . $ . . . .
Transcripts . . . . $ . . . .
Telegrams and long distance telephone . . $ . . . .
_____ $ . . . .
_____ $ . . . .
_____ $ . . . .
TOTAL FOR CASH ADVANCES $_____

Total for Our Services and Use of Facilities;
For Merchandise Selected; and For
Cash Advanced For Your Convenience

$_____

(Space for insert)

The foregoing memorandum has been read by (to) me and I hereby acknowledge receipt of a copy of same and agree to pay the above funeral account and such additional services and materials as ordered by me, on or before_____, 19____
The liability hereby assumed is in addition to the liability imposed by law upon the estate and others, and shall not constitute a release thereof.
Legal rate of interest will apply to past due accounts. Any charges incurred after this date will be billed later.

By . . . .
. . . . (L.S.)
. . . . (L.S.)
. . . . (L.S.)
Date . . . . , 19 . . . .

THIS IS AN AGREEMENT

It is suggested that the agreement be completed and signed first by the funeral director offering to serve as stipulated and then by those responsible for payment as approving and accepting the responsibility for payment. This is important because of the possibility of death or impairment of any of the participants to the contract before the contract is executed or performed completely.

Statement

At the time of making funeral arrangements those who are responsible for payment of the expenses should be advised that a *Statement of the Funeral Account* will be furnished shortly after the service is completed and all charges are finalized for items which may not be determined at the moment of arranging the funeral, i.e., cash advances for accommodation of the family, for certified copies of the death certificate, cemetery charges, transportation charges, and honoraria, which are to be paid by the funeral director and added to the funeral account. This accommodation practice by funeral directors is changing due to governmental interpretation and social and economic pressures.

The *Statement of the Funeral Account* should follow the form used in the *Funeral Agreement* and should contain all the provisions of the agreement including the method, manner, source and responsibility for payment.

If several members of the family desire to pay proportionately, the agreement should be binding on each member for the entire purchase price, the division being an agreement between family members and not between the funeral director and each guarantor for his or her portion.

Tax Consequences

Funeral expenses are not deductible at this time for income tax purposes as are medical or dental expenses. However, funeral expenses are deductible in Federal Estate and State Inheritance Tax Returns. To the extent of the tax rate and depending upon the taxable estate there is a benefit to the beneficiaries of the estate. Recently there have been efforts made by congressmen to have the income tax laws amended to provide for deduction of funeral expenses, but at the time of this writing none of the proposed legislation has been adopted.

Small Estates

In many states the laws provide for payment of claims which would be first class, that is, last illness and funeral expenses, without the necessity of probate proceedings when the size of the estate is under a stated amount such as $1,000, $3,000, or $5,000, as provided in the state statute regulating the disposition of small estates.

Assignments

Extension of credit for funeral service is becoming more complex due to changing attitudes, social and economic conditions, as well as other factors present in the business world. Insurance assignments are sometimes warranted because of differences between family members. N.F.D.A. Form 1 is available for this purpose. It is reproduced on page 175.

The use of assignments of any sort—insurance, wage and benefits of all types—must be dictated by the good judgment of the funeral service practitioner. Discretion is advised in the use of such collection procedures.

Outside Agencies

The use of collection agency services in the satisfaction of funeral service charges is not usually necessary because for the most part funeral accounts are paid for in a single payment. If adequate precaution is used at the time of making funeral arrangements, difficulties in making collection of the account are minimized. Funeral directors who find it necessary to avail themselves of collection agency services should have a distinct understanding of what the agency charges are for such services and under what conditions these charges exist.

Insurance

A simple definition of the word insurance is "a contract whereby one party agrees to indemnify or guarantee another against loss by some contingent event." Another way to look at the subject is a method of protecting real and personal properties as well as intangible assets.

In this section on insurance we shall consider only the economic consequences of circumstances and situations which need to be insured against.

In this category we find the following:

Fire
Lightning, hail, windstorm
Liability for property damage or bodily injury
Explosion, malicious mischief, riot, strike, smoke, water damage
Vehicles, aircraft
Theft, dishonesty
Workmens compensation and employers liability
Malpractice, mental anguish
Libel and slander
Motor vehicle coverage, all facets
Funeral procession, liability of the funeral director
Medical and hospital expense caused by accident
Use and occupancy of business premises
Employee group hospital and medical, and life and income protection

Protection through insurance is essential in every type of venture. The manner of "writing" insurance today has changed to a broader form than the practice of only a few years ago. Insurance protection must be programmed for each individual business to make certain that all exposures have been sufficiently covered. There have been costly instances of damage incurred beyond liability limits.

Care should be taken in the selection of the insurance agent and/or broker as he becomes your representative in case of a loss. The agent/broker is the servicing agent in the insurance program and your guide and counsellor as the occasion requires.

Physical items to be insured include buildings, furnishings, funeral equipment, office equipment and records, motor equipment, yard equipment, merchandise, money and securities. Individuals in your employ must also be insured for various exposures including liability, property damage, theft, dishonesty, health and income protection.

Make sure your heating and air conditioning equipment is covered and also that exposures from motors and other operating parts are covered.

Policy Exclusions

If you do not understand any clause in your insurance policy, write for a written interpretation of the particular point you desire clarified. Read the policy exclusions carefully. These are the "fine print" items that in reality govern what is *not* covered under your policy. If a clarification is desired make sure the insurer or carrier makes the clarification; do not accept a general statement from the agent.

Valuations

Cost of replacement and current values are constantly changing and every firm should have an appraisal of the value of property covered at regular intervals. If co-insurance clauses are written into your policies, be sure you understand the manner in which a settlement would be made in case of a loss. Co-insurance is a method of gambling with the insurance carrier; you bet your coverage is within a certain percentage (usually 80% to 90%) of the current insurable value of the property insured.

It must be remembered that there are appraisals of properties for many different purposes and an appraisal for one purpose may not be satisfactory for any other purpose. There are appraisal methods for buying, selling, current replacement, insurable value (current value less depreciation), tax valuations and others.

Income Protection

The business may be insured to provide for business interruption, sometimes referred to as use and occupancy insurance. Just what is covered and to what extent it is covered must be clearly understood.

Both employer and employee may be insured for income protection in case of prolonged illness. In this area also fall the pension, profit-sharing and deferred income plans. These should be tailored to the needs of the business and should be studied carefully before selecting any program. There are many alternate coverages.

Procedures

Before buying any insurance program, obtain the advice of a recognized insurance broker or agent and get his outline of proposed coverage. Then call in your attorney and tax consultant together with your accountant if they are separate individuals. This team can then coordinate your needs with your insurance program and afford you the proper consideration of all aspects before you buy.

The successful business or professional man will carefully understand and provide coverage for all reasonable exposures. These will differ from place to place depending on many factors.

THE FEDERAL TRUTH IN LENDING LAW

Thomas H. Clark

When Act Does Not Apply

Where there is no finance charge as part of a funeral transaction, where the funeral bill is to be paid in four or less installments and where there is no discount for early or prompt payment, no charges for late payment, and where no interest is charged for payment after a certain date, the Truth in Lending provisions will not apply to such a transaction.

Act Applies to All Consumer Credit Transactions

The Act requires disclosure of the terms of a consumer credit transaction and regulates the advertising, if any, done in regards thereto. Consumer credit, for the purpose of the act, includes all credit extended to an individual for personal, family or household purposes. Sales credit is a credit given for a specific period of time where the total amount, number of payments, and due dates are agreed upon between the customer and the creditor. It also includes single payment loans and demand loans which for the purpose of the act are deemed to be of six months' duration.

Thirty-, sixty- and ninety-day open account transactions are to be considered for the purpose of the act as a cash sale and not subject to the credit disclosure requirements except in those cases where a delinquency charge or late payment penalty is imposed, or where the sale reverts to an installment account divided into more than four payments, or where a discount is given.

Business Loans and Fiduciaries Not Covered by Act

By definition business purposes are excluded and also by definition persons other than natural persons are excluded. Under law a fiduciary is not a natural person. Therefore, the act and its provisions do not apply to trustees, guardians, administrators or executors of an estate. If your funeral statement indicates the obligor to whom you look for payment to be the estate of the decedent, the Truth in Lending Act is not applicable. However, where you could or might seek to hold one of the next of kin, or the person who made the funeral arrangements, personally liable, the funeral service bill is covered by the act if there is any form of finance charge or discount applicable, or if a funeral bill is by agreement to be or may be paid in more than four installments.

In those instances where the funeral director does or could look to an individual for the payment of his bill and where there is or could be a finance charge, a discount, or more than four payments, the transaction is subject to the Truth in Lending Act and in particular to its very definite disclosure requirements.

These disclosure requirements of the act vary depending on the type of credit involved, but because we are here concerned with funeral service and credit given by funeral directors we will only look to the disclosure requirements which deal with credit generally extended by sellers of services and/or merchandise.

The Truth in Lending Act does not in any way affect the rate that may be charged in any transaction covered by it, nor does it affect the rate of discount that may be given for the early payment of any credit bill. In states which do not have a pre-need law so that the seller may receive benefit from the transaction either by way of principal, interest or indirect use of the funds prior to the time that the services and/or funeral merchandise have been rendered, pre-need sales are governed as a credit transaction by the Truth in Lending Act.

Disclosures Required

In regard to funeral bills the required disclosures are some 14 in number and are as follows:

1. The cash price of the service and/or merchandise purchased, using the term "cash price."

2. The amount of the down payment, using the term "cash down payment."

3. The difference between the "cash price" and the "cash down payment," using the term "unpaid balance of the cash price."

4. All other charges individually itemized which are included in the amount financed but which are not a part of the finance charge—cash advances.

5. The sum total of the "unpaid balance of cash price" and the amount of all other charges set forth in item number 4, using the term "unpaid balance."

6. Any amount that might be deductible because of an escrow account for the benefit of the customer. (Example: an amortized pre-need contract that is inadequate to finance the selection made by the family.)

7. The difference between the "unpaid balance" and the amount set forth in item number 6 hereof, using the term "amount financed."

8. The total amount of the finance charge set forth in terms of dollars, using the term "Finance Charge." "Finance Charge" includes any amount that could be "deducted" or "discounted" for early or prompt payment.

9. Use of the term "deferred payment price" which is the sum of the "cash price" plus all other charges listed in item number 4, plus the total amount of the "Finance Charge."

10. The finance charge expressed as an annual percentage rate specifically using the term "Annual Percentage Rate" except in the case of a finance charge which (a) does not exceed $5.00 and is applicable to an amount financed not exceeding $75.00 or, (b) does not exceed $7.50 and is applicable to an amount financed exceeding $75.00, or (c) where the only funeral charge is a discount and the discount is 5% or less.

11. The number, amount and due dates of payments scheduled to pay the indebtedness, and the sum of such payments using the term "total of payments." If any payment is more than twice the amount of an otherwise regularly scheduled equal payment the creditor shall identify the amount of such payment by the term "balloon payment" and shall state the conditions, if any, under which the payment may be re-financed if not paid when due.

12. The amount or method of computing the amount of any default, delinquency or similar charges payable in the event of late payment.

13. A description of the type of any security interest retained by the creditor in connection with the existence of credit. In this regard special consideration should be given to those instances where a cognovit note is used.

14. The method of computing any unearned portion of the "Finance Charge" in the event of prepayment of the obligation, including computation of a discount or other prepayment deduction, all of which shall be stated in dollars and as an A.P.R.

All of the 14 disclosures where applicable must be clearly typed or written and must be listed in an order which will be meaningful to your customer. The "Finance Charge" and the "Annual Percentage Rate" are really the two most important disclosures required by the regulations. They tell your customer at a glance how much he is paying for his credit and its relative cost in percentage terms.

Finance Charge and Annual Percentage Rate

"Finance Charge" is defined as the total of all costs imposed by the creditor and paid either directly or indirectly by the customer as an incident to the extension of credit. These include interest, service charge, carrying charge, loan fee, binder fee or similar charges, time price differential, credit life insurance premiums, credit report and amounts paid as a discount allowed for early or prompt payment. A cash discount for early or prompt payment is a "Finance Charge" which the customer must pay if he does not take advantage of paying a lesser amount on or before a specified date. This applies only to so-called customer sales in which funeral service and/or funeral merchandise are included. Certain items not part of the "Finance Charge" are taxes, license fees, registration fees and the like.

Use Federal Reserve Table to Determine A.P.R.

In computing the "Annual Percentage Rate" the actuarial method has to be used. Payments are first applied to interest due and any remainder is applied to reduce the principal. The actuarial method is very complicated and recognizing this the Federal Reserve Board has prepared tables showing the annual percentage rate based on the finance charge and the number of weekly or monthly payments to be made. These tables are available from your nearest Federal Reserve Bank or the Federal Reserve Board, Washington, D. C. 20551, at a nominal cost. The most applicable one to funeral directors is FRB-100-M, Volume 1, which covers interest from 2% to 61.75% and payments up to 60 months.

For credit of $100 for one year at a 6% add-on charge, the annual percentage rate would be 11%. If a $100 credit were provided for one year at a 6% discount in advance, the annual percentage rate would be 11½%.

Practice Will Simplify Determining Necessary Figures

The "Finance Charge" will be readily discernible after you have worked it out several times pursuant to the regulations contained in the Truth in Lending Bill. Insofar as the "Annual Percentage Rate" is concerned, it is not too difficult because of the tables.

In using the tables in determining the "Annual Percentage Rate" it is important to know the total amount financed and the "Finance Charge" because the chart is made up of a list of the number of payments together with the finance charge for $100 of the amount financed. The "Finance Charge" per $100 of amount financed is arrived at by dividing the total amount financed into the financial charge and multiplying that result by 100.

The words "Finance Charge" and "Annual Percentage Rate" must conspicuously stand out as against the other specified requirements. Authorities generally suggest that these two items be in capital type letters or bold type and that the other disclosures be in regular letters and regular type.

Special Provision for Discounts

Where the transaction is not otherwise covered by the act and there is a discount for early payment, the transaction is covered by a special provision of the act. Whether the discount is in terms of a percentage or dollar amount, it is considered a discount and the following information only need appear on the invoice or statement if the discount is 5% or less:

1. Terms of sale
2. Date of sale
3. Net amount of sale
4. Discount rate in percentage
5. Amount of discount in dollars
6. Date the discount period expires
7. The date on which the net amount due is to be paid
8. The finance charge which is also the amount of the discount.

If the discount for early payment is more than 5% in addition to the 8 items listed above, there should also be listed the annual percentage rate which is to be determined as follows:

Divide the amount of the finance charge by the least amount by which the obligation can be paid in full and multiply that quotient expressed as a percentage by a fraction in which the numerator is 12 and the denominator is the number of whole months (but not less than one) between the first day of the billing cycle in which the transaction is consummated and the first day of the monthly billing cycle in which the obligation becomes due. As an example, a $1,000.00 funeral which has terms of 6%/10 days, net 30 days, results in a finance charge of $60.00, a least amount payable of $940.00 and an annual percentage rate of 76.56%. The formula is $\frac{60}{940} \times \frac{12}{1}$

Disclosure Must Be on Face Side of Note

The disclosures must be made together on the face side of the note or instrument evidencing the obligation which in the case of the funeral director would be his bill, and if the bill is required to be signed, on the same side of the page and adjacent to the place where the client is to sign the bill. Where desired the disclosures may be on one side of a separate statement which clearly identifies the transaction. This separate statement should be signed by the obligor. (The person to whom you look for payment.) The disclosures must be given to the purchaser prior to the time that the services and/or merchandise are contracted for and therefore it would seem to be beneficial for funeral directors to have the bill or statement which contains the information signed by the purchaser prior to performing any services and supplying any merchandise unless the credit is extended solely to the decedent's estate in which event the transaction is not covered by the Act.

Act Covers Advertisements

The act itself also covers advertisements. An advertisement may not state the amount of a down payment required, or that none is required; may not state the amount of any installment payment; may not state the dollar amount of any finance charge; may not state the number of installments or the period of payment, or may not state that there is no charge for credit, nor may it state the rate of finance charge unless said advertisement also contains the cash price or the amount of loan as applicable, the amount of down payment required, or that none is required, the number, amount and due date for period of payment needed to pay the indebtedness if credit is given, the amount of any and all "Finance Charges" expressed as an "Annual Percentage Rate," the deferred payment price, the sum of the payments and the amount of discount where the discount is applicable.

In advertising the trouble area is going to be in making only a partial disclosure, that is disclosing less than that which is required. Anyone intending to advertise any of the foregoing disclosures must set forth all the disclosures in the advertising piece.

Customer's Right to Rescind Certain Transactions

The most serious problem which is faced under the Truth in Lending Act is the provision which permits the customer the right to rescind certain transactions. When a credit sale such as giving a funeral on credit or providing a funeral with a discount provision in it is made and the seller obtains a security interest in the purchaser's residence, the purchaser has the right to rescind the credit transaction within three working days without giving any reason for his having done so. This is important because it has been stated by representatives of the Federal Trade Commission, who have the obligation to enforce the Truth in Lending Act insofar as funeral directors are concerned, that where a cognovit note is signed it gives the basis for the creditor to obtain without notice an interest in one's residence and therefore a transaction involving a cognovit note is a transaction where the customer has the three-day right of recision.

A cognovit note is a negotiable instrument whereby the obligor authorizes any attorney to confess judgment in case of default against the obligor without notice to the obligor.

This deductive reasoning has been taken one step further and according to the FTC representatives, right of recision applies even where the customer presently does not own a residence but might acquire one in the future. Therefore, in all cases where a cognovit note is used the customer has the right to rescind the transaction within three working days without giving any reason for having done so. The three days commence from the time that the required disclosures have been presented to the customer. If a customer decided to cancel the transaction, it is incumbent upon the seller, the funeral director, to repossess the funeral merchandise which has been delivered.

The customer has no obligations to see to it that it is returned to the seller. This might seem very harsh particularly where a funeral is involved, especially so where the funeral has already taken place. But nonetheless it is true. The person liable for the funeral where his right of recision is exercised must nevertheless pay for the cost (funeral director's) of the merchandise if repossession has not taken place.

The transaction can be cancelled in three working days if a cognovit note was used. A client or customer has the option, however, to waive the three day recision right for urgent personal reasons which would include the requirement of funeral and burial for a member of the family within the three-day period.

Recommend Funeral Directors Do Not Use Cognovit Notes

Therefore, we first suggest that cognovit notes not be used. If they are then a sample form should be on hand at the funeral home that would permit the customer to waive the three-day recision right based on the urgent need concept. The form must be used only as a guide because you cannot supply a printed form for the customer to sign. The customer must voluntarily write out the waiver.

The problem with the waiver is that a court at some future date has the right to determine if in fact there was an urgent need, making sure that the urgent need was not just in the mind of the customer and/or the creditor. An enforcement of the transaction will depend on the court agreeing with the creditor (the funeral director) and the customer that there was in fact an urgent need, otherwise the customer would have the right at that time to cancel the transaction and get his money back, or, if it had not been paid, to be relieved of any further obligations.

Penalties under the Truth in Lending Act provide that a client or family may sue for twice the amount of the finance charge, a minimum of $100 up to a maximum of $1000, plus court costs and attorneys' fees. The amount of attorneys' fees in some cases can be much more than the actual amount of recovery to the customer. If the violation is willful and you are convicted, you could also be fined up to $5000 or be imprisoned for one year, or both. If asked by the proper agency, the FTC, you must show your records relating to disclosure and evidence of compliance.

Copies of all contracts or bills which are covered by the Truth in Lending Act must be kept for at least two years as evidence of your compliance with the Act. The regulations do not require monthly statements to be sent to the obligor, but if they are sent monthly or otherwise periodically such statements must contain the "Annual Percentage Rate" and the date within which payment must be remitted to avoid late payment charges or to receive a discount.

Examples of the Application of the Provisions of the Truth in Lending Act to Funeral Homes and Related Forms

1. A funeral bill totaling $800 including cash advances is given to the customer. Terms of that bill are net thirty (30) days—6% per annum if not paid within 30 days. The bill is to be paid in one installment. Such a bill is covered by the Truth in Lending Act because interest is charged, and all of the required disclosures must be included on the statement. In this example the "Finance Charge" is $24 and the "Annual Percentage Rate" is 45%, that is because demand obligations or obligations not having a particular due date or installment date are deemed to be payable in six months.

If the above bill was addressed and applicable only to an estate, and the funeral director did not look to the next of kin or the person who selected the funeral, then the Truth in Lending Act does not apply. The same would be true if the funeral selected would be by a corporation such as an airline—then the Truth in Lending Act would also not apply.

2. A funeral bill of $1100 is rendered. Terms: net amount due when paid. The bill for the service and merchandise provided by the funeral director is addressed to one of the next of kin who selected the funeral, and the next of kin had to sign a non-cognovit, demand, non-interest bearing note. In this case the Truth in Lending Act does not apply. However, it would apply if any one of the following existed:

(a) If interest were due after a specified number of days.
(b) A discount were given for early payment.
(c) If the obligation was to be paid in more than four installments.
(d) If the cognovit feature existed in a note.
(e) If the note called for interest.

3. F ⟶ situations having discounts of less than 5% the following may be used:

(a) Discount 2%/10 days (finance charge $____).
(b) Interest to be charged for late payment.
(c) Net 30 days–6% per annum.

4. A funeral bill amounts to $800 including costs advanced. The terms permit a discount of 6% or $48 if paid within 30 days. Such a bill is covered by the Truth in Lending Act and certain disclosures must be presented on the bill or on a separate paper which adequately identifies the transaction, as follows:

1.	Date of sale–	5.	Date discount expires–
2.	Net amount–$800	6.	Date net amount due–
3.	Discount rate–6%	7.	Finance charge–$48
4.	Amount of discount–$48	8.	Annual percentage rate–76.60%

In this example the "Finance Charge" or discount is $48 and the "Annual Percentage Rate" is arrived at by dividing the $48 "Finance Charge" by $752, the amount to be paid in the first 30 days, and that result of .0638 is multiplied by 12. Since the transaction is intended to be a single installment payment transaction, the "Annual Percentage Rate" of this transaction is 76.60%.

If the use of a discount is advertised by the funeral director, all the necessary disclosures, including the "Finance Charge" and the "Annual Percentage Rate" must be included in the advertising. If the discount was 5% or less, the APR need not be given.

5. In our fourth example we shall consider a funeral bill of $800 not including cash advances of $200 and dated August 1, 1970. Terms to be 6% after 30 days. The Truth in Lending Act applies and the following is a list of the items which must appear on the statement and be given in writing to the person responsible for the payment of the funeral bill prior to the time that the funeral services and/or merchandise are provided:

1. Cash price	$800.00
2. Less down payment	0.00
3. Unpaid balance of cash price	800.00
4. Other charges: Cash advances	200.00
5. Amount financed	1000.00
6. Finance Charge: 6% for 6 months	30.00
7. Total of payments	1030.00
8. Deferred Payment Price (1 plus 4 plus 6)	1030.00
9. "Annual Percentage Rate"	6.00%
10. "Finance Charge" to commence September 1, 1970	

In a transaction which has other features, one or more of the following items might also be required:

(a) Burial policy to be the down payment.
(b) Number, amount and due date of payments.
(c) Identification of security interest if acquired.
(d) Name of creditor not necessarily the seller–one who actually is given the credit–use in pre-need sales.

(e) Prepaid "Finance Charge" if any.

(f) Required deposit balance.

(g) Balloon payment—amount and due date.

(h) Default and/or delinquent charges.

*   *   *   *

For examples concerning possible installment payment of a funeral bill we list the following three examples with the terms of the transaction appearing at the top of the column and the financial data appearing thereunder:

EXAMPLE ONE

Date: July 1, 1970

Seller's Name and Address

Purchaser's Name and Address

Contract No._____

Funeral Bill—$600
Cash Advanced—200
6%—1 year
12 installments

1. Cash price	$600.00
2. Down payment	0.00
3. Unpaid balance of cash price	600.00
4. Other charges	200.00
5. Amount financed	800.00
6. "FINANCE CHARGE"	48.00
7. Total of payments	848.00
8. Deferred payment price (1 plus 4 plus 6)	848.00
9. ANNUAL PERCENTAGE RATE	10.8%

Purchaser hereby agrees to pay to Mathers Funeral Home at their offices shown above the "TOTAL OF PAYMENTS" shown above in eleven monthly installments of $70.00 and one final payment of $78.00, the first installment being payable August 1, 1970, and all subsequent installments on the same day of each consecutive month until paid in full. The "FINANCE CHARGE" applies from July 1, 1970.

(Signed) . . . .

*   *   *   *   *   *

EXAMPLE TWO

Date: July 1, 1970

Seller's Name and Address

Purchaser's Name and Address

Contract No._____

Funeral Bill—$600
Cash advanced—200
Down payment—100
6%—1 year
12 installments

1. Cash price	$600.00
2. Downpayment	100.00
3. Unpaid balance of cash price	500.00
4. Other charges	200.00
5. Amount financed	700.00
6. "FINANCE CHARGE"	42.00
7. Total of payments	742.00
8. Deferred payment price (1 plus 4 plus 6)	842.00
9. ANNUAL PERCENTAGE RATE	10.8%

Purchaser hereby agrees to pay Mathers Funeral Home at their offices shown above the "TOTAL OF PAYMENTS" shown above in eleven monthly installments of $61.00 and one final payment of $71.00, the first installment being payable August 1, 1970, and all subsequent installments on the same day of each consecutive month until paid in full. The "FINANCE CHARGE" applies from July 1, 1970.

(Signed) . . . .

*   *   *   *   *   *

EXAMPLE THREE

Date: July 1, 1970

Seller's Name and Address

Contract No._____

Purchaser's Name and Address

Funeral Bill—$600
Down payment—100
Cash advanced—200
6%—2 years
24 installments

1. Cash price	$600.00
2. Down payment	100.00
3. Unpaid balance of cash price	500.00
4. Other charges	200.00
5. Amount financed	700.00
6. "FINANCE CHARGE"	84.00
7. Total of payments	784.00
8. Deferred payment price (1 plus 4 plus 6)	884.00
9. ANNUAL PERCENTAGE RATE	11.25%

Purchaser hereby agrees to pay to Mathers Funeral Home at their offices shown above the "TOTAL OF PAYMENTS" shown above in 23 monthly installments of $32.50 and one final payment of $36.50, the first installment being payable August 1, 1970, and all subsequent installments on the same day of each consecutive month until paid in full. The "FINANCE CHARGE" applies from July 1, 1970.

(Signed) . . . .

*   *   *   *   *   *

In the event that you deem it necessary to have a note executed to evidence or better secure the payment of a funeral bill, the following is a recommended form of such note:

PROMISSORY NOTE

_____   _____
(City)   (State)

Date _____

For value received undersigned maker(s), jointly and severally, promise to pay to the order of_____ at the above place_____ Dollars ($___ ____) in_____consecutive monthly installments of $_____, each beginning one month from the date hereof and thereafter on the same date of each subsequent month until paid in full. Any unpaid balance may be paid at any time, without penalty, and any unearned "FINANCE CHARGE" will be refunded based on the "Rule of 78's." In the event that maker(s) default(s) on any payment, a charge of_____ may be assessed.

(Signed) . . . .

The bottom of the note should contain all the information required to be given with the original bill as set forth in the above examples.

In the event that you deem it necessary that a cognovit feature be included, the following is the form which must be tendered to the customer, notifying him of his right of recision:

. . . .
(Identification of Transaction)

NOTICE TO CUSTOMER REQUIRED BY FEDERAL LAW

You have entered into a transaction on_____(date) which may result in a lien, mortgage, or other security interest on your home. You have a legal right under federal law to cancel this transaction if you desire to do so, without any penalty or obligation within three business days from the above date or any later date on which all material disclosures required under the Truth in Lending Act have been given to you. If you so cancel the transaction, any lien, mortgage, or other security interest on your home arising from this transaction is automatically void. You are also entitled to receive a refund of any down payment or other consideration if you cancel. If you decide to cancel this transaction you may do so by notifying_____(Name of Creditor) at_____(Address of Creditor's place of business) by mail or telegram sent not later than midnight of_____(date).

You may also use any other form of written notice identifying the transaction if it is delivered to the above address not later than that time. This notice may be used for that purpose by dating and signing below.

I hereby cancel this transaction_____(date)
_____(Customer's signature)

In the event that you wish to have the three days recision period waived, we would like to suggest the following wording which, however, may not be by means of a printed form, but must be in the hand writing of the person waiving the recision.

"I_____hereby certify that it is necessary that the funeral of_____ _____ for the cost of which I admit personal liability, must take place as soon as practicable, and that a delay of three business days in the performance of the Mathers Funeral Home's services will jeopardize the welfare of the undersigned and next of kin of the decedent, and therefore the undersigned waives his right to rescind the transaction wherein the Mathers Funeral Home is to supply services and/or merchandise for the funeral of _____."

Adapting Truth in Lending to Agreement Forms

The funeral agreement forms earlier illustrated in this chapter are for some basic funeral pricing methods. Form 1 is for the single unit method. Form 2 is the bi-unit and Form 3 is the multi-unit. (See pages 52, 53, 54).

The forms can be adapted for use by a funeral home. Such adaptations must take into consideration the Truth in Lending law where applicable. In order to set forth further recommendations as to these forms the following examples are given of inserts that can be used in compliance with the law when applicable.

Example 1. If the transaction is a single cash payment with no discount and if it can be reasonably expected that the payment will be made within a stated period of time, the following wording should be inserted:

> This is a cash transaction and after 30 days (or 60 or 90 as the case may be) if unpaid, interest at the rate of _____% per annum will be charged.

Example 2. Discount of 5% or less for prompt single payment where no other finance charge is imposed then insert:

1. Cash price on funeral $_____
2. Down payment (Cash or Burial Policy) _____
3. Unpaid balance of cash price _____
4. Other charges (Cash advances) _____
5. Unpaid balance _____
6. Amount financed _____
7. FINANCE CHARGE (Amount of Discount) _____
8. Time sale price (1 plus 4 plus 7) _____
9. Time payment balance (6 plus 7) _____
10. ANNUAL PERCENTAGE RATE _____
11. Beginning date of FINANCE CHARGE _____

Example 3. In all funeral arrangements where "truth in lending" is applicable and the provisions in example 1 and 2 will not be used, the following should be inserted:

1. Cash price of funeral $_____
2. Down payment (Cash or Burial Policy) _____
3. Unpaid balance of cash price _____
4. Other charges (Cash advances) _____
5. Unpaid balance _____
6. Amount financed _____
7. FINANCE CHARGE _____
8. Time Sale Price (1 plus 4 plus 7) _____
9. Time payment balance (6 plus 7) _____
10. ANNUAL PERCENTAGE RATE _____
11. Beginning date of FINANCE CHARGE _____

Example 4. Where installment payments are a part of the funeral agreement regardless of the number of installments if the "truth in lending" law is applicable, the following wording should be inserted:

1.	Cash price of funeral	$_____
2.	Down payment (Cash or Burial Policy)	_____
3.	Unpaid balance of cash price	_____
4.	Other charges (Cash advances)	_____
5.	Unpaid balance	_____
6.	Amount financed	_____
7.	FINANCE CHARGE	_____
8.	Time sale price (1 plus 4 plus 7)	_____
9.	Time payment balance (6 plus 7)	_____
10.	ANNUAL PERCENTAGE RATE	_____
11.	Beginning date of FINANCE CHARGE	_____

The undersigned hereby agree to pay or cause to be paid the sum set out in UNPAID BALANCE (Item No. 5 above) within____days of the date hereof, and in the event the said UNPAID BALANCE is not so paid, then the undersigned agree to pay the_____or order, or their assigns, the TOTAL OF PAYMENTS shown above in____monthly installations of $____(final installment to be $____), the first installment being payable_____, 19____ and all subsequent installments on the same day of each consecutive month until paid in full. In the event of default of any payment when due the entire balance shall become due and owing at the option of the holder thereof. This agreement shall draw interest after maturity at the same rates set out opposite the ANNUAL PERCENTAGE RATE in Item No. 10 above.

Default payments: Each installment delinquent for more than ten (10) days shall bear one delinquency charge of 5% of such installment or $2.50, whichever is lesser.

Example 5. Where more than one but fewer than five installments are part of the funeral agreement and the "truth in lending" law does not otherwise apply, only the following wording need be inserted:

The undersigned hereby agree to pay or cause to be paid the sum set out above within____days of the date thereof, and in the event the said UNPAID BALANCE is not so paid, then the undersigned agree to pay the_____or order, or their assigns, the TOTAL OF PAYMENTS shown above in____monthly installments of $____ (final installment to be $____), the first installment being payable_____19____ and all subsequent installments on the same day of each consecutive month until paid in full. In the event of default of any payment when due the entire balance shall become due and owing at the option of the holder hereof.

Example 6. Where one installment with a discount of 5% or less and where a late payment percentage charge is made, and where the truth in lending does not otherwise apply, only the following wording need be inserted:

Net____days. ____% per annum interest to be charged for late payment.

The multi-unit form (No. 3) is not specifically applicable in states where there is an itemization law. Funeral directors in those states must be guided by regulations or opinions of the pertinent governmental agency of their state.

CASKET SELECTION ROOM EVALUATION

Glenn H. Griffin
and
Robert C. Slater

It is generally agreed that 14 to 16 units (caskets) are required to give each family an adequate representation of material, design and quality from which to make its selection. The average number of units per selection room throughout the country is 20-22 units. Some larger funeral homes may provide from 36 to 40 units. Funeral directors realize that too many units not only cause duplication, but can also confuse a family in making its selection.

All units should be displayed in one room or adjoining rooms open to each other. To group caskets in separated rooms can lead to confusion, misunderstanding and criticism by the funeral selecting public. All prices should be clearly displayed, easily readable and as inclusive as possible as to what the price includes. The various methods of pricing are discussed in detail elsewhere in this chapter.

The number of units available from which to make a selection and the presentation and pricing of those units are the personal responsibility of the funeral home. There are organizations and individual consultants to guide, advise and counsel in these areas. However, each funeral director is ultimately personally responsible to the community and those he serves to provide a selection room that will meet the needs of each and every family as was pointed out in the chapter on "Income and Expense Patterns."

The public today expects the funeral director to receive fair and adequate compensation for his personal professional services and the merchandise he provides. They also expect him to provide services and merchandise for those unable to do so, as well as for those who must depend on charity or governmental assistance at such a time. To fulfill these several functions the selection room must meet the needs of all families that use it while providing a fair return for the funeral home. It is this responsibility that each funeral director must accept and fulfill to the best of his ability.

Just as there are many ways of planning a selection room, there are many ways of evaluating its effectiveness. Many funeral directors develop their own plan and evaluation. Others use procedures developed by management organizations or individual consultants. It is our intent to detail here a plan that can be used by any funeral home regardless of the annual case volume that it serves.

The example used here is based on a typical funeral home that had a case volume of 95 services in the calendar year 1968. We will use it to develop step by step an evaluation procedure that can be adapted by the individual funeral director.

> *Step 1*—Compile a record of selections (see Figure 1) for a given period of time. It is usually easiest to develop this record by date and total selections which would include only services and casket. For those using the single unit method it would be the price which takes into consideration the services and the casket. If the bi-unit method is utilized it would be the total of professional services and casket. Under the multi-unit method it would be the total of professional

Record of Selections

Typical Funeral Home

(Includes Services and Casket)

January		April		July		October	
January	1 — 1225	April 3 — 237		July 6 — 1085		October 1 — 1085	
	11 — 975		4 — 605		7 — 237		10 — 375
	17 — 76		5 — 1165		8 — 1125		26 — 76
	18 — 975		5 — 450		8 — 525		27 — 735
	19 — NC		5 — 1465		8 — 89		27 — 975
	20 — 525		10 — 1035		10 — 605		29 — 1225
	25 — 1925		14 — 976		16 — 450	November	6 — 945
	26 — 1005		17 1225		22 — 525		7 — 1165
February	4 — 176		21 — 795		26 — 1165		15 — 795
	6 — 525		26 — 1165		28 — 795		24 — 450
	8 — 45	May 1 — 375		29 — 735		27 — NC
	11 — 795		10 — 237		30 — 450		28 — 795
	12 — 1465		16 — 735	August 2 — 525	December	1 — 875
	25 — 1165		26 — 375		10 — 945		5 — 735
March	3 — 605	June 1 — 76		11 — 1925		10 — 375
	6 — 237		3 — 450		12 — 605		15 — 680
	9 — 850		3 — 525		24 — 1165		15 — 525
	12 — 1225		10 — 1165		26 — 1035		15 — 176
	15 — 680		10 — 975		28 — 95		16 — 375
	18 — 76		19 — 945	September 6 — 795		20 — 1465
	21 — 525		21 — 1465		10 — 945		22 — 975
	26 — 975		24 — 735		21 — 525		28 — 1165
	26 — 735		26 — 795		21 — 945	December	29 — 1225
March	27 — 1165	June 30 — 795	September 22 — 450		

Figure 1

services, facilities, personnel, livery and casket. Under the complete itemization method the funeral director would have to determine those items which make up the total selection price.

For a funeral home in the 100 annual services category a once a year evaluation is suggested. In the 200 services annually category, an evaluation should be made every six months. In other words it is a good practice to evaluate the effectiveness of the selection room after every 100 services are selected.

Step 2—On a Frequency Chart (see Figure 2) each selection made should be plotted. The first column is made up of $50 increments. The second column has listed the various units available. The main section provides a square for each selection. The fourth column permits a recording of the number of units available in each quartile. The fifth column can be used to record the percentage of caskets provided in a certain category.

Special Note: Figure 2 reflects the plotting of the 95 selections made and recorded on Figure 1.

Step 3—All services provided for families in which no casket selection was made in the selection room shall be separated from those made in selection room. On Figure 2 these services are separated by the diagonal line. You will note that in the example used 15 out of 95 services were in such a category.

Step 4—The remaining selections should be divided into *four equal* groupings. Each grouping is then known as a *quartile*. In Figure 2 the 80 such services are therefore divided into four equal groups of 20 each.

Step 5—Review carefully for each quartile:

    a. the number of units provided from which the families in each quartile can make their selection (Figure 2, column 4).

    b. the percentage of total units available from which a selection can be made (See number on Figure 2, column 5).

    c. the total dollar income for each quartile. (See Figure 2, column 6.)

    d. the average selection (indicated by the figure A871 on the bottom of Figure 2) and the median selection (indicated by the figure M850 on the bottom of Figure 2).

Special note: The significance of the Median Selection is evidenced by the fact that it is that group *below* which 50% of the families made their selection and *above* which 50% of the families made their selection. It is determined by ascertaining that group which is exactly "in the middle" when the selections are arranged in order of progression from lowest to highest. In Figure 2 it is determined by counting the 40 (one-half of 80) selections starting with the first square on the 375 unit line. Selection 40 is on the 850 unit line. Using Figure 2 on the basis of our evaluation we can conclude:

Twenty families in the first quartile made their selection from three different units representing 15% of the total selection in the selection room, producing $9,300 of income.

Twenty families in the second quartile made their selection from four different units representing 20% of the total selection in the selection room, producing $14,450 of income.

Figure 2. SALES FREQUENCY CHART

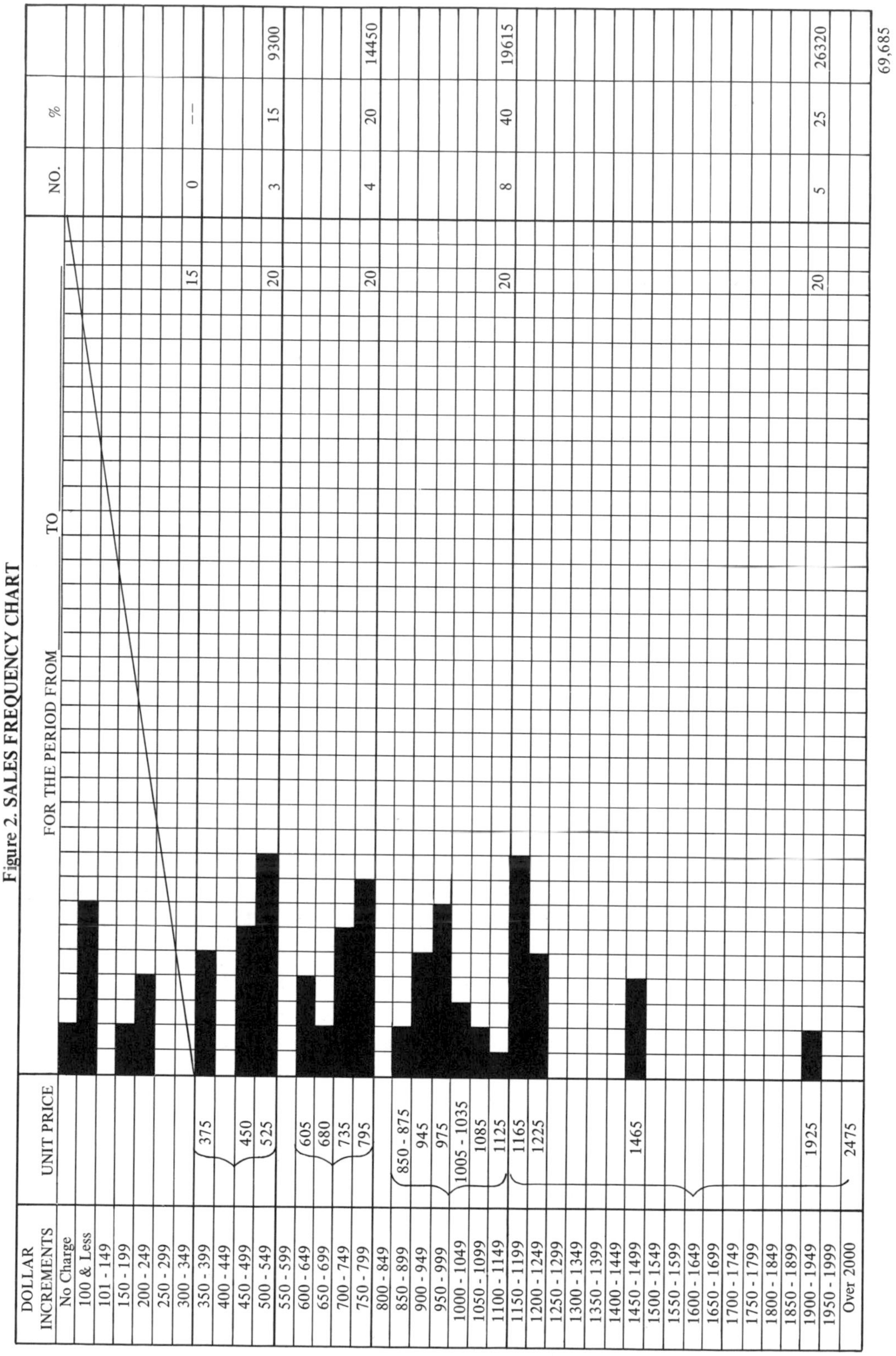

FOR THE PERIOD FROM _____ TO _____

DOLLAR INCREMENTS	UNIT PRICE		NO.	%	
No Charge					
100 & Less					
101 - 149					
150 - 199					
200 - 249					
250 - 299					
300 - 349					
350 - 399	375	15	0	--	
400 - 449					
450 - 499	450				
500 - 549	525	20	3	15	9300
550 - 599					
600 - 649	605				
650 - 699	680				
700 - 749	735				
750 - 799	795	20	4	20	14450
800 - 849					
850 - 899	850 - 875				
900 - 949	945				
950 - 999	975				
1000 - 1049	1005 - 1035				
1050 - 1099	1085	20			
1100 - 1149	1125				
1150 - 1199	1165		8	40	19615
1200 - 1249	1225				
1250 - 1299					
1300 - 1349					
1350 - 1399					
1400 - 1449					
1450 - 1499	1465				
1500 - 1549					
1550 - 1599					
1600 - 1649					
1650 - 1699					
1700 - 1749					
1750 - 1799					
1800 - 1849					
1850 - 1899					
1900 - 1949	1925	20	5	25	26320
1950 - 1999					
Over 2000	2475				

69,685

Twenty families in the third quartile made their selection from eight different units representing 40% of the total selection in the selection room, producing $19,615 of income.

Twenty families in the fourth quartile made their selection from five different units representing 25% of the total selection in the selection room, producing $26,320 of income.

The total income produced by 80 families comprising the four quartiles was $69,685.

It is important to point out that the number of units provided per quartile from which a family makes its selection is the prerogative of the funeral director. It has been determined statistically and by economists that where such a selection process is provided, a practical guide to use is that 10% of the total selections be available in the first quartile, 27% in the second quartile, 40% in the third quartile, and 23% in the fourth quartile. Funeral directors may vary these percentages depending upon the communities they serve, but in the final analysis the percentages will usually approximate the above suggestion. (In Figure 2 this funeral home showed a higher percentage in the first quartile, a lower percentage in the second quartile, an identical percentage in the third quartile, and a slightly higher percentage in the fourth quartile.)

The determination of the design, quality and price of each unit within a quartile remains the responsibility of the individual funeral director. Likewise the placement of each unit within a quartile in the selection room is left to the discretion and judgment of the funeral director. If the periodic selection room evaluation reveals deficiencies or problems an adjustment that is satisfactory to the selecting families and the funeral director should be made.

Conclusion

The arrangement conference and the casket selection each play an integral role in funeral service. The ultimate success of the funeral home, not only financially but even more importantly by service and reputation, will be dependent on the competence and ability of the funeral director to function adequately in each of these areas. Successful funeral service management demands evaluation and knowledge that can be obtained by using the procedures outlined in this chapter.

6

FUNERAL SERVICE PRICING

AN INTRODUCTORY OVERVIEW

William L. Bustard

Many methods of funeral service costing and pricing are used. This is healthy. It is as it should be in a free and competitive society.

The funeral director's "product," if use of that word is permissible, is the funeral which is a most complex admixture of services, facilities, equipment and merchandise. It is a thing of infinite variation, related to individual human beings and influenced by a multiplicity of religious, social and psychological customs and traditions. Costing thus becomes involved with many factors, not the least of which is that day-to-day demand on the individual operation is totally unpredictable. Yet supply must equal demand at all times.

In handling this involved matter the funeral home owner or manager faces problems. Among them, by a gigantic paradox, is the service-oriented nature of the funeral director himself. Another is the residue of customs accumulated during funeral service's evolution. Still another is the wide diversity of costing information and mis-information entertained by many enterprisers in all fields which may lead to the adoption of the errors of others. And these are not the only problems, merely some of the more difficult ones.

Those arising from the service related outlook of the funeral director are truly paradoxical. Both by nature and training the typical funeral director is intensely service-oriented. He may lack the specialized knowledge necessary to cope with costing problems so difficult that they challenge the experts. It is possible for him to concern himself so wholeheartedly with service that he may fail to realize the importance of the economics of his operation. In that event he may either proceed to deal with costing using only rudimentary knowledge, or he may delegate this responsibility to, or be influenced by, those whose only abilities may be financial. In either case the result could be unfortunate. If the funeral director lacks the necessary skills and knowledge he must carefully seek qualified counsel, but the ultimate decision must be reserved to top funeral service management because *costing is a part of the service function,* not an unrelated business activity.

One example of antiquated customs should suffice—the practice of relating the price of the funeral entirely to the cost of the merchandise. This has not been logical for well over a century, though it may have been when the early-day undertaker was, in fact, only a casket merchant. This is a vestige from our evolutionary past. It attempts to impose the methods of the retail merchant, who buys a product at wholesale and sells the same product at retail, on the practices of a functionary who produces today's complex admixture of services, facilities, equipment and merchandise.

That which he purchases for resale, the casket, is only a relatively small part of that which he offers for selection. He creates the balance with time and people and investment. To base his total fee on the cost of one minor component would be as ridiculous as setting the value of an automobile from the cost of its unfinished sheet metal. Today this method is found very rarely among funeral directors, but it is surprising how often this superficial thinking appears among outside critics who demand costing reforms without adequate knowledge of the problems involved.

When we come to the matter of widely diverse information and misinformation we see clearly what the homespun philosopher meant when he said, "It's not the ignorance that does the damage. It's knowing so much that ain't true."

There is a built-in conviction of some in funeral service that somewhere there is to be found a magical, mathematical computation which solves all costing problems. There is no such formula and belief in it is today's equivalent of yesterday's search for the mythical touchstone.

Frequently this manifests itself in the naive assumption of many in most fields of endeavor that "cost" plus "reasonable margin" equals a "fair price." This is perhaps the most widely believed bit of misinformation in America today. Cost alone does not determine the proper price. It never will. Cost *influences* pricing decisions, but it does not give the whole answer.

The purpose of pricing is not simply to guarantee to the supplier the return of a bundle of costs created and controlled by that supplier, plus a profit. This would grant the supplier complete freedom from responsibility for costs and obligate the purchaser to accept, without question, any expenditure the supplier chooses to designate as cost. Obviously this would not be compatible with the free enterprise system and could do serious damage to the basic concept of "a fair return for a fair value." The theory of an inviolate "right" to cost-plus is invalid, disregards the basic rules of pricing and, in a free economy, is used only with governmental contractors whose cost computations, it must be remembered, are rigidly regulated. Valid costs must be recovered but not necessarily in neat packages mathematically assigned to each specific funeral.

One of the reasons for the fallacy of this concept is that an exact cost for any product cannot be finally and firmly determined. An exact cost which could satisfy all criteria is elusive beyond description. Typical accounting systems are inappropriate for precise cost determining purposes, although the necessary information can be extracted from their data. Some accounting systems are nothing more than financial diaries. Most of them are intended for financial reporting purposes. While they serve these purposes well, they do not necessarily produce the information necessary for cost analysis, yet all too frequently they are relied upon for this purpose.

Further, any accountant and most amateurs can produce and "prove" many different costs from the same set of figures. . .and each may be as reliable as the others.

Sometimes this search leads to a most dangerous delusion. There are some who believe that by dividing total expenditures for a given period by the number of services directed there is produced an incontrovertible and exact dollar cost. This is referred to as the "average overhead cost per service." This, some say, cannot be supported by any economic or accounting logic as it attempts to impose an inflexible cost in an invariable manner on an extremely variable service. It also disregards basic costing or pricing principles as well as certain social and ethical considerations.

Those who disagree with this approach maintain one *begins* by calculating such overhead figures. They, however, use the results as only one of their guides. They are valuable in reviewing expense patterns. But such figures are only the beginning, not the end. Therefore the experts set them aside while they analyze the other factors, both financial and non-financial, which are a part of the pricing decision.

These include supply, demand, desirability, competition, competitive prices, marginal cost, marginal revenue, the effect of price on volume and the effect of volume on price to mention only a few, in addition to the equally important social, ethical and moral elements of fair pricing. All of these are added to the arithmetical computation and from this complicated mix must be drawn the correct pricing decision. All of these elements are present in every field of endeavor. Their degree of importance is variable but no one is immune to them. The rapidity with which faulty judgments can be recognized has great variations. It may be a day or a decade but it is certain.

In funeral service the relative importance of some of these factors is so low as to appear almost non-existent. As examples, total demand changes very slowly, general desirability is almost completely lacking while specific desirability is very important. Various relationships between price, volume and market move so slowly that the casual observer fails to see them, yet this movement does exist and is as irreversible as that of a glacier. On the other hand, because funeral service is a basic human necessity, non-optional and non-postponable, the social, ethical and moral elements of pricing play a far more important role than in many other endeavors.

I must risk belaboring the obvious by pointing out two special reasons why it is a fallacy to rely on what should be a preliminary guide to provide a final answer. These apply so directly to a funeral service that although they are mentioned in Dr. Charles Nichols' material which follows, I believe they are worthy of repetition.

Contemporary funeral service is geared to the needs and desires of the vast majority of the public. This is logical and proper. The response of this majority has proven their desire and ability to make expenditures consistent with that which has been created for them predicated on previous experience with needs, desires and demands. On the other hand, if today's standards had been created to meet the needs of the minority which includes the less fortunate, the average costs would be substantially lower. Therefore, insistence that the total costs be equally divided among all clients demands that the minority, including the less fortunate, subsidize the desires of the more fortunate majority.

Secondly, the "average" cost is applicable only to the "average" funeral—and there is no such thing. The exact costs for specific funerals can be measured after the fact, in terms of staff time, use of equipment, occupancy, supplies, and the like. On such a basis they will be found to fluctuate remarkably from funeral to funeral. The majority will group close to the theoretical average but the extremes will show substantial variations, both above and below the average and median range. This remains true even after giving weight to the necessary cost of constant availability.

Unquestionably, the price must be firmly quoted in advance, so this internal variation must be accepted as a fact together with the equally inescapable fact that it is utterly impossible to anticipate such variations or to relate them in advance to any stable component of the funeral. They do exist but are wholly unpredictable. They have no relationship to any other factors, such as merchandise, other costs or total price. Nevertheless, this should be taken into account in considering whether a completely rigid and inflexible allocation of an exact pro rata portion of total costs is truly logical, just or equitable.

If one generalization may be permitted, it is this: *Only a part of the answers to funeral service costing and pricing can be found in accounting ledgers. An equally important part must come from the exercise of social responsibility.*

Records and computations are vitally necessary, of course. They provide a guide to intelligent and equitable costing, but they cannot supply the total answer. Anyone, in any occupation, who buries his head so deeply in his books that their pages cut off his view of people will inevitably make faulty judgments.

Costing cannot be solely an accounting procedure. Too many other factors are involved. The mechanical and statistical must be fitted into the philosophical and ethical, rather than the other way around.

Dr. Charles Nichols' discussion of "variable allocation" and "graduated recovery" appearing in the pages following this overview presents some very worthwhile information for those interested in wholesome costing and pricing methods. His discussion is accurate and well presented. I agree with the things he has said but wish to make some additional comments. (This does not imply any disagreement with the balance of his material, only that I limit my comments to those specific portions.)

The two approaches, "variable" and "graduated," are very similar in origin and effect. Both seek to meet the needs of all segments of society in a socially responsible manner. Both recognize the fallacy of seeking a total answer from arithmetic alone. Both provide for total recovery of total costs, which most other methods fail to do. Both see justice in allocating recovery of costs in accordance with a balanced blend of need and necessity, ability and desire. In short, both see pricing policy as a part of the service function; both require acceptance of social responsibility by both the funeral director and the community. Beyond these similarities, Dr. Alfred Rappaport's illustration of one possible method is superior for several reasons.

It must be emphasized that all examples of either approach are illustrative of principles only. They are not intended for transplantation intact into any funeral home operation. Before creation of any range the basic information must be developed from the individual's own records.

These illustrations are extremely simplified, almost rudimentary, for teaching purposes. They are subject to many variations. Much more elaboration and sophistication can be employed, depending on the capability of management and its advisors. As only one example, it is possible to distinguish between direct productive costs and the expense of general operation, such as administrative, general insurance and informational expenses and assign recovery on a different scale. Variation is a constant in competent costing.

The important point is that the examples are illustrative of wholesome principles but that there is more than one way to reach a result beneficial to all concerned.

At first glance the examples may appear to be completely arbitrary in their allocation or graduation to recovery. This is not true. Given the same basic data as that used in creating the illustrations the recovery curves can be established by management judgment, by mathematical computation, or by mechanical graph and the results will be substantially the same. As a practical matter many have found it helpful to translate the curve, no matter how it was created, to a graph as a convenience for ready reference.

It should be noted that need and necessity are equitably balanced with ability and desire. In all examples the majority returns the majority of total costs in very similar amounts. It should also be noted that those whose contribution of costs is greater receive a correspondingly greater increase in the proportion of the stable, or "direct variable" items. (Note that in the Rappaport example the increase in selling price from bottom to top is 7.38 times while the increase in casket cost rises 11.58 times.)

There may be those who will say that the variable or graduated recovery methods cannot be used with the fragmented methods of quotation, frequently referred to as "functional." This is only partially true. They cannot be used if the purpose is to eliminate modestly priced funerals and if the quotation is presented in a manner which confronts the purchaser, before selection, with a floor below which he cannot go without having charity thrust upon him. They can be used if the only purpose is to outline the various categories of costs involved in establishing the total fee. This is best done in an explanatory manner after the fact although it is possible to approach it in other ways, provided great care and discretion are used.

If confrontation with charity is not the intent, there is no more reason for strict adherence to an inflexible "cost" in fragmented quotation than in unit quotation. A full range for free selection can still be maintained. If variations are questioned, a simple explanation of the principles of graduated recovery will satisfy all reasonable persons. In fact, if the funeral director says he gives his personal charity to all who cannot pay his uniform package of "costs," the thinking person may be caused to suspect the reliability of the cost computations. There is a considerable hazard, particularly when we remember that Dr. Rappaport has said that there is no economic or accounting logic to support a single cost figure which can be equitably and inflexibly applied to all sorts and conditions of funerals.

Some might argue that the decision to depart from the arithmetic of averages is arbitrary in itself. Such a decision is not an arbitrary action. A better description is "value judgment" based on socially responsible behavior. The alternative is the imposition of an inflexible figure which cannot be supported by logic, economic or accounting practices. If funeral service costing must be criticized as being based in any degree on value judgments, it is better that these judgments be made in recognition of funeral service as an essential human need and that the fees to be charged therefor be related as equitably as possible to the known needs, necessities, abilities and desires of the total community served.

There is no purpose in my dwelling on methods or mechanics. The examples discussed by Dr. Nichols are more than adequate for any funeral director to develop a method which fits his specific circumstances and makes proper use of the data drawn from his own history and records.

The principle is the important thing. This principle is that funeral service costing shall equitably serve all of society; that it be related to people; that it not be imprisoned in mechanical computations; that it permit all persons to maintain their self-respect while burying their own dead.

Cost and price decisions are the prime responsibility of the funeral director even though the advice of outside counsel is used.

Pricing and service go "hand in glove" in a service institution. An institution's pricing policy is a clear expression and example of its philosophy of service. It must be responsive to human needs. If it is not, service could be diminished, damaged or destroyed. The most delicate understanding and most competent counselling of those served, the ultimate in expertise in preparation of the body, the finest facilities, and the greatest attention to detail can all be ruined if pricing is insensitive to its service function.

AN ANALYSIS OF PRICING METHODS

Charles H. Nichols

Pricing has been a major concern of funeral service for many years. The succession of basic methods adopted and subsequently abandoned by the field, the variety of methods being utilized by funeral firms at any given time, the current search for more satisfactory methods—mutually satisfactory to both client and funeral director—all bear evidence to a continuing interest. The social responsibility of the funeral director to make available a wide range of prices to accommodate all of the families of his service area adds to his concern. Criticism is frequently based upon misconception or failure to grasp the total situation. This serves to sharpen the issue.

The matter has been complicated by fears of violating the antitrust laws in any recommendation of pricing formulae or uniform pricing techniques. Legal counsel for groups in funeral service has often advised that decisions on methods of pricing must be predicated on individual judgment, not on collective action of any form.

In August of 1969 the Federal Trade Commission issued a letter of advisory opinion to the National Selected Morticians enabling funeral service associations to make available sound, basic information which can be used in funeral service costing. This could prove to be a breakthrough regarding a substantial problem.

Review of Pricing Procedures—Past and Present

In order to have a set of simple, easily grasped, rounded figures with which to illustrate various methods please assume that we have a funeral service firm which handled 100 standard adult services and grossed $100,000 in funeral sales over the past year. Bear in mind that we are talking about funeral service income only—not income from burial vaults, garments, urns, mileage, ambulance, or any other source.

Assume further that annual casket costs were $20,000; that the costs of rendering service and providing facilities and equipment (somewhat loosely referred to by funeral directors as "overhead") were $65,000; and that profit *before taxes* in the operation was $15,000.

Now simply hold these figures in mind as we review pricing methods, past and present.

"Historical" Pricing

The earliest known pricing procedure of the field has been termed the "historical method" of pricing. It was a simple mark-up of three times the casket cost—once for merchandise, once for service, and once for profit. Dating back before the turn of the century, when facilities were extremely limited or non-existent and the service pattern was slight, this formula worked. It returned enough dollars to do what it was supposed to do. Actually, it was born of the early casket manufacturers and represents a first application of a simple multiple applied to the casket.

It wouldn't work today—for obvious reasons. Our pattern of service has increased in complexity and cost. Our facilities have, of necessity, become more elaborate than in the days of home funerals. The method would no longer return enough dollars—not even enough to cover out-of-pocket costs. In our example, this method would bring in $60,000 (i.e., three times the $20,000 cost of caskets). Just the cost of service, however,—never mind the caskets—amounted to $65,000; and we need $100,000 in funeral sales to maintain the operation on an economically respectable basis. So "historical pricing" broke down and gradually gave way to another method.

Itemization

The method which replaced it, by far and large, was itemization. Some of the critics now advance this as a "new" method, an "improved" method over what we have. In its simplest form it meant an item-by-item listing of merchandise and service—each one individually. You might think of it as "a la carte" pricing—and it had the same disadvantages from the consumer's point of view. In the restaurant, for example, a full meal, a la carte, invariably costs more than a full meal from the complete standard offerings—what are known as "table d'hote."

The same might be said of funerals, for the typical family desiring a conventional funeral would normally be better off with a standard, inclusive price than if obliged to select a large number of different items of merchandise and service, each at a separate price. Not only would their total cost, in all probability, be higher, but their task of selection would be more complicated. Moreover, being generally unfamiliar with funeral arrangements, they might not know what items to select, with resultant dissatisfaction. Bills would be, as they were, long, cumbersome and confusing. The allocation of overhead, depreciation and profit, moreover, on an item basis, would not only be difficult for the funeral director, but misleading to the client—very much the problem of the hospital today when it is accused of charging "fifty cents for an aspirin tablet" in what is usually a non-profit operation.

Those who for any reason urge itemization by law could well be unwittingly eliminating low-cost standard funeral offerings. Thus a situation which may encourage their activity for itemization could probably be exaggerated by their insistence upon reviving a long discarded method.

To sum up this point, absolute itemization did *not* work—either to the satisfaction of the client or of the funeral director—and it was subsequently abandoned. Results of its recent revival by several states remain to be seen.

Standard or Unit Pricing

About the mid-twenties we find the beginnings of what has been variously called "standard," "unit," or "package" pricing. This method consisted of establishing a single price, based upon the casket selection but including the so-called standard or necessary items of service to meet the needs and customs of a given locality. This method became almost universal throughout the field and continues to be the most prevalent method of pricing. A study by the Batesville Casket Company, for which the field work was done in 1968, reveals that 84.7% of the funeral firms in the United States were then using a unit method, although there was a slight trend away from it. The remaining firms were using: bi-unit, 8.2%; semi-itemized or functional, 5.4%; and itemized, 1.7%. Even though the use of a unit price is fairly widespread, however, there is considerable variation in the methods by which that unit price is calculated. Let us consider a few of the more common methods.

Straight Multiple

One method is the application of a multiple determined by the ratio of funeral service sales to casket costs. In our sample figures this ratio would be $100,000 to $20,000 or 5 to 1. In our example, therefore (and this is *only* an example, nothing more), the multiple would be 5. The casket cost would be multiplied by 5 to determine the funeral price. Now obviously with this system the *spread* between casket cost and funeral price, in actual dollars, increases as casket cost goes up. This places a great burden upon the casket and has been criticized because of the highly variable charge on services represented in that spread.

Against these disadvantages and criticisms two considerations must be weighed. When the ratio is properly determined from the figures for any one funeral service operation, the method, uniformly applied, returns the funeral gross required by that business. Furthermore, the low end selections do not pose too great a problem—for such a multiple applied to a minimum casket does not normally result in too high a funeral price for the starting point of a line. The critics, when looking at the spread in a single price offering, are using a "per funeral" approach; the logic of the method rests upon total funeral service selections.

Essentially, this method employs what might be called a "per dollar" basis. In our example, 20% of every funeral service dollar is allocated to casket cost; 65% of every such dollar is allocated to cost of service ("operating costs" or "overhead," as the field is inclined to use these terms); and 15% of every dollar is allocated to profit before taxes. The approach of this method, therefore, is funeral service gross, as distinguished from "per case" considerations.

Ratios Applied to Predetermined Price

Another common method, closely akin to what has just been described, is the application of the pertinent ratios to a predetermined price. Suppose, for example, that the funeral director wanted to offer a service at precisely $860 to fit a particular level of his offerings. He simply establishes that price arbitrarily. Then, again using the figures of our example, 20% of $860, or $172, can be spent for the casket. This particular ratio, incidentally, whatever it might prove to be in a particular business, is sometimes referred to as the "MVR"—the Merchandise Value Ratio. Of that same $860 price, 65% or $559 would go toward cost of services; and 15% or $129 would go toward profit before taxes.

This method has all the advantages and disadvantages of the one just described, but it starts with the selling price rather than the casket cost, which is an aid to balancing the line. It must be recognized that both these methods—straight multiple and application of pertinent ratios—can be adjusted on a sliding scale MVR, with the MVR increasing as quality and price increase in the line. However, this cannot be done capriciously! Frequency of selection at each price level must be carefully considered, for the particular practice still must generate a certain gross as determined by its level of operation—in the case of our example, $100,000. Moreover, the *overall* constancy of the MVR (that is, over the entire sales experience) must be maintained, in our example, 20%. To be specific, $10,000 of sales at a lower MVR, say 18%, would have to be offset by $10,000 of sales at a compensatingly higher MVR, 22%. This is where sliding scales become tricky and require careful scrutiny and calculation. Notice, particularly, that the figuring must be based upon selections—not upon a particular price offering.

Markup on Casket, Plus Recovery Factor

Another method in use is the application of what is regarded to be a reasonable markup on the merchandise only—say 100% on the casket, comparable to a normal furniture markup—plus a recovery and profit factor designed to bring in the additional needed gross. This is somewhat abstract, so let's examine an illustration, using the figures of our example.

If we were to mark up our caskets 100%, using our sample figure of $20,000 for casket costs, we'd bring back $40,000 into the operation. But we still need that $100,000 gross, so we have an additional $60,000 to bring in. Since our hypothetical firm has an annual volume of 100 funerals in which selections will be made, we divide that needed $60,000 by 100. This gives us $600 which would become our "add-on" factor—not an average cost of service or average overhead, but simply a calculated "add-on." The pricing formula would then be casket cost times two plus $600 in terms of the sample figures we have been using.

This method relieves what some feel is the load upon the casket and spreads service costs and profit more evenly over the entire volume being handled. However, it poses the usual problems in low end selections. A minimum casket, say $50, using this formula with our sample figures, would mean a funeral price of $700. It is difficult, if not impossible, to start a line at $700, meet our social responsibilities, and remain competitive. On the otherhand, a $200 casket cost would then mean a $1,000 funeral price; a $400 casket cost, a $1,400 price; a $600 casket cost, a $1,800 price. It is easy to see what is happening. The MVR keeps increasing as you move up the line—from 7%, to 20%, to 28%, to 33%, in the examples cited.

Casket Cost Doubled, Plus "Average Overhead"

A method somewhat akin to the one we have just considered is the formula: casket cost times two plus average overhead. Funeral directors use this "average overhead" concept, essentially, as their total cost of service divided by funeral volume, usually confined to regular adult services. The method returns a profit equivalent to merchandise cost. In our sample figures, for example, cost of service is $65,000; divide that by the number of adult funerals, 100, and you have an "average overhead"—really an average cost of service—of $650. A casket cost of $100, therefore, would result in an $850 funeral price—$100 times two equals $200, plus $650.

The use of this method is not uncommon. It is an easy concept, easy both to understand and to explain, but it does, of course, have both the advantages and disadvantages of the other method just described, i.e., markup on casket plus add-on.

Markup on Merchandise and Service

One method which does make special provision for the low end is the markup on both merchandise and service, with provision for a supposed low-end "loss." To illustrate this method we are going to have to add one more figure to our sample set, namely, a "loss" figure, let us say $10,000. This is not an actual operating loss we are talking about, but it represents the cumulative "loss" on sales below the average unit so-called "break-even" point. Within the framework of this method, anything sold below casket cost plus average overhead represents a "loss." We are assuming, therefore, that the total loss of this kind, from low-end selections in our supposed operation, is $10,000.

Now the chief argument of this method is that the funeral price should represent a markup not only on cost of casket, but on cost of service as well, with a built-in provision for recovering the aforementioned "loss." The working formula is this:

Profit *plus* "Loss" *equals* x% of Casket Costs *plus* Service Costs. In our sample figures, substituting in this formula:

$$15,000 \ plus \ \$10,000 \ equals \ x\% \ of \ \$20,000 \ plus \ \$65,000.$$

Simplifying: $25,000 *equals* x% of $85,000. The answer, of course, is 29 plus percent, say 30% in round numbers.

Now this is how you would use that percentage. Obviously, you will wish to recover 100% of the cost of both casket and service. Additionally, in our example, you will wish to bring in 30% of casket and service costs—to cover "loss" on low-end selections and to provide the desired profit. Therefore, you will use as your multiple 130% or 1.3, applied to casket cost plus average cost of service. Again, using our sample figures, average cost of service would be $650. Assume a casket cost of $200. Casket cost, $200, plus average cost of service, $650, would be $850; $850 times 1.30 would give you a funeral price of $1,105.

Under this system you would arbitrarily provide several services below your unit "break-even" point, in order to offer a balanced range of selection to meet the needs of all, but then you would compute and recover "losses" in the manner explained.

So much, at the moment, for "unit" or "standard" pricing methods. There are more recent refinements which will be discussed later in this chapter because their underlying concepts are relatively new, even though they are essentially unit pricing.

Service Charge or Bi-Unit Method

Another method that should be mentioned is the service charge or bi-unit approach. This approach divorces merchandise from service—but, in practice, we do not find it extensively used. To be perfectly logical in its application, a charge would be made at least comparable to the actual cost of service, up around the $600 mark on an average basis. Most funeral directors who use some modification of this method, perhaps for competitive reasons, perhaps for fear of inability to justify, or who knows whatever other reasons, are afraid to go this high. More often, they will arbitrarily establish a service charge at some level they feel to be suitable and acceptable.

Now remember this: whatever pricing method is used, it must recover all costs plus a profit, and this is equally true of the service charge method. Let's assume the funeral director decides upon a $500 service charge. Again, using our sample figures, 100 funerals would mean the recovery of $500 times 100 or $50,000 in service charges. But the operation needs $100,000 in funeral sales, so there is $50,000 yet to get in income. The question now becomes—what is the ratio of that added needed amount to casket costs? The ratio is that of $50,000 to $20,000, or two and one-half, or 2.5. This then becomes the multiple applied to the casket cost. The formula, in this example and using these sample figures, would become casket cost multiplied by 2.5 to arrive at a price for the casket; then, in addition, the $500 service charge would be made.

The service charge focuses public attention upon what they are primarily paying for—service, as distinguished from the unit or standard price being erroneously viewed as the price of the casket. It must be admitted, however, that more than merchandise and pure personal service is involved. There is the use of facilities, representing a considerable investment in the funeral home or mortuary. There is the use of equipment, particularly automotive equipment, which again constitutes a heavy investment by the funeral director.

Functional Pricing

These latter considerations have led to a recent emphasis upon so-called "functional pricing" (or "multi-unit"). Upon analysis this seems not so much a new method as modification of unit pricing with some aspects of itemization. What you have, normally, is a breakdown or itemizing of the unit price into several components—three or more, but quite typically four, including casket, service, facilities and automotives. When reassembled into a total, therefore, you have a unit price.

Invariably under this method the casket is sold separately and usually with a realistic markup such as would apply to an item of furniture. Then the average cost of rendering service plus the average profit sought (both usually calculated on the basis of functional services only) is broken down into the functional components on the basis of the firm's applicable ratios. This breakdown might read, for example (apart from the casket as selected):

Professional and Staff Services	$331.00
Use of Funeral Home and Facilities	274.00
Use of Automotive Equipment	105.00

The important addition of this method, therefore, is the descriptive breakdown. It lets the client know what he is paying for—how many dollars for the casket, how much for the service, how much for the use of the facilities, and how much for the funeral cars. It adds informational utility.

As with unit pricing, there can be considerable variety of approach in determining the dollar breakdown of components (or "functions" performed and/or provided by the funeral home). The basic approach is to determine the total number of dollars to be generated by functional selections, divide by the number of functional selections anticipated, and then break down this resulting quotient, as determined by the applicable firm ratios, into specific component prices. For example, if a firm determined that it needed $71,000 from functional sales (i.e., from service, facilities and automotives) to provide for cost of operation and desired profits; and if that firm was doing 100 cases annually on a functional basis; then $71,000 divided by 100 would equal $710 to be charged for each of these functional services (apart from merchandise). If, further, from its accounting records and appropriate computations, the firm calculated that 46.6% of this $710 should go for service, 38.6% for facilities, and 14.8% for automotives, then the breakdown resulting would be approximately that of the example cited above.

The key figure, therefore, is the total number of dollars to be generated by functional selections. Frequently this is determined simply by deducting from projected gross sales *all* income that is not to be ascribed to the functional components, including, however, casket sales. This means that such items of income as casket sales, income from unit sales, children's funerals, welfare, vault, clothing, and forwarding services involving no merchandise, would all be deducted. Profit, of course, is included in the projected gross, and the projection is based upon the firm's actual selections experience coupled with any forecast change.

As with any pricing method, there seem to be both advantages and disadvantages. Casket value becomes obvious when merchandise stands alone. Service is perhaps properly elevated in importance. But the low end is still a problem. There is still the matter of the funeral director's community obligation. To meet this some funeral directors will offer several selections, perhaps as many as four or five, on a unit price basis, below that level where functional pricing goes into effect. Income from such unit sales is then deducted from the projected gross, in the manner explained above. However it is done, some provision must be made for the less fortunate families without causing them to feel humiliated, incapable of paying their own way, or objects of the funeral director's charity. The system rather implies that one is in this category if he cannot pay for the casket selected plus the component prices for services, facilities, and automotives. And there are such families. The long-term public relations effects of the method therefore must bear careful watching.

Normally there is no expectation by the funeral director that the client will exclude any one of the major components and expect a corresponding reduction. Literally, the term implies pricing according to specific functions—and if a client were to reject any one or more of the functions, what alternative would the funeral director have? The answer probably lies in the inclusion of only *necessary* services in the standard, or unit, or functional price. For example, some kind of casket is normally required on every service. The use of funeral cars is essential for transportation of the body. At least some minimal use of the funeral home is involved in every instance, if nothing more than a central point from which to operate. The same is true of services, even with some exclusions; there are permits, arrangements, notices, and counselling. And the factor of readiness or availability should not be overlooked. It is costly to have staff and facilities standing by every hour, day and night, week in and week out, Sundays and holidays not excluded, ready to serve when needed. What we are saying is that there are certain justified charges for basic services which simply cannot be eliminated. Such, then, are the justifications for functional pricing or unit pricing when components are challenged. As long as people want to exercise choices as to facilities, services and merchandise, all except the less fortunate must share in the cost of making such choices available.

Objectives of Pricing

At this point it might be well to pause and raise the question, "What do we seek in a pricing method?" We have reviewed so many possibilities that the net result might be sheer confusion. The critics of the funeral haven't helped matters either. Usually without any real knowledge of our pricing procedures—without any understanding of the problems involved—they are sharp and glib in their criticisms, but they never suggest any solutions! We can approach an answer to this question from two points of view—that of the public, and that of the funeral director.

Where funeral prices are concerned, certainly the public has a right to choose from an adequate range of selection with complete freedom of choice. The public is equally entitled to equitable charges for services received. The public expects and is entitled to receive fair merchandise value in terms of the price paid. Finally, the public has the right to understand funeral prices, to know what prices they are paying, what those prices include or do not include, and how they are established. Fulfillment of these reasonable expectations, it certainly seems, would result in public satisfaction where funeral service pricing is concerned.

Now, from the funeral director's point of view, there are these equally logical and reasonable expectations. First, the price must certainly recover the cost of the funeral merchandise provided. Second, in addition, the price—if not individually, at least on an over-the-line basis—must recover all of the costs of providing service. The service costs include those of "using up" both facilities and equipment, usually termed depreciation. Depreciation must be recovered in order to perpetuate the operation. Third, the price should provide a reasonable profit; and considering the substantial investment and capital risk involved, certainly 15% before taxes would be a fair and reasonable profit. This should not be confused with defensible salaries paid to active owners, partners, or corporation officers for these are part of the cost of rendering service.

In all these things, from the funeral director's point of view, funeral prices should provide satisfaction to those he serves, and for a very selfish reason. He wants those families to come back to him on future occasions of need. Satisfaction, therefore, is a mutual objective both for the public and for the funeral director.

Public Wants in a Funeral

Change is inevitable, but those things of value are not likely to change in essence. Pricing is not likely to be changed by such considerations as: whether the casket is open or closed; whether there are shifts in public preference where time of the funeral is concerned; whether the remains are taken to the cemetery or to the crematory: whether Humanist services replace religious rites for the non-church-connected; whether there is a resurgence of church funerals in contrast with some recent trends; whether the eulogy gives way to a revitalized funeral sermon. All these changes and others have been suggested by some critics of the modern American funeral. Most do little to alter the essential ingredients of the traditional pattern because such ingredients are proving to be functional and contemporary.

For most people, therefore, a unit price will probably seem best. Any of the unit methods satisfactory to the firm and its clientele might be used—although some of the more recent refinements, discussed later in this chapter, should be considered. Not only should the method meet the expectations of both public and funeral director, as previously developed, but it should be independently determined. In our competitive free-enterprise system the funeral director sets his own prices. As pointed out previously, the law prohibits collusion, so price levels become his private affair. Competition remains the controlling factor, as it is intended to be.

That leaves us with the limited few who do not want, or who think they should not have, the conventional funeral. These are the people who object to the standard approach, who don't want the whole package. They are a minority, but they must be served and served fairly, both where their interests and those of the funeral directors are concerned. For this group there is probably no other approach than some form of deduction from unit price, or some form of itemization, based upon what they want and freely select. This, whether a deletion from unit price or an addition in itemization, might involve: embalming at a flat professional fee; casket at a defensible markup apart from service; service at a man-hour rate; livery at prevailing local scales and facilities as selected on a predetermined rate basis. If a unit method of pricing is employed by the firm it would seem more logical to use a system of deduction from unit price rather than itemization. It is important, however, regardless of which, that this kind of limited service and pricing not be grudgingly offered, or it will be self-defeating. Neither should it be forced upon the worthy poor. It should be intended only for those well able to pay, but who do not wish that which has been called the conventional or the customary or the traditional funeral.

Obviously, too, such cases should not be figured in totals for establishing unit prices. They are in effect partial services and should be so considered and so treated. Needless to say, they should carry their own weight for the limited services involved. It would be well to repeat here that *all who are selecting a funeral should be able to choose the aspects of service they want. In doing so all except the less fortunate must share in the cost of making the choices available.*

Variable Allocation of Overhead or Cost of Operation

Many of the pricing methods presented up to this point are historical in the sense that they were introduced some time ago, even though still being used, with modification, up to the present time. Recently, however, in recognition of the continuing problems where funeral pricing is concerned, some interesting and valuable new concepts have been introduced.

One of these, the idea of a variable allocation of overhead over the line, is the concept of W. L. Bustard with whom I share this chapter. The terminology and explanation here presented, however, is strictly that of the author who assumes any and all responsibility for shortcomings in the presentation.

The rationale of this concept is very thought provoking. Many funeral directors will attempt to apply their "average overhead"—more exactly, their average cost of rendering service—as a pricing factor at every level of their offering. In other words, they attempt to treat their average cost of services as an actual cost of service on every funeral. The facts in many instances do not justify this, for some funerals require much in the way of service and use of facilities, others relatively little. Admittedly, however, it is difficult to pinpoint these variations in terms of selection, in advance, for pricing purposes. Essentially some should be paying more, and others less, than the average would indicate.

When serving a "mixed" clientele as most funeral homes or mortuaries do, the funeral director must gauge the level of his operation to the needs, wishes and often demands of the majority of people in the community served. The location and excellence of his facilities and its appointments and the comprehensiveness of his service, including the competence of his staff, are all a part of this picture. Now, when a family which could not be looked upon as being in that "majority," because of less ability to pay, experiences a death it should not be expected to pay more than it can afford. What the family is provided in essence was not planned for it and the family should not be financially penalized therefore. It should be given a price advantage.

Looking at this another way we could call this a "noblesse oblige" situation. As the needs and wants of those who can afford them are met in an appropriate manner, some of what these persons pay for their funerals helps make services and facilities available to the less fortunate at prices they or friends or an agency of the government can afford. Therefore, according to this rationale, let the so-called overhead or cost of service be allocated in some manner from low to high.

As an example of just one possibility, consider this hypothetical illustration:

Annual Volume—200	*Annual Overhead—$100,000*			*Average Overhead—$500*
Selection Category:	$200–$450	$451–$650	$651–$1100	$1101–Up
% of Volume in Category:	10%	20%	55%	15%
No. of Funerals in Category	20	40	110	30
% of Total Overhead Allocated:	5%	15%	. . . . 80%	
$ of Total Overhead Allocated:	$5,000	$15,000	$80,000	
$ of Overhead per Service:	$ 250	$ 375	$ 570	

The above categories of selections should not be interpreted as fixed or representative of every firm. It would be incumbent upon each funeral director to analyze his own experience and thus determine what allocation best fitted his own clientele. Interpreting the above example, even though 10% of the selections fell between $200 and $450, the firm was going to attempt to recover only 5% of its total overhead in this category of business; 5% of $100,000 would be $5,000 and this is divided by the 20 cases in the category to arrive at a $250 overhead allocation per funeral. With precisely the same procedure the other allocations worked out at $375 and $570 for higher levels in the line. In this example, the lower 30% of volume receives a break on the average overhead of $500, and the upper 70% of volume pays something more than the average. This is in keeping with the rationale and certainly enables the funeral director to meet his community obligation more effectively.

In the actual pricing—with the resultant unit price—a markup for profit would be applied to the total of overhead allocation and casket cost. Continuing the illustration we find the following application. Again, these are sample figures and no more:

Selection Category:	$200–$450	$451–$650	$651–$1100	$1101–Up
$ of Overhead per Service:	$250	$375	. . . . . . $570	
Casket Cost—Example:	50	75	150	
Casket Cost Plus Overhead:	300	450	720	
Plus 15% Profit:	45	67.50	108	
Offering Price	$345	$517.50	$828	

The variations in approach to this method of arriving at a unit price could be numerous, but its central principle is constant—the idea of varying the overhead allocation over the line. Nor is it simply a sliding scale markup on the merchandise for the markup is made on a combination of casket cost plus allocated overhead. The possibilities of this approach are not only intriguing, but rationally defensible.

Using the sample figures given earlier in this chapter, here is another sample application of the concepts involved.

VARIABLE OVERHEAD ALLOCATION
(Variable by management decision)

EXAMPLE: Given—100 sales, $65,000 Total Overhead, Overhead per Service $650.

Sales Analysis –

Bracket	$200–$500	$501–$700	$701–$1200	$1201–Up
Percentage of Sales	10%	20%	55%	15%
Number of Sales	10	20	55	15
Ascribed Percentage of Total Overhead	5%	15%	60%	20%
$ of Total Overhead	$3,250.00	$9,750.00	$39,000.00	$13,000.00
Overhead per Service	325.00	487.50	709.09	866.66
Assume –				
Casket Cost – Example	$ 60.00	$ 90.00	$ 160.00	250.00
Cost of Service	325.00	487.50	709.09	866.66
Total Cost/	385.00	577.50	869.09	1,116.66
Desired Profit @ 15%	57.75	86.63	130.36	167.50
Selling Price	$ 442.75	$ 664.13	$ 999.45	$ 1,284.16

Graduated Recovery Approach

Dr. Alfred Rappaport of the Graduate School of Management at Northwestern University, who has been called "an accountant's accountant," has proposed a "graduated recovery approach" to funeral service costing. It is based upon a frank recognition of the funeral director's social responsibility to provide low cost funerals for the economically underprivileged of his community—a policy decision which cannot be based upon cost accounting logic. Quoting him directly, "Essentially a graduated recovery approach suggests that to make available to the public the desirable wide range of price categories, recovery of costs should be graduated in a manner which takes into account a need and necessity balanced with ability and desire."

He regards this approach as not only socially valid, but economically valid as well. Because of economic diversity within a community, facilities of the funeral home tend to be geared to an average or better than average economic level, rather than that of the lower economic group. So graduated recovery seems a fair concept.

An infinite number of plans, each embodying this concept, is possible. For ease of understanding, however, the approach will be stripped to its bare essentials, treated one by one, and reassembled into a meaningful example.

As the term implies, the heart of the approach is the graduation of recovery; so as a matter of priority we tackle this principle first (although it is but one part of the total concept). Assume that we are applying this principle to an average "overhead"—i.e., average operating expense or average cost of rendering service—$620. For this simplified example, then, we want to graduate this figure over our line—successively lower as we move toward the low end from our median, successively and compensatingly higher as we move from the median scale toward the high end of the line. Obviously, frequency of selection at each level of the offering is going to be a consideration. Obviously, too, we wish to recover the total amount of our overhead or operating expense. To illustrate, again extremely simplified, study the following example which assumes 36 selections from 11 offerings distributed in a perfect bell-shaped curve. (Of course, nothing quite so simple or so perfect is likely to occur.)

Average Overhead—$620

Total Overhead—36 x $620 = $22,320

1. Offering (Low to High)	2. Projected Selections	3. Allocation Factor	4. Unit Overhead Recovery	5. Overhead Recovery (Col. 4 x Col. 2)
A (lowest)	1	.5	$310	$ 310
B	2	.6	372	744
C	3	.7	434	1,302
D	4	.8	496	1,984
E	5	.9	558	2,790
F (median)	6	1.0	620	3,720
G	5	1.1	682	3,410
H	4	1.2	744	2,976
I	3	1.3	806	2,418
J	2	1.4	868	1,736
K (highest)	1	1.5	930	930
Total	36			$22,320

Reviewing the example, in Column 1 eleven caskets of the line, designated by letters, are arranged progressively from the minimum, Casket A, to the top offering, Casket K. In Column 2 we have projected our anticipated sales at each level of the offering—only one *expected* selection for Casket A, two for Casket B, on up to six anticipated selections for Casket F; anticipated selections then decline with each higher offering above the middle of the projection (Casket F) till we are back to just one anticipated selection for our top offering, Casket K. Altogether, there are 36 anticipated selections.

Column 3 is critical to the approach, what has been designated the "Allocation Factor." Notice that a factor of 1.0 has been assigned to the anticipated median selection, Casket F. This means "one average overhead" or, in the example, $620, specified in Column 4 as *"Unit* Overhead Recovery." As we drop below median, to accommodate our below median families, we successively lower the allocation factor. As we move above the median, however, note that the allocation factor is raised—but just enough to compensate for the below median reductions. To illustrate, for Casket E, one notch below median, the allocation factor is .9. This means that we have reduced the average overhead at this level by .1 (one-tenth) of an average overhead. Five selections are anticipated at this level, making for a total of .5 (five-tenths or one-half) of an average overhead. We must compensate for this, so please note that at the level of Casket G, one notch above median, where five selections are also anticipated, we have raised the allocation factor to 1.1 (one and one-tenth) of an average overhead. This, in a sense, evens the score. Reductions below median, with frequency or number of anticipated selections taken into account, are offset by corresponding increases above median, likewise taking frequency into account.

Column 4, is simply a unit calculation of overhead to be ascribed. Casket A, for example, with an allocation factor of only .5 (one-half of an average overhead) shows one-half of $620 or $310 as the "Unit Overhead Recovery." Casket B shows 6 (six-tenths of an average overhead) or $372. The very top line, Casket K, shows 1.5 (one and one-half average overhead) or $930.

Column 5 is an extension—a simple multiplication of the ascribed unit overhead recovery (Column 4) by the number of anticipated selections at that level (Column 2). It shows the number of overhead dollars to be recovered at each level of the offering, considering the anticipated number of sales. Note that the grand total of this column, $22,320, does indeed equal the total amount of overhead needed to be recovered in the operation.

This particular illustration of graduated recovery is in no sense a pricing method. It says nothing about prices. It deals just with lumped overhead or operating expenses, on an average basis, and illustrates a graduated means of recovering them in full, based upon anticipated sales. Dr. Rappaport suggests a somewhat different application, as we shall see.

This leads to a statement of the next principle, projection of selections. In order to recover costs and expenses we must have some idea of what they are going to be. A first consideration in getting such an idea is estimating the number of selections we may reasonably expect—*and where in the offering these selections are most likely to occur.* The statement in italics represents a step beyond what is normally done by most funeral directors. It is not enough to estimate total anticipated selections for the purposes of this approach; the distribution of these selections must also be estimated and this is what Dr. Rappaport refers to as the "service mix." Naturally we look to our immediate past experience, that of the last year, probably, as a guide to establishing the service mix. But we must also consider any and all other factors that are likely to affect anticipated sales and their mix.

Probably the next principle to hold in mind, for application of Dr. Rappaport's approach, is that computations are based upon gross sales rather than just funeral selections per se. This sets the approach apart from just about every method discussed earlier in this chapter. The chief reason for doing so is simply that much of the expense for generating sales other than funeral service—for example, burial vaults, garments, urns, extra mileage, and others—is already covered in the provision for funeral service expense. Therefore, miscellaneous income is, in effect, handled as a credit to Operating Expense; or it may be regarded as a reduction of profit, the end result being the same. To illustrate, assume that a firm received $14,000 in revenue from sales of vaults, boxes, urns, clothing and other items and that the merchandise costs for this miscellaneous merchandise amounted to $7,000. The difference, $7,000 (i.e., $14,000 less $7,000) would be regarded as net miscellaneous income. This $7,000 would be used to reduce operating expense.

In accord with this same principle, profit, too, is based upon gross sales. The firm's management must decide what number of dollars it expects to realize as a return on its gross, considering also the relation of this return to its investment. This figure, whatever it may be, becomes one factor in the computation, as we shall see later. It is up to management to decide what figure is fair and reasonable, all circumstances considered.

The next principle involves a somewhat different classification of expenses than most funeral directors are accustomed to in their thinking. Dr. Rappaport draws a distinction between "direct" expenses and "common" expenses. In addition he distinguishes between two kinds of direct expenses—"variable" and "fixed." Altogether, therefore, you are dealing with three kinds of expenses.

Direct Variable Expenses are out-of-pocket costs incurred for individual funeral services, such as casket costs, embalming materials, funeral printing and supplies, fees to other funeral homes, outside services, gas and oil, and others. They are direct in the sense that they apply directly to funeral service, but variable in that their total increases with volume.

Direct Fixed Expenses are those which cannot so readily be attributed to particular funerals but which *can* be attributed to funeral service as a general category, such as building occupancy, funeral automotive equipment, salaries for *direct* performance of funeral service functions (licensed staff), and others. Again they are direct in the sense that they can be applied to funeral service as a category, but fixed in that they are there and must be met regardless of volume.

Common Expenses are necessary, but they are not attributable to funeral service either specifically or generally, such as office and administrative, advertising and promotion, insurance and taxes, dues and subscriptions, miscellaneous.

As a hypothetical example, we might postulate the following figures:

```
REVENUE   — Funeral Service . . . . . . . . . . . . . . $104,000
          — Miscellaneous . . . . . . . . . . . . . . . .   14,000

          — Total . . . . . . . . . . . . . . . .                         $118,000
MERCHANDISE COSTS   — Caskets . . . . . . . . . . . .     20,000
                    — Miscellaneous . . . . . . . . .      7,000
                    — Total . . . . . . . . . . . . .                       27,000
                                                                            91,000

EXPENSES  — Direct Variable (except Mdse.) . . . . . . .    5,000
          — Direct Fixed . . . . . . . . . . . . . . . .   45,000
          — Common . . . . . . . . . . . . . . . . . .     22,000

          — Total . . . . . . . . . . . . . . . . . .                       72,000
TOTAL OPERATING RETURN . . . . . . . . . . . . . . . .                      19,000


NET INCOME   —FUNERAL SERVICE. . . . . . . . . . . .                        12,000
             —Miscellaneous . . . . . . . . . . . . . .                      7,000
                                                                            19,000
```

For further clarification—	Revenue	Costs & Expenses	Net Income
Funeral Service Revenue	$104,000		
Direct Variable (Caskets & Other)		$25,000	
Direct Fixed Expense		45,000	
Common Expense		22,000	
Operating Return			$12,000
Miscellaneous Revenue	14,000		
Merchandise Costs		7,000	
Miscellaneous Net Income			7,000
TOTALS			
Gross Receipts	$118,000		
Mdse. & Expenses		$99,000	
Net Operating Return			$19,000

The next pertinent principle is the concept of budget. It is perhaps best understood in terms of an estimate, based upon past performance, reasonable expectations and sound management judgment. The approach requires that all costs, all categories of expenses, all projected income, and the desired return be provided for in the total budget. As a preliminary it would be necessary to establish what Dr. Rappaport calls a "Budgeted Service Mix and Direct Variable Expenses," all of which the following might be an example of:

BUDGETED SERVICE MIX AND DIRECT VARIABLE EXPENSES

Offering	Projected Sales	Unit Casket Cost	Other Unit Direct Variable Expense	Unit Total Direct Variable	Total Direct Variable Expense
No. 1.	6	$ 60	$50	$110	$ 660
2	5	75	50	125	625
3	5	90	50	140	700
4	7	110	50	160	1,120
5	9	130	50	180	1,620
6	13	150	50	200	2,600
7 (Med)	15	175	50	225	3,375
8	14	215	50	265	3,710
9	9	260	50	310	2,790
10	6	300	50	350	2,100
11	4	365	50	415	1,660
12	2	435	50	485	970
13	2	475	50	525	1,050
14	1	555	50	605	605
15	1	620	50	670	670
16	1	695	50	745	745
	100				$25,000

It will be noted that other direct variable expense, earlier postulated at $5,000, has been averaged over an anticipated volume of 100 services at $50 per service. These expenses are of such a nature that this averaging is equitable; actual usage of the items involved would be about the same for each service. You will notice that the "Unit Casket Cost" plus "Other *Unit* Direct Variable Expense" for each level of offering adds up to "Unit Total, Direct Variable." This figure, multiplied by "Projected Sales" gives "Total Direct Variable Expense" for each level in the last column. The total of this last column, $25,000, is then our budgeted figure for Direct Variable Expense. This is now used for creating a "Total Expense Budget" of which the following is a much abbreviated hypothetical example, based upon our earlier figures.

TOTAL EXPENSE BUDGET

Direct Variable Expenses (from foregoing)	$25,000
Direct Fixed Expenses	
Salaries (direct)	
Building Occupancy	
Automobile (other than gas and oil)	45,000
Common Expenses	
Office and Administrative	
Insurance and Taxes	
Advertising and Promotion	
Dues and Subscriptions	
Miscellaneous	22,000
	$92,000

Without careful and intelligent budgeting there simply cannot be any basis for a projected cost and pricing structure. The importance of the principle is as simple as that.

Now I believe we have arrived at the point where we can put all of these principles to work in an overall plan—assembling these various elements, so to speak, into a complete whole. Upon careful analysis the following relationships seem to be valid:

Required
Dollar
Income = Direct   Direct
           Variable *plus* Fixed   *plus* Common *minus* Misc.   *plus* Budgeted
           Expenses   Expenses   Expenses   Income   Return

All that we are saying in the above is that we need enough dollars to meet all categories of expenses, less miscellaneous income (which we are thus crediting to expenses), plus the return that we wish to budget. Remembering that we earlier postulated $7,000 in miscellaneous income (to be credited toward operating expenses) and a budgeted return of $19,000 (our desired overall return), we draw upon our "Total Expense Budget" for the other needed figures. Then, substituting in the above equation:

Required Dollar Income = $25,000 *plus* $45,000 *plus* $22,000 *minus* $7,000 *plus* $19,000
Required Dollar Income = $104,000

Since we have determined that a total of $104,000 is needed in *funeral service* income to meet all anticipated expenses and return the desired profit, and since we shall incorporate direct variable expenses of $25,000 into the pricing structure, we now know that the difference, or $79,000, must also be recovered on the 100 services. Moreover, we want to provide a wide range of prices, adapted to the service area, so we shall employ a graduated recovery factor. To do this, we divide the required total recovery margin, $79,000, by the anticipated volume, 100, to arrive at an average recovery of $790. To this figure, $790, we assign a recovery factor of 1.0 and apply it to the median cluster of anticipated sales. Below that we shall graduate the recovery factor down to a level designed to fulfill the needs of low end families—our social responsibility; above it, we shall graduate the recovery factor up to a level sufficient to return the needed total recovery margin, over the entire projected sales experience. This can only be done on an individual firm basis, more or less unique to that firm in its own particular community. Moreover, it must be carefully computed, by trial and error, to balance recovery dollars below median with those above, to arrive at the total recovery margin. This approach is illustrated in the following sample figures.

SAMPLE CALCULATION OF RECOVERY MARGIN

Offering	Projected Sales	Recovery Factor	Recovery Margin Per Service	Total Recovery Margin
No. 1	6	.3	$ 237	$ 1,422
2	5	.5	395	1,975
3	5	.7	553	2,765
4	7	.8	632	4,424
5	9	.9	711	6,399
6	13	1.0	790	10,270
7 (Median)	15	1.0	790	11,850
8	14	1.0	790	11,060
9	9	1.1	869	7,821
10	6	1.3	1,027	6,162
11	4	1.4	1,106	4,424
12	2	1.6	1,264	2,528
13	2	1.8	1,422	2,844
14	1	2.0	1,580	1,580
15	1	2.1	1,659	1,659
16	1	2.3	1,817	1,817
				$79,000

So far we have established the direct variable expense to be allocated to each price level of the line offering; we have also established for each such position in the line progression the graduated recovery per service. Now all that remains is to put them together, as in the following example, to arrive at price.

SAMPLE CALCULATION OF UNIT PRICES, WITH GRADUATED RECOVERY

Offering	Projected Sales	Unit Allocation of Direct Var. Expense	Unit Allocation of Fixed and Common Exp. Plus Profit	Unit Selling Price	Total Sales
No. 1	6	$110	$ 237	$ 347	$ 2,082
2	5	125	395	520	2,600
3	5	140	553	693	3,465
4	7	160	632	792	5,544
5	9	180	711	891	8,019
6	13	200	790	990	12,870
7	15	225	790	1,015	15,225
8	14	265	790	1,055	14,770
9	9	310	869	1,179	10,611
10	6	350	1,027	1,377	8,262
11	4	415	1,106	1,521	6,084
12	2	485	1,264	1,749	3,498
13	2	525	1,422	1,947	3,894
14	1	605	1,580	2,185	2,185
15	1	670	1,659	2,329	2,329
16	1	745	1,817	2,562	2,562
	100				$104,000

It is obvious from this last tabulation that the plan does return the required number of income dollars in our hypothetical example, namely $104,000. This total meets all categories of expenses, takes into account miscellaneous income (i.e., income from sales other than funeral service) as a credit toward expense, and returns the desired number of profit dollars. The plan is based upon projected sales at each level of offering. If they do not materialize, or if other contingencies occur such as increases in casket costs, decline in local mortality, higher operating costs than anticipated, etc., then adjustments must of course be made. Such possibilities should be taken into account at the time of budgeting the various categories of expense which comprise the basis for this pricing approach.

The principle of graduated recovery may be applied in an infinite number of combinations. Some change of terminology and some change in the order of presentation has been made in the interest of brevity and clarity, but the essence of the procedure is unchanged.

Partial Service Pricing

When the forwarding or transfer of a body is necessary for the completion of the funeral service two funeral directors most times are necessary. In this regard the Code of Professional Practice of the National Funeral Directors Association spells out the following pertinent advice:

> When death occurs in a place other than where the funeral and/or burial are to take place, most times the services of two funeral directors are necessary. Under such circumstances the family should not pay for a complete service both where death occurred and also where the burial or cremation is held.
>
> The forwarding funeral director should make an allowance or adjustment for those of his services not required and should notify the receiving funeral director thereof. Likewise the receiving funeral director should not charge the family for the services already provided by the forwarding funeral director unless there is a duplication thereof desired by the family.
>
> The family should pay for only one complete service plus any additional charges incurred because the place of death and the place of final disposition require the services of two funeral firms.
>
> As soon as the details and schedule in the transporting of remains are known to the forwarding funeral director, he shall immediately notify the receiving funeral director thereof.

Pricing Infants' and Children's Services

The pricing methods discussed to this point all deal with adult services and nothing has been said about pricing infants' and children's services. Usually these adult methods have been based upon so-called "merchandisable" cases, where the service situation is fairly normal and the client is economically able to make some kind of standard selection. Other categories, very often, are handled as "credits" to overhead, that is, to reduce the overhead total allocated to standard services. Such categories would include not only infants' and children's cases, but welfare, partial services not involving merchandise, and other cases not regarded as standard or merchandisable.

Service on infants' and children's cases may approach, many times, that of regular adult funerals, but most funeral directors feel some reduction of price level is in order. There is, admittedly, much variation and, to some degree, arbitrary decision on pricing method is necessary. A common practice is to use casket size as a basis. One recommendation is to classify with a 6" differential as follows:

Casket Size	% of Adult Overhead	Multiple of Casket Cost
2'0"	10%	2
2'6"	10	2
3'0"	15	3
3'6"	15	3
4'0"	20	3
4'6"	20	3
5'0"	25	3.5

Pricing of Vaults and Clothing

The pricing of a funeral service as such normally bears the burden of fixed and common costs, because such service is basically the reason for the funeral home. But what of optional or convenience items—burial vaults, burial garments, others?

The prevailing practice is a markup on cost, but individual management must determine that markup percentage. Many variables affect the decision. Competition is one. Selection frequency is another; vaults are used on 61% of all funerals, but individual firm usages could vary from nearly nothing to almost 100% depending upon region, cemetery vault regulations, or cemetery competition. Burial garment selection also fluctuates markedly but accounts on the average for only 1% of total charges. Still another variable is firm policy on optional item income: will it, in whole or part, augment profit or be credited to operating costs?

Conclusion

I have made no recommendation for a single or preferred pricing method. Rather, after reviewing various methods I would conclude with these tests as to funeral pricing:

1. Is it logical—is it consistent with the funeral service practice for which it is designed?
2. Is it understandable—does the funeral director believe in it and can he outline its merits for others?
3. Is it defensible—can the funeral director stand behind it point by point right down the line?
4. Is it unique to the funeral home—is it predicated on sound management principles in the light of the community being served?
5. Will the funeral director explain it to all he serves so that the good that comes from understanding will exist instead of the harm that comes from misunderstanding?

7

FORMS TO ASSIST
THE FUNERAL DIRECTOR

Howard C. Raether

There are many component parts of a funeral service all of which in their own way are important to the period of the funeral and to the mourners, especially the immediate family. Additionally, life is becoming more detailed and more is expected of those in service professions. Therefore, forms to be used as guides or as a check, or to record authorizations, are often essential. This is especially true in a funeral service practice.

Basic Forms

For many years most of the information relative to a funeral service was recorded in a large funeral journal or record book. One page was devoted to the particulars of each service with a copy of the newspaper death notice pasted in. These were kept on an annual basis, and given the date of death and name a funeral director could find all the facts regarding a service in a few minutes.

The funeral director market for these books was so general they were manufactured in large numbers.

There are still many funeral directors that use a funeral journal or record book, but it is no longer enough for record keeping purposes. It often is supplemented or replaced by a manila folder or envelope, one to be used for each funeral conducted. The envelope does not have a flap. One end is open. An acceptable size of this folder is 9½ x 10¼ inches. On the upper left hand corner—depending on how it is filed—there is printed:

Name _____

Date of Death _____

Funeral _____ — _____

The entries to be made as to the name of the deceased and the date of death are self-explanatory. The information as to "funeral" codes that service for the funeral home. Before the dash the year should be given. After the dash, the number should be that of the funeral for that funeral home for that year. For instance, the 24th funeral a firm had in 1970 would be listed as 1970–24.

It is in this folder that all or most of the following can be filed for each funeral conducted at a funeral home.

First Call Form

In the chapter which follows, "Person-to-Person Professional Service," the first call seeking the services of a funeral home following a death is discussed. Often times, especially in a funeral home with a sizable number of funerals annually, this call is received by someone other than the person who will personally serve the family. Also, often the call will be placed by someone other than a member of the immediate family. The following form or record completed for each death call received will prove helpful always and necessary many times.

Name _____Age _____

Home Address _____

Home Telephone _____

Date of Death _____Time _____

Place of Death _____

Doctor _____

Next of kin _____Relation _____

Address of next of kin_____

Telephone of next of kin _____

Name of person calling _____

Will there be an autopsy Yes (_____) No (_____)

If yes, when will body be available _____

Personal belongings _____

_____

_____

Remarks _____

A General Form

A folded card which allows for information on four sides is handy and useful to many funeral directors. It can be made up to include most of the information needed for a funeral. It should be small enough to fit in a suit pocket so that the funeral director can carry it with him on the first call if he is going to see the family then and/or to the arrangements conference.

The cardboard should be firm enough so the funeral director can write on it without a desk or table beneath.

The four sides of a 4¾ x 7 inch card being used by some funeral homes are shown on the following pages.

SURVIVING RELATIVES AND ADDRESSES

Father

Mother

Husband

Wife

Sons

Daughters

Brothers

Sisters

Grandchildren (No.)

Newspaper Notices

Name

Residence

If Non-Resident, Give City & State

Place of Death

Date of Death

Sex   Color   Single   Married   Widowed   Citizen

Husband of (Maiden Name)

Wife of

Age of Husband or Wife if Alive

Birthplace of Deceased   City   State

Date of Birth   Age

If Veteran, Specify War & Unit   Service No.

Entered Service   Discharged

Rank or Rating

Occupation   Soc. Security

Place of Business

Date Deceased last worked

How long in hospital   In City   In U.S.

Doctor   Last Visited

Cause of Death

Informant   Tel.

Informant's Address

Father's Name

Father's Birthplace

Mother's Maiden Name

Mother's Birthplace

Cemetery   City

Funeral at

Date   Hour   A.M.-P.M.

WORK SHEET

Check each item as accomplished.

Casket	$	Outside Case Delivered $
Vault	$	Cemetery Equipment $
Opening Grave	$	Grave Marker $
Hair Dresser	$	Clothing $
Death Certificate	$	Burial Permit $
Newspaper Notices	$	Telephone & Telegrams $
Flowers	$	Door Spray $
Bearers	$	Lodges Notified $
Hearse Hire	$	Police $
Extra Limousines	$	Flower Car $
Clergyman	$	Prayer Cards $
Church Expense	$	Acknowledgment Cards $

INSTRUCTIONS

Hair-Styling

Coloring

MEMORANDA

SERVICE DETAILS

Clergyman

Church .... Call for

Pallbearers

Orders & Societies

Music

Grave No. .... Plot No.

Range No. .... Section No.

Lot Owner

N W S E

The basic data to be recorded on this form can be adapted to the needs of a particular practice. Similar forms or "work sheets" have entries to show if the deceased was an aid recipient, to indicate notification of newspapers, radio and television stations, and the listing of honorary or paid pallbearers.

Clergyman's Record

Clergymen are busy professionals. Anything that can be done to assist them in their ministry following a death will be helpful to them and appreciated by the family. These are the reasons a funeral home should prepare a brief record for the religious officiant at each funeral.

The following form can be printed in advance on paper of a size that will conveniently fit an inside coat pocket. The details can be typed or printed by the funeral director and given to the cleric.

CLERGYMAN'S RECORD

Name _____

Residence _____

Family Telephone _____

Place of Birth _____

Date of Birth _____

Place of Death _____

Date of Death _____

Age _____ Years ____ Months ____ Days ____

Single ____ Married ___ Widowed __ Divorced __

Date of Service _____

Time of Service _____

Place of Service _____

Interment _____

Church Affiliations _____

Remarks _____

The information this form provides is essential for all funerals where a clergyman is involved. It is especially important where the cleric had a limited acquaintance with the deceased, or did not know the deceased at all.

Automobile List

The automobile list is important. The lining up of cars should not be a mechanical procedure. If properly done, it adds to the overall satisfaction of the family. If a mistake is made or there are delays the family could be upset and the funeral director embarrassed.

There are numerous lists published in booklet form small enough to fit easily in a suit coat pocket. A format which has proved helpful is the following:

Page 1—Data as to name of deceased and day and time of the funeral.

Page 2—Miscellaneous general information such as cemetery, clergyman, musicians, and any special instructions as to route and so forth. This page should spell out special treatment if it is to be given to anyone.

Page 3—Place to list active and honorary body- or pallbearers. Indicate whether a funeral home furnished vehicle will be used for them or whether they will be driving their own car. If their own car or cars are used give license or make of car and name of driver for each car.

Then pages should follow sufficient to list at least twenty cars in the following suggested manner:

1st Car

License or make of car   *Driver*

_____   _____
_____   _____
_____   _____
_____   _____
_____   _____
_____   _____

The car list usually can be completed with the help of some member of the family. Much of this is done the evening before the funeral, especially as to the cars of the family and close friends. The balance is taken care of as the people arrive for the funeral.

Sometimes there are those who use public transportation to the funeral home and who would like a ride to the church and/or cemetery. A couple of pages in the booklet captioned "Memoranda" or "Other Information" can be used to list these people who will be "assigned" a place in a car as the funeral leaves the funeral home or mortuary.

When the funeral service is in church and there is to be no procession from the funeral home, a "curb card" is helpful. It simply lists the name of the deceased and the details as to the driver and car for the clergyman, the active bearers and the honorary bearers. Then there is room for about twenty lines—one line per car—giving only the name of the driver and the make or license of each of the cars.

Sometimes the back side of the curb card is used to list the names and addresses for whom a car is to be sent and the time that person or persons are to be picked up.

Check List

In spite of and in addition to other forms many funeral directors use a master check list. Its purpose is to help discipline their own conduct and that of their associates for each funeral they have. Some lists have as many as 75 entries on them. Others do not go into as much detail.

The check list not only is a reminder of things to do, it is a progress report of what has been done.

In preparing a check list either of two methods can be followed. One lists items chronologically. And in the other the items are grouped under certain categories such as the following:

I Service to Family
    A. Number in immediate family
    B. Seating in funeral home.and/or church

       C. Transportation
          1. Local—police escort
          2. To another city
       D. Special attention for individual members
       E. Memorial book
       F. Acknowledgment cards
       G. Personal belongings
          Disposition of jewelry

II Additional Services and/or Merchandise
       A. Cemetery or crematory
       B. Outside receptacle or urn
          Vault key
       C. Clothing
       D. Clergyman
       E. Other church arrangements
       F. Soloists
       G. Organist
       H. Pallbearers
          1. Active
          2. Honorary
       I. Flowers
          1. For family
          2. Delivery after funeral
          3. List of those received
       J. Special organizations participation
          1. Lodge
          2. Veterans
          3. Other

III Certificates and Forms
       A. Death certificate
          Certified copies wanted
       B. Social Security
          1. Form 719
          2. Form 721
       C. Veteran's applications
          1. Allowance
          2. Flag
          3. Headstone

IV Notification of News Media
       A. Obituary (news story)
       B. Death notice (paid)
       C. Radio station(s)
       D. Television station(s)

The items given hereon are not all-inclusive nor are they mutually exclusive. They are adaptable for a comprehensive check list if one is desired.

Special Forms and Envelopes

Release of Personal Effects

When a death results from an accident, or a crime, or is otherwise sudden and it becomes the subject of an investigation by the coroner's or medical examiner's office, the emergency nature of the incident often finds the deceased wearing jewelry and having a purse or wallet and/or money in a pocket.

If the family wants the funeral director to secure the personal effects a close relative should sign a statement directing the personal effects to be released to a representative of the funeral home.

Release to Communications Media

The time element often results in the report of a death being given over the telephone to a newspaper, radio station, or television station. But sometimes the effort required to fill out a form and deliver it to the media, even if it supplements the telephone report, is worth the accurate reporting which should result therefrom.

The information can be given on a properly arranged and printed 8½ x 13½ inch sheet of paper. (See a sample on the following page.)

Check on Death Certificate and Certified Copies

The death certificate and certified copies thereof are legal documents essential to the disposition of a dead body, to vital statistics, and necessary for the filing of numerous claims.

The status of a death certificate is always important and is especially so following certain deaths. In funeral homes with a large number of services annually there should be a central source with this information. A *check* or *status sheet* has been developed to allow for an orderly, routine *recording* of each certificate in a practice. The headings of the columns on the sheet are: Name of Decedent, Doctor, Date to Doctor, Date Returned, Cause of Death, Date Filed, Where Filed, Remarks.

Funeral directors report that people will call at all hours to order certified copies of death certificates, and also call almost any time to find out when they can get the copies they ordered.

This is not a problem in all funeral establishments. But where it is, a "certificates ordered" *status sheet* with the following headings has proven helpful: Name of Deceased, Number of Copies Requested, Sent To, Where Filed, Remarks, Delivered.

Floral and Remembrance List

A printed floral and remembrance list is helpful for those funeral directors who wish to do more than put the cards from the flowers and remembrance in an envelope.

For those interested in having such a list printed to be filled in for each service conducted the sheet can be captioned "Floral and Remembrance List." Then the statement at the top of page 111 is recommended.

DEATH REPORT

Name _____   Date of Birth _____ Age _____

Address _____   Place of Birth _____

_____   Early Life _____

Date of Death _____   _____

Time of Death _____   Came to State _____

Place of Death _____   _____

Cause of Death _____

Length of Illness _____   Came to City _____

Occupation _____   _____

_____

Military Service _____   Achievements _____

_____   _____

Organizations _____   _____

_____   _____

_____   _____

_____   _____

SURVIVORS

Relation	*Name*	*Address*
_____	_____	_____
_____	_____	_____
_____	_____	_____
_____	_____	_____
_____	_____	_____
_____	_____	_____
_____	_____	_____
_____	_____	_____
_____	_____	_____
_____	_____	_____
_____	_____	_____
_____	_____	_____
_____	_____	_____
_____	_____	_____
_____	_____	_____

Funeral Services   *Pallbearers*

Date and Time _____ _____   _____

Place _____   _____

Minister _____   _____

_____   _____

Interment _____   _____

Arrangements made by _____   _____

_____   Father's name _____

Music _____   Mother's name _____

_____

_____

_____

This list of flowers and other remembrance tributes received for the funeral of _____ is for your convenience in identifying the various tributes with the senders. Many cards contained several names. However, only the first name on the card is listed here.

Two columns equally divide the balance of the sheet. The left-hand center column is headed "Sender." The right-hand column, used to describe the remembrance, is headed "Floral Piece or Other Tribute."

This list then can be placed in a clasp envelope 7½ x 10½ inches or larger. On the envelope the following can be printed: "This Envelope Contains the Cards from your Floral and Remembrance Tributes."

Envelope for Transit Permit

Many people are dying at a place other than where their funeral and/or burial will take place. Most times their body is forwarded via a common carrier. Inasmuch as a transit permit must accompany the body and be accessible, a strong clasp envelope should be used for the permit. The envelope with the permit should be placed at the *head end* of the forwarding container.

It is useful to have "Head—Permit Enclosed" printed on the flap of a 6 x 9 inch envelope. On the same side the following should be printed, to be filled in by the forwarding funeral director:

Body of_____

Destination _____

Via_____ to_____

Via_____ to_____

Accompanied by_____

Receiving Funeral Director_____

Social Security Information Card

Each year well over a million lump-sum death payments are paid by the Social Security Administration. This payment and other benefits are important to survivors. A way to remind such survivors of the Social Security program is to give them a card with something like the following printed thereon:

_____   _____
Name of Deceased   Social Security No.

We will report the above social security number to the local District Office of the Social Security Administration.

In some cases you will have to go to the Social Security Administration (give address) to make application for any benefits to which you may be entitled.

If possible you should phone the local Social Security office before you go as in some cases widow's benefits are automatically paid if the widow has been receiving checks.

Also, a phone call gives the Social Security office an opportunity to advise you if other documents, such as birth or marriage certificates, are needed.

In some cases there are no benefits payable and they can give you this information by phone.

The telephone number of the (name of city) Social Security office is_____.

Name of Funeral Home on All Forms and Envelopes

In describing or suggesting various forms and envelopes it was not continuously suggested to print the name of the funeral home and its address, or addresses, and telephone number or numbers.

This should be done. It is a reminder type of "advertisement" as well as a place or places to contact in case the individual form and/or envelope with its contents are lost.

Other Forms Suggested

There are other forms which should be a part of every funeral-home practice. They are reviewed and illustrated in other chapters. These forms are:

1. Embalming report.
2. Consent for autopsy.
3. Authorization to transport remains.
4. Release of next of kin when body is kept in a church or other place overnight.
5. Guarantee by church or other place having temporary custody of the body.
6. Assignment of proceeds of insurance.

8

PERSON-TO-PERSON
PROFESSIONAL SERVICE

Howard C. Raether

More people living today than ever before have not been intimately associated with the arranging of a funeral service. Millions of the half of America's population who are 27 years of age or less—including hundreds of thousands of young adults—have never seen a dead body except perhaps in a movie, on TV, on a highway or on a battlefield.

Derogatory publicity about the funeral and the funeral director has become prime material for many who are a part of the death denying culture of our day. To some the person most closely associated with death and symbolic of it—the funeral function-ary—is regarded as someone to be "stoned" in print and in conversation, as those who disposed of the dead were physically stoned hundreds of years ago.

The results of this "stoning" give formative young minds negative thoughts about the funeral. It also provides older minds with a vehicle to take the easy but often unhealthy way out when they are involved in funeral arrangements. This has resulted in some trends away from aspects or facets of the funeral as a public event.

The funeral is good as it meets the needs of most of those who mourn. Therefore it is necessary for the funeral director first to have knowledge about the good there is in what he does and how he does it. Then he must put that knowledge into practice step by step through all the stages he walks and/or guides those he serves.

The most important of these stages are:

1. The first personal contact with the family following a death.

2. The arrangements conference with the family.
3. The selection of the casket.
4. The first time the family views the body of the deceased.
5. The "visitation" or "calling hours."
6. The last time the family sees the body of the deceased.
7. The funeral service.
8. The funeral procession.
9. The committal.
10. Post funeral services.

The First Personal Contact

Most deaths do not occur at home as they once did. Across the country about 65% occur in hospitals or semi-medical institutions, on highways, or on battlefields. In some areas this percentage of deaths away from the residence of the deceased is as high as 90%. In other places it is below 50%.

The telephone call to the funeral home telling of a death and requesting the services of the funeral director is generally made by someone other than the next of kin. And at times it is received by someone in the funeral firm other than the individual who will personally serve the family.

This telephone call is *never* to be looked upon as something routine. It might be the hospital, or doctor, or clergyman, or business associate, or friend calling. But it could be a very upset and distraught member of the family. Or it could be someone requesting a summary disposition of the body without any services at all.

When the call comes from a member of the family, such person must be talked to in a reassuring and comforting manner—reassuring but not terse; comforting but not syrupy.

If the request is for summary disposition of the body and no funeral it should be diplomatically pointed out that such decision could result in some second thoughts or afterthoughts of regret. Or there might be embarrassing questions asked or situations develop. The person attempting to arrange for immediate disposition over the telephone should be informed that even for this the funeral director is going to need information for the death certificate and for other records and that a conference would be in order to discuss the entire matter.

Many "death calls" can be taken properly by a courteous staff member. Some "death calls" are of such a nature that they should be regarded as requiring special attention.

The First Face-to-face Meeting

The first face-to-face meeting with a member or members of the family following the telephone call announcing a death is most important. If death occurred in a private residence, a properly attired and groomed member or associate of the funeral establishment should be the first person from that firm to see the family. This usually is a traumatic experience for one or more members of the family. The employee of a service company, or the driver of the first call vehicle, should not be the first person to be seen as a representative of the funeral home. Nor should an associate or driver go with the funeral director to the door with the cot on which the body is going to be removed.

If the funeral director is known to the family, his initial presence will often result in a visible expression of grief. This is good for the survivors. He should listen and be comforting. But he should not be artificial. Sometimes the clergyman will be present also. This is a good place for the funeral director and the clergyman to start their united service in the interest and good of the bereaved family.

Only after some conversation should the funeral director get to the matter of securing various details from the family. (A form to help record the information is in Chapter 7.) He should do this casually and in a manner of discussion, not question by question like a census taker, or an opinion-poll surveyist. If information is not readily available the family should be told they can furnish it later, such as bringing it with them when the detailed arrangements are made for the funeral.

Some people may be in the room where death occurred while the body is placed on the cot. Others may leave. Often those who stay do so because they don't want to let go of the body. Because they are there they see how the funeral director treats the body of the person who just hours before was alive and was someone they loved and who loved them in return. They feel that the way the body is handled initially is the way it will be cared for from that point on.

When death occurs at a medical institution, or is the subject of a medical examiner or coroner investigation, the body is usually in a morgue at the hospital or at some public facility where it is called for by the funeral firm. Seldom does the funeral director see the family at the medical institution or morgue and hardly ever in the presence of the body. Therefore, if more than six hours will elapse between the time of the death call and when the family is coming to the funeral home, a personal visit by the funeral director to the family, or at least a telephone call prior to meeting them at the funeral home is appreciated and wise. Evidence of the concern of the funeral director and an offer of his availability is often helpfully reassuring to the immediate members of the family. When the first meeting takes place away from the funeral home, the advice previously given is applicable.

The Arrangements Conference

When the funeral director did not see the family at their home, or at the hospital or morgue shortly after death, generally his first meeting with them is at the funeral home.

By this time the death took place some hours ago and the reactions and responses to the funeral director are more controlled. But before any funeral arrangements are made the funeral director should determine, if he does not know, who is the minister, priest or rabbi of the deceased and/or of the family. The funeral director should ascertain if such clergyman has been notified of the death. If this has not been done the funeral director should suggest it be done and should offer to do so for the family.

After a brief conversation on matters relating to the death, the funeral director must get down to the task at hand. And he *should not* do this from behind a desk.

If he does not have an arrangements room without a desk in it, he should use his office but sit *with* the family away from the desk—not on a swivel chair behind it from which he may seem to be communicating in an authoritarian fashion.

If he has not secured the vital statistics up to now, he should do so. Then, before attempting to determine the details of the funeral, he should discuss the significance and values within a funeral. The funeral experience, or lack of it, and the attitude of those to whom he is talking usually will determine what should be said. Following this he can explain his services and those of his staff, the use of his facilities and equipment, and the method of pricing he uses. He should also go into other facets of the funeral over which he has no control such as cemetery or crematory arrangements and expense, memorialization regarding a monument or marker or urn, and miscellaneous items such as newspaper notices, flowers, and the like. The funeral director should review for the family the various death benefits and/or burial allowances that may be available to them such as those involving Social Security, the Veterans Administration, a labor union, fraternal and other organizations.

Before the specifics as to any and all aspects of the religious part of the funeral are decided, they should be discussed and cleared with the clergyman. This can be done either by the family or the funeral director as their representative, or by both.

There are a small but growing number of persons who are unchurched. Often they want the funeral they are arranging *not* to include any religious rites or overtones. A secular or humanistic service should be arranged for them. The values of the funeral should not be lost to them because a religious service would be dysfunctional.

The funeral director's actions must be positive and engrossing. He at no time should be dictatorial. Nor should he be defensive and apologetic. He should welcome questions and answer them completely. Then when he thinks he has provided all the information the family needs to know he should reiterate the pricing method he uses and the range of prices of funerals he has available, and then prepare to take the family in the casket selection room.

Before this time it may become apparent that the family is thinking about a funeral which omits some of the parts traditional or customary or contemporary to the community. Or perhaps they are thinking about no funeral at all, such as immediate disposition of the body.

At this point the best suggestions that can be made are those included in a brochure of the National Funeral Directors Association called "Someone You Love Has Died: Some Thoughts and Suggestions About Funerals." Its excellence merits its being quoted in entirety.

> Someone you love has died. You are about to make funeral arrangements. You must consider many things. After the funeral, you *cannot then do* what you should have *done,* but didn't. After the funeral, you *can't undo* or change what *was done.*
>
> If you are like most people, you are sad and you will go through a trying time, because for most persons there is no more difficult period than that encountered immediately after death and separation.

The person who has died was also a member of a group, large or small. The funeral can provide that *group* as well as the *community* an opportunity to acknowledge and to respond to the change that the death has brought about. In the process, some of your needs will be met as well. But experience indicates this will not be accomplished by getting things over with as fast as possible.

We have served many families during their time of crisis and loss. We want to help you as we have helped them. This brochure can assist you as it offers thoughts and suggestions while you start the period of the funeral you are arranging.

The Funeral

The funeral is a ceremony during which relatives, friends and associates pay their respects to the deceased and comfort the survivors. It usually covers a period of two to four days and takes place in the presence of the body of the one who has died.

The period of the funeral generally begins with the "visitation" or "wake" or "calling hours." Most times, this occurs in the funeral home. And there are instances, like in the new liturgy of the Roman Catholic rite, when a religious service is conducted during the wake or visitation.

The visitation is followed by the funeral service. For many this includes religious or other rites conducted either in a church, funeral home, or public or fraternal building.

Following the funeral service, there is the committal at the grave, mausoleum, or crematory.

The actual period of the funeral is usually concluded with a gathering at the house of worship, at the home of the deceased, at a restaurant or public meeting place, or at the home of a member of the family.

The "Visitation" or "Wake"

When you have a "visitation" or "wake," or what some refer to as "calling hours," you permit family and friends in the presence of the viewable body to express their feelings about the deceased. This sharing experience can be important to you in your grief. When you are by yourself, you are alone with your grief. When you are with others, "one touch of sorrow makes the whole world kin."

You and others should be able to express your own emotions. At the same time it is helpful for you to hear what the life of the deceased has meant to others, some of whom you may not even know. The visitation in the presence of the viewable body provides a proper setting and climate for these expressions.

There are those who believe that the wake, visitation or calling hours is outmoded or unnecessary. They suggest other approaches or even elimination of this custom. But nothing has proven to be as meaningful. In fact, some alternatives are totally lacking in those elements which experience and research have shown to be helpful to normal recovery from the loss a death creates.

The Body Present and Viewed

You may feel you want to deny the death which has occurred. It is not unusual to try to do so. However, it is necessary to admit to yourself death's presence, even though this can be a painful experience for you.

One of the ways some attempt to eliminate a confrontation with death and hope to avoid the pain that loss brings, is to resist viewing the body of the deceased. They say that they wish to remember the deceased as he or she appeared alive. However, for you to view the body is an important first step toward accepting the death.

If the death was violent or the body wasted away, our skills will be employed in such a fashion as to modify or erase the scars of violence or the ravages of disease. This preparation will allow for an acceptable recall image of the deceased.

It must be remembered that the period of the funeral, from the first announcement of the death to the committal service, is a declaration that a death has occurred. Viewing, when possible, is an essential part of the affirmation.

The Funeral Service

If you are religiously oriented, the funeral service is a spiritual occasion. "Weeping may endure for the night, but joy cometh in the morning" (Psalm 30:51). Most likely, you will want the service conducted at a church or funeral home with your clergyman officiating. You probably have already notified him of the death. If not, we can assist you by doing so.

The religious funeral is directed toward meeting your spiritual needs. You will want it to be public, not private, so that the members of your religious community can share with you their emotional and spiritual support and participate in the affirmation of belief.

If you do not profess a specific religious belief, you may want to consider having what is called a "humanistic" or "secular service". This should also be public to grant to your family and friends the opportunity to share their love and sorrow with you.

The Committal

Soon you will say your final farewell to the person whose funeral you are arranging. Although it will be painful to do this at the place where your earthly relationship ends—at the grave, at the mausoleum, or at the crematory, this is where the committal service should be. If it is, you will find that like other temporary "hurts" you will have during the period of the funeral, it will also be a hurt that heals.

Children at the Funeral

If you are wondering whether your children or those of other members of the family should be involved in the funeral, authorities agree that even as early as age three, children have awareness of and respond to death. They must know the truth the funeral tells and should be allowed to attend the services if they desire. They should not be denied the experience of this significant part of their life. If they are, it might have future troublesome emotional implications because they could develop a sense of abandonment instead of belonging. However, no unwilling child should be made to participate.

Some Concluding Thoughts

This brochure indicates that there is no *one* prescribed form for a funeral. You and your clergyman, if you have one, and we as your funeral director will arrange the kind of service that best meets your needs.

If you are concerned about dress, wear the type of clothes you normally would to attend a funeral other than the one you are arranging. Today there is very little use of mourning clothes, as such, by the members of the family.

You should know that there are a variety of ways in which people will share in your loss and express their love, respect and grief. Some will come to both the visitation and funeral service. Others will be at just one. Most who are at the funeral service will want to be with you at the committal. Some of those whom you will see during the period of the funeral, and others who are unable to attend, may wish to further show their affection with a tangible expression such as flowers or another form of remembrance.

The funeral is *of* the person who died and it is *for* those who live on. That is why it is important to you as well as to your relatives, friends and associates that you do not try to prevent them from showing their sympathy and offering you comfort at this time. Such expression and consolation—freely given and freely received—are beneficial to both you and the giver.

The funeral you are arranging can be an experience of value as it meets your needs. As your funeral director, we want it that way.

The Selection of the Casket

Many persons react emotionally when they first walk into the casket selection room. Some of them will be seeing a display of burial merchandise for the first time. Therefore it will be helpful to them if the funeral director tells them what to expect before they go into the selection room.

The reaction often is predicated on a subconscious picturing of the deceased in a casket. This is all a part of facing up to what has happened. It is a hurt or pain that will eventually be healed because it was felt and adequately expressed.

The casket has many functions. It is a receptacle in which the body is placed for viewing for the visitation period, for the funeral service itself, and for transporting the body to the place of final disposition. And if final disposition is earth interment or entombment, as over 90% of them are, it is the receptacle which most times encases the body in or above the ground.

There is another function of the casket. Sociologist Robert Fulton once said that the dead body is a gift both given and received. The availability of the deceased body for a funeral allows those who survive to have a service with the body present during which the body is in the last material gift such survivors can give—the casket.

The casket also adds to the esthetics of the funeral setting and if properly selected, to the repose of the casketed body.

There are many funeral directors who go with the families into the casket selection room to talk about the funeral merchandise and to answer questions. They stay with the family until a selection is made.

There are other funeral directors who will take families to the selection room and after some explanatory remarks will leave them alone to rejoin them there at their request to answer questions, or to meet with them after they have made their decision as to the kind of casket they want.

Regardless of the procedure followed, because the price of the funeral is related to the casket selection, a price card should be on each casket in the selection room. Such card or brochure should outline the services offered by the funeral home. Services and merchandise not included where a unit price method is used should be listed on the card or brochure as separate items or given in a verbal explanation.

Representations of the funeral director with respect to caskets should be as to material, construction, design, hardware, mattressing and interior. The use of an outside receptacle in which the casketed body is placed should be fully explained. Facts should be given regarding the requirements of cemeteries where they exist as to such receptacles. The various kinds of receptacles and their materials, construction and design should be reviewed and representations made as to the degree of protection each provides to the casketed body.

When a family decides on the kind of service desired the funeral director should provide a memorandum or agreement for the family to approve or sign showing: (1) the price of the service that the family has selected and what is included therein; (2) the price of each of the supplemental items of service and/or merchandise requested; and (3) the amount involved for each of the items for which the funeral director will advance monies as an accommodation to the family. See the forms in Chapter 5 which can be adapted to an individual practice.

The Family Sees the Body for the First Time

Most families will view the body if it is at all possible to make the body viewable. A tension builds among many of the immediate family for this moment. This is especially true if the survivor had not seen the deceased for some time, if death was sudden or violent, or if the deceased had succumbed to a lingering, body-withering illness.

The family should see the body for the first time in privacy except for their clergyman and other close associates they might want with them. The funeral director should take them to the casket, slowly withdraw, and then leave the room.

After the first emotional reactions he should unobtrusively return to the family's presence and inquire if the body is properly casketed. He should welcome suggestions and if they can be complied with, he should do so.

If the body is to be repositioned, or the hair changed, or some further cosmetizing done, the funeral director should ask the family to leave momentarily while he makes the changes. After he has done this, he should ask the person or persons making the suggestion to see the body again. Only if the changes are satisfactory, or if there is nothing else that can be done, should the visitation, or wake, or calling hours begin.

The Visitation or Calling Hours

During the visitation, or the wake, or the calling hours, the funeral director should be available but unnoticed. When the family knows he is there and the visitation is underway, unless called by the family, he should not come into their midst and ask if everything is alright.

Many times some floral pieces will arrive after the visitation is begun. They should be placed but with the least possible interruption to the overall scene. It is best for all the floral pieces which are a part of the casket setting to be placed before the family arrives. After that the casket setting should be disturbed only at the request of, or with the permission of, the family.

The funeral director or a member of his staff should check occasionally for petals or leaves from flowers or plants that may drop or for water that might be leaking from a flower container. Tidying up is important, but it should be done as unnoticed as possible and certainly not with a vacuum cleaner or carpet sweeper while there is someone present.

By this time in the funeral period the funeral director will know if any family member is overwrought with grief, or is upset to the point where he may become hysterical or faint, or get "trance" like. He should be alert to such a situation and tell his staff. He also should tell the clergyman who may want to minister to the person or persons. In unusual cases a physician might have to be called.

Of course, during the entire period of the funeral the funeral director will be looking for a member of the family or a friend who has a supportive attitude and talent that can be enlisted.

Seeing the Body of the Deceased the Last Time

A growing number of authorities are recommending that when the funeral service is a religious rite the viewing should be completed before the religious service begins and the casket closed for the service and from that point on. Others believe in the custom of keeping the casket open during the religious service and closing it after a final reviewal of the body.

Whatever the situation, the family usually will want to have an opportunity to see the body of the deceased for the last time. Sometimes they will want their "leave taking" in private.

The final viewing should be encouraged. It aids in establishing the finality that death brings to that person's life on earth. It should not be hurried. Nor should it be drawn out. Some family members may by word or action try to stop the funeral director from closing the casket. But it must be closed and the funeral director must be courteously resolute in the process.

The Funeral Service

If the funeral service is a religious rite, regardless of where it is held, the wishes of the clergyman should prevail subordinate only to those of the family in those areas where choices are available.

The same general advice as given in the section on visitations applies to the conduct of the funeral director in dealing with the sensitivities of the mourners. Beyond that there is the matter of promptness, overall courtesy, ushering, and other tasks involving a sizable number of people.

The funeral director should not strut, nor should he appear mousey. His demeanor should show dignity, concern and confidence.

The funeral director should not talk loud, nor should he whisper secretively. He should speak in a subdued voice.

The funeral director should not walk around unnecessarily in the funeral service room in his funeral home, or in the church. And above all he should not snap his fingers or hiss to get attention.

The Funeral Procession

In the section immediately following there is a brief discussion on the committal.

The committal at the cemetery, mausoleum or crematory is important. The easiest organized way to get from the place of the funeral service to the cemetery, mausoleum or crematory is by a procession. Therefore the funeral procession remains an integral part of the funeral. It was one of the first and still remains one of the grandest of all parades for men of renown (the Kennedy brothers, Cardinal Spellman, General Eisenhower). It also is meaningful to others. And in some places the procession is planned with justification to go by the residence, place of business or employment, or some other place special in the life of the deceased.

Funeral directors must never underestimate the place of the procession and what it helps to accomplish.

The Committal

In his book *The Funeral and the Mourners,* Paul E. Irion writes:

> The committal service provides, as nothing else...does so graphically, a symbolic demonstration that the kind of relationship which has existed between the mourner and the deceased is now at an end.

Men and women of learning concur with Reverend Irion. They point out that when a survivor turns his back to walk away from the grave or a mausoleum, or a crematory, the setting is such that there is the feeling that the deceased is dead, to walk the earth no more. On the other hand the survivor is alive. Just this realization will help the survivor to resolve grief.

Funeral directors can play a helpful role during this traumatic but meaningful experience.

After the clergyman has talked with the immediate family, the funeral director should let them linger awhile if they want to. Their sensitivities are more important than the mechanics of lowering of the casket, or the tasks involving the vault or the mausoleum. If someone needs physical support the funeral director should give it or see that it is given. At this point many mourners need other people badly.

When Less Than a Complete Funeral Is Desired

This chapter assumes that most persons will arrange a complete or total funeral to the extent that such is possible. There will be times when there will be less than the kind of funeral most people have in the community where the service is held. Sometimes circumstances dictate this. Other times it is the result of the beliefs and attitude of the surviving family or one or two members thereof.

When the latter situation develops, the funeral director has fulfilled his obligation to the family when he reviews with them what he thinks their needs might be based on the experience he has had. If they do not concur, he should serve them as they want to be served. He should not assume an attitude of "either or else" or "take it or leave it."

The matter of cost may enter into the discussion. When it does, the advice of Dr. Charles Nichols in Chapter 6 is sound. He writes that less than complete funerals should "carry their own weight for the limited services involved. It would be well to repeat here that *all who are selecting a funeral should be able to choose the aspects of service they want. In doing so all except the less fortunate must share in the cost of making the choices available."*

Post Funeral Counselling and Services

In those sections of the country where a gathering is held at which a meal sometimes is served, the funeral director should attend, if invited, if only to talk with the family for a few moments.

As life becomes more complex there are more things the funeral director has to do long after the funeral is over. There are insurance forms to fill out, certified copies of the death certificate to get, Social Security forms to prepare, veteran's allowance request to be submitted, union death funds to be reviewed, and many other things. The amount to be done depends on the benefits available to the deceased or his family, the circumstances of his death, and the extent to which the family needs assistance.

The funeral director can render many post-funeral services but he should not try to practice law. Nor should he try to practice psychiatry. Some of his care taking comes about by doing what he can and then recognizing when the advice of a professional in another field is needed.

But one last thing a funeral director can do. Regardless of whether the bill for his services is or is not paid, on the tenth day, and about the 90th day, and about six months after death he should telephone the surviving spouse if there is one, or the next of kin, unless he sees them socially or otherwise. He should ask how things are going. If the answer is a sincere "fine," then chances are things are fine. But if the answer indicates some difficulties, he should probe further and see if he can be of some help himself, or by recommending someone else who can.

9

PUBLIC INFORMATION PROGRAMS

Howard C. Raether

A well-known sociologist told those at a symposium on death, grief and bereavement that most people usually think about death only when prompted by events such as an accident, illness or death of another. He indicated that death was a taboo subject but the nature of the taboo is changing and that soon eight out of every ten adults will be doing something about their own death by writing a will, or by getting insurance, or selecting a cemetery lot, or by thinking about or planning their future.

The elimination of the taboo is brought about for many by increased education, by an overall desire for information, by many new books, pamphlets and articles on death and the funeral both pro-funeral and anti-funeral, and by a lack of actual experience involving a death and the period of the funeral which follows.

Some of the desire for information is negatively oriented. Much of it is based strictly on a "show me" attitude. Regardless of the motivation, millions of people are interested in funeral matters today. And those in funeral service cannot look to communications media to help tell the story of the funeral positively as part of regular news coverage, feature articles, documentaries and the like. It is a fact of life that good funeral and good funeral director publicity is hard to get. The only consistent exception is the coverage of state funerals and the burial rites for other noteworthy individuals. But even in these instances developments can be given a negative twist or implication as "the high cost of dying" label is given them or implied.

A need for information exists because things are the way they are in our death denying culture. This need must, in the main, be met by funeral directors as they go about day after day meeting the publics they serve.

The Publics Served

A death creates situations which must be handled properly. Sensitivities and dispositions are as numerous and varied as there are people. Properly caring for them helps those who survive get back into the mainstream of life. Improper handling could do irreparable harm.

Funeral directors know this. They also know there are publics they serve beyond the families that call them. Among them are their staff, the professional and business men with whom they deal routinely, and those in other aspects of the funeral field.

These "publics" are served by and serve with the funeral director and help him meet the needs of those who mourn.

Clergy and Religious Groups

This group is of such importance that Chapter 10 is devoted to clergy–funeral director relations. Later in this chapter there will be some suggestions on church and ministerial association meetings.

The Medical Profession

The doctor in all but a very few instances signs the death certificate. About 65% of all deaths occur in a hospital or at a quasi-medical institution. There are autopsies and occasionally the gift of a body to medical science. Often times a member of a family will need medical attention during the period of the funeral. Sometimes someone will need the help of a doctor (perhaps a psychiatrist) days, weeks, or even months after the funeral.

Cooperation is needed between those in all facets of medical care and those in funeral service. They must have an awareness of each other's functions and problems. When a decision involving both groups is required it should be reached at a special conference, not in discussions before the family. This will avoid making a trying time for the bereaved even worse.

Agencies of Government

Agencies of government at all levels seem to be getting involved in more of every person's life. This is true as to certain things done and/or funds provided following a death.

At the federal level there are Social Security matters, veterans' programs and allowances, armed forces funerals and allowances, vital statistics data and railroad retirement funds—to name but a few.

State governments license funeral functionaries and administer the laws. Many times they also provide funeral and/or burial allowances for indigents and wards and are interested in vital statistics and other health matters. There are also county and/or municipal governments that get into licensing, allowances and vital statistics.

Department heads and their staffs, and sometimes case workers, are in key positions to facilitate procedural matters in the interest of the survivors. Funeral directors should cultivate these people individually and collectively and provide them with data that can be useful to them.

Veterans Groups, Labor Unions, Fraternal Groups

Many different organizations and groups are at times involved in the funeral and/or in payments toward its cost. Members of veterans' groups, lodges and other fraternal organizations often participate in the funeral ritual or ceremony. Membership frequently provides a death or funeral or burial benefit. Additionally a growing number of labor unions have pension programs or other fringe benefits which include the payment of all or some funeral expenses for deceased members. In most of these organizations there is a ceremonial officer, a death clerk, a benefits administrator, or some other individual whose primary or collateral duty involves deaths and funerals. These persons should be kept knowledgeable about the funeral.

Communications Media

A death is always news to someone. Some deaths are more newsworthy than others. Some are of such a nature that the publicity about them and the funeral which follows is extensive.

The funeral director's public in this area ranges from the person who takes the death notice or the information for the obituary to the radio or television commentators who are covering the story.

The funeral director is the logical person to have accurate information on the funeral arrangements. Likewise, he is the one who can pass it on promptly and accurately to the communications media. Also, if the newsworthiness or sensationalism of the death is such that much attention will be given the funeral, the funeral director should cooperate with the news media. However, in doing so he should act diplomatically as a buffer for the family during their time of tribulation. Under no circumstances should he use his position for personal publicity purposes.

In Summary

The persons who make up the publics reviewed can help families surviving a death. This is done in most cases through the funeral director because usually those in these publics are never seen by the bereaved, nor are they known to them personally.

The persons in these publics can also be important to the future of the funeral. If they feel the funeral meets needs, they can directly or indirectly speak and act for it. On the other hand if they do not think the funeral has a place in present-day America, they can openly or subtly initiate its depreciation and deterioration or go along with others who might.

The thoughts expressed or implied thus far in this chapter are best spelled out by suggesting:

1. Funeral directors individually and collectively maintain communications and rapport with the publics they serve and with whom they serve.

2. Funeral directors individually and collectively provide pertinent data on the funeral to those who make up these publics.

3. Funeral directors personally on a social basis and associationally through a meeting or meetings iron out differences and agree on procedures for cooperation.

Advertising

Advertising in many forms is much used to give the public information about a broad spectrum of products, services and events. The discussion regarding advertising herein will be general. No attempt will be made to suggest ad formats or to analyze the pros and cons of the use of advertising in various media. This is for the specialist to do, taking into consideration the customs of the community being served, the potential of the area, whether the funeral home has competition, and the purpose of the advertising.

However, there are some things which should prove helpful.

The Uniqueness of Funeral Advertising

Some of the basic reasons for advertising are not applicable to a funeral practice.

Advertising of funerals or a funeral home does not create a demand for the basic product. There must be a death before there is a funeral.

Funeral advertising cannot expand the market for the same reason. A funeral director operating in an area without competition can advertise all he wants to, but his funerals are going to be limited to those who die in the community, plus those who die elsewhere and who are brought back home for the funeral and/or burial.

Advertising can shift the "market" between existing firms.

The "loss leader" theory is not applicable. It would be unethical for a funeral home to advertise some item of service or merchandise "within" the funeral at a loss to sell another item as part of the same transaction. Some may argue the cause of the loss leader in hopes of getting immediate repeat business, but it could be twenty years before there is another death in the same family. And in many instances the family will have moved away by then.

But advertising of funeral homes is an accepted practice and its facets should be reviewed.

Types of Funeral-Home Ads

There are numerous types or kinds of funeral-home ads. Some are strictly the "reminder" type. The purpose of such an ad is to "remind" the community of the presence and service of a funeral home. Sometimes just the name, address and telephone number of the firm is given.

There are funeral homes that build on this basic information by adding the year they were founded or by stating the number of years they have been in the community.

Other firms go still further hopefully to add interest by featuring a series of famous hymns, historical facts, Biblical quotations, other famous verses or quotations.

Some advertisements go into data on government allowances, such as the Social Security lump-sum payment and the V.A. burial allowance. The basic format is "reminder–knowledge" unless the ad directly solicits veteran's funerals or implies that funerals are available within the amount of the veteran's and/or Social Security payments.

There are ads which go beyond reminding the reader of the presence of the funeral home in the community. These may stress physical plant and equipment and display their specialized services or plans. Examples of these "features" include: "Wall to wall carpeting"; "fleet of air-conditioned Cadillacs"; "burial insurance available"; "funerals prearranged"; and "62 individual items of service."

Other ads emphasize the members of a funeral home's staff and often list their names and pictures. Some combine facilities and staff presentations.

All ads have an aura of competition to them. But some are much more competitive as they get into prices and such areas as offering free funerals for public servants killed in line of duty; making statements about being the oldest or best firm in town or having the finest facilities; or pointing out that they have some service or facility no other funeral home has.

There is a trend toward a reminder–informational type ad which makes statements on the funeral, its purpose, its meaning and its value. The text runs over the firm's name or logo, address and telephone number. Copy which can be adapted for such ads is found in Appendix I. It consists of a series of twelve institutional ads which public-relations–advertising expert George DeGrace originally prepared for use by funeral director associations. They have been revised for inclusion in this book.

Some reminder–informational ads have a conventional makeup. In other words the message is written in letter form and "signed" by the funeral director. Another method used to convey the message is the question and answer format.

Radio and Television Advertisements

There are funeral homes, especially in smaller cities, that utilize radio advertising. Often these commercials are quasi-public service in nature because they sponsor the reading of the names of people who died, following which the funeral details are given. When this is the format, all deaths should be announced, not just those of individuals for whom the firm advertising is conducting the funeral.

Some firms advertise on television. Considerable expense is involved even for a spot TV announcement. The expense is greater if a well-known program is sponsored solely or jointly with others advertising services or products.

The information for a radio commercial must be prepared solely for listening. When television is used some form of visual aids must also be employed. In both instances the material in this chapter on the text or copy for ads also applies for broadcast commercials with three added considerations:

    1. The radio or television commercial is short and timing must be exact.

    2. The voice for the radio commercial must not be funereal. Neither should it be syrupy. The same thing is true of the voice for the television commercial. If the man or woman whose voice is used is also seen on TV, proper appearance and dress becomes a factor. Above all, the dress should not be funereal.

3. Readers of a newspaper can scan over a funeral-home ad or avoid it without any negative reaction if they are not interested. Radio and television commercials are different. The listening or viewing audiences are "captive" to that station or channel. They must change the station or channel quickly to avoid the funeral-home commercial. This makes everything connected with the commercial especially important because it could result in hostility instead of good will.

What Advertising Message Pays?

Studies indicate that only a small percentage of funeral homes are chosen just because of the firm's advertising. Here are the reasons given just a few years ago by families as to why they called the particular funeral director they did for the last funeral they selected, in the order of frequency: (1) Reputation and character, and church connections of the funeral director, (2) past experience with the firm; (3) availability; (4) other considerations including "had seen his advertising."

However, this is changing somewhat. More people are living and dying in cities where they have limited acquaintances. And often they and their friends have had little or no experience with a funeral firm. Previous service and location remain important. But in a youth-influenced and mobile society many of those who will be selecting funeral homes and funerals will be younger and better educated. Therefore funeral-home advertising could grow in importance and the format and copy for the ads become vital.

The research which has been done indicates there is a growing appreciation of informative ads on the funeral and the services of the funeral director. College men and women are especially critical of self-praise advertisements and dislike what they feel are "puffy" statements about the facilities and equipment available at a funeral home. Announcements dealing with a new funeral home or remodeled facility would be exceptions.

The Funeral Home as a Source of Information Programs

Authorities feel that the continuation of the contemporary funeral is essential to the success of most of today's and tomorrow's funeral homes. They insist that the need for more information on the values of the funeral and the role of the funeral director in it can be partially met by the funeral director himself with the help he gets from his associations. It is in line with this thought that the remaining material in this chapter is presented.

Before citing individual programs it should be pointed out that every person associated with a funeral home and every member of his or her family should speak for the funeral. Any and all opportunities should be used to say what the funeral has been, what it is, and what it can do.

This recommendation does not mean that those in funeral service should have a series of "canned" statements that they have memorized, ready to recite at a second's notice. This would have the opposite effect of what is desired. Rather, all should be knowledgeable about the funeral and welcome conversations in which death and the funeral are the subject matter. Questions should be answered positively—not with a chip-on-the-shoulder attitude.

In other words, when death and the funeral are being questioned or discussed those in funeral service should not become "conversation drop-outs." When they do they add to the suspicion or mystery that exists in the minds of some and they dispel or shake confidence in the minds of others and eventually in themselves.

Handout Literature and Books in the Funeral Home

All funeral homes should have a rack or table to display literature on the funeral. This display should be at a point of "traffic flow" in the funeral home, but it should not be over-conspicuous or in the way. It should be dignified and kept neat and in supply at all times. The following brochures and booklets are recommended for distribution from such a display:

"Teaching Your Wife to be a Widow" by Oscar Doob ——— (Good Reading Rack Publication)

"How to Meet a Family Crisis" by Dorothy Diamond ——— (Good Reading Rack Publication)

"The American Funeral—Caring for the Dead—Serving the Living—Giving Dignity to Man" ——— (NFDA Brochure)

"What About Funeral Costs?" ——— (NFDA Brochure)

"Some Thoughts to Consider When Arranging a Funeral" ——— (NFDA Brochure)

"Funerals are Good for People—M.D.'s included" by William M. Lamers, Jr., M.D. (Reprinted from *Medical Economics*)

Most funeral homes have a lounge or a smoking room. There are times when people want to do something besides sit, or sit and smoke in these rooms. They will often pick up anything available and thumb through it, stopping to read that which might interest them.

There should also be three or four books in the room at a place which would invite perusing. *History of American Funeral Directing* (Bulfin) and *Funeral Customs the World Over* (Bulfin), both by Lamers and Habenstein; *You and Your Grief* (Meredith) by Jackson; and *Talking About Death* (Beacon) by Grollman, are recommended. Sometimes individuals will ask to borrow a book to read. The request should be complied with even at the risk of losing the book.

On the other hand, funeral journals should not be in this room or area. These publications and the advertisements in them are written for those within funeral service, not the lay public. However, copies of some or all of the booklets and pamphlets listed for the display above should also be in the lounge or smoking area.

Books in the Funeral Director's Office or Arrangement Room

People are sometimes impressed with the appearance of books in the office of a professional.

There is good literature about death and funerals that many people don't know about and that others doubt exists. Some of the books are:

The Christian Funeral—by Dr. Edgar N. Jackson (Meredith)
Funeral Customs the World Over—Habenstein and Lamers (Bulfin)
The History of American Funeral Directing—Habenstein and Lamers (Bulfin)
You and Your Grief—Dr. Edgar N. Jackson (Meredith)

*Funeral—Vestige or Value—*Rev. Paul E. Irion (Abingdon)
*Telling a Child About Death—*Dr. Edgar N. Jackson (Meredith)
*Explaining Death to Children—*Dr. Earl A. Grollman (Beacon)
*For the Living—*Dr. Edgar N. Jackson (Channel Press)
*The View From a Hearse—*Joseph Bayly (David C. Cook)

All funeral directors should first read these books and then prominently place them in their office or arrangements room. They are impressive and "decorative."

Each arrangements room or office also should have a plaque, card or easel on a desk, table, or framed on the wall with the following message or an adaption of it:

> We invite you to discuss freely and frankly with us questions you may have regarding any and all aspects of the funeral, including our services and our fees. Funeral directors serve best when such service is based on a mutual understanding between them and those who seek their services. This should prevail during the arrangements for the funeral and until all the needs and desires of the survivors have been satisfied.
> We serve the living while caring for the dead. As we do this we help give dignity to man.

Visitations

"Visitation" means two things to most funeral directors. First, it is the period during which for a day or two before the funeral service friends may call to pay their respects to the deceased and to the survivors. In this sense, "visitation" is synonymous with "calling hours," "wake" and "reviewal."

The second use of the word is when a group from an organization visits a funeral home or mortuary at a prescribed time to go through it, to learn about the funeral, and to ask questions of the funeral home staff member or members. Church groups and other religious bodies, ladies organizations, senior citizen clubs and youth organizations are interested in arranging a visitation.

A visitation is an effective public information vehicle if limited to a number that can be conveniently handled at one time; if scheduled when it won't interfere with calling hours or a funeral; and if a program or procedure is outlined and followed.

A suggested program for visitations is the following:

1. All gather in the funeral service room or chapel for a statement by the funeral director on the purpose of the visitation and some basic data on the funeral. (See Appendices II and IV for ideas.)
2. Show a film on the funeral or on the funerals of noteworthy persons.
3. Divide those in attendance into small groups with a staff member with each group for a tour of all the facilities, including the preparation room if no body or bodies are in it.
4. At a stipulated time gather again in the room where the meeting started. Encourage questions to be directed to the funeral director.
5. Adjourn after expressing appreciation for the attendance of those who were there. Give each a neatly prepared packet of material selected from the list of booklets and pamphlets in Appendix VII.

There are two aspects of a visitation program on which there are different opinions. One is the extent to which the sponsoring firm should "hard sell" its facilities and services, as against a "soft sell" presentation on the needs and problems that come with death, and how the firm and its staff can help meet these needs and solve the problems.

On this point, present-day thinking favors the "funeral can be an experience of value" approach with a "soft sell" or subtle presentation by the sponsoring firm.

The other difference of opinion is whether to pay an organization a specified amount for each person who makes the visitation. It is this writer's opinion that if the funeral firm wants to give money to an organization it ought to be an outright gift with no strings attached. Likewise, people will benefit by the knowledge they will acquire on a visitation. This should prompt their attendance and interest, not the fact that an organization to which they belong is going to get a per capita payment if they are there.

Dedication, Open House and Anniversary Programs

There are special occasions which a funeral firm may wish to commemorate such as the opening of a new or a remodeled establishment, or an anniversary of the business.

When a new business is started or a new or remodeled building of an established business is ready for use, one or two days on a weekend may be set aside to introduce the new facilities to the public. Sometimes a formal dedication is held with a clergyman participating. When this is the case the dedication service becomes a religious service and the officiant should be consulted as to its content.

A "business" anniversary celebration can be a one- or two-day affair.

All of these events are benefited by a planned program. A dedication with or without a religious officiant should focus attention on the purposes of the structure and what services its facilities will offer to the community.

Regardless of the type of events, a definite program should be presented at stipulated times. It can be patterned after the one for a visitation outlined earlier, without the question period.

If the opening is a two-day affair one format would include an open house on late Saturday afternoon and evening, the formal dedication early Sunday afternoon, followed by an open house for the balance of the day. The "open house" invitations can be printed and mailed and/or published in a newspaper ad.

A typical schedule for such an opening could be:

Saturday – Open House—4:30 P.M. to 10:00 P.M.
     Presentation of a program at 5:00–7:00–9:00 P.M. in the Chapel
     Showing of the film "Too Personal to be Private"
       All are welcome

Sunday – Dedication Service—1:00 P.M.—Reverend Frank Smith officiating.
       Invitation only.
     Open House from 2:00 P.M. to 10:00 P.M.
     Presentation of program at 2:30–4:30–6:30–8:30 P.M. in the Chapel.
     Showing of "Too Personal to be Private"
       All are welcome

When there is a dedication the control factor requires personal invitations. For all other commemorations a newspaper announcement suffices except for those for whom a special invitation is desired.

An open house celebrating an anniversary usually is a Saturday or Sunday afternoon and evening affair. The same advice as to invitations and a planned program is applicable.

At any commemorative event some literature on the funeral should be given to everyone attending.

Speaking for the Funeral

Funeral directors should accept invitations to speak before groups interested in the funeral. Pertinent advice follows concerning appearances before each of the kinds or categories of organizations interested in such programs.

There are also suggested manuscripts for speeches in the appendices. They are meant to be models or guides. They should be adapted especially if the speaker knows the audience before whom he is appearing has had a funeral director speak before it using the same or similar text.

Ministerial and Church Organizations

Funeral directors are often asked to participate on a panel with clergymen or at a ministerial association meeting to talk about the funeral and clergy—funeral-director relations. Sometimes they are asked to appear before religious bodies at a local, state, district or even national level. However, most requests involve individuals or groups in their immediate area.

Clergymen are important people. They are opinion makers as well as ministers. Likewise religious groups can be instrumental in promoting a good or bad image of funeral service. Therefore, when a request is received to speak to clergymen or a church group the funeral director or funeral director association contacted should ascertain the answer to these questions:

    1. What is the nature of the group making the request?
    2. Is there any special reason for the discussion on the funeral?
    3. What sources of material are there available to use?
    4. Are there any films which should be considered for showing?
    5. What should be said?

When all the preliminary facts are known the funeral director should decide on an overall presentation of the funeral highlighting facts of special interest to his audience. The text of a talk adaptable to most religious groups is found in Appendix IV. The following is a list of material that can be considered for distribution to church and other religious organizations following a general type of presentation.

    The Significance of the Christian Funeral—Jackson (Channel Press)
    Appointed Once to Die—(The American Lutheran Church)
    The Funeral—An Experience of Value—by Rev. Paul E. Irion
    A Funeral Is for the Living—by Harold W. J. Earley (The *Lutheran* Magazine)
    Bible Light on Modern Funeral Service Customs—by Roderick Sheldon

Some Thoughts to Consider When Arranging a Funeral—NFDA brochure
What About Funeral Costs—NFDA brochure

A ministerial group generally wants more specific information related to the religious aspects of the funeral. The statement making up Appendix V is a good starting point.

There are some seminaries which each year invite a person outside of their seminary, religious order or denomination to discuss death, grief and bereavement with them. If the invitation asks the funeral director to make a brief statement to be followed by a discussion period in which local and/or denomination practices are to be reviewed, a suggested statement in Appendix V will prove helpful.

If the seminary administration wants an authority on phases of death, grief, bereavement, religion, theology and pastoral counselling of the bereaved and the funeral, funeral directors should look to associations to which they belong for assistance in arranging such a program. They should not attempt this kind of presentation themselves because only a very few have the background to make an adequate presentation of this scope and depth.

Appearances before religious groups though worthwhile are necessarily limited. However, a gift of printed matter on the funeral will live on in the offices and libraries of clergymen and seminaries. A list of suggested books in addition to those previously given that could be appreciated by most men of the cloth and their teaching institutions is in Appendix VII under the caption "College—University—Community Libraries."

Religious groups like films. "Too Personal to Be Private," available from NFDA has been excellently received by all denominations. "Of Life and Death" deals with the new Catholic funeral liturgy. It is especially welcomed by Catholic audiences.

Civic, Service, Veterans' and Other Groups

There are service clubs—Rotary, Kiwanis, Lions, Optimists, Exchange, Sertoma and others—that meet regularly. Most of them generally have a 20- to 35-minute speaking program. Funeral directors are often invited to give a "classification" talk, or if they desire to show a film in lieu of a speech.

Numerous lodges, fraternal orders, civic groups, veterans' organizations and religious luncheon clubs have regular or special meetings which ordinarily or occasionally schedule a speaker or a film on a subject of general interest. Funeral directors have also been invited to participate in these.

Other special groups of a business or professional nature are interested in listening to a program on the funeral.

All such invitations received should be accepted with the text of the talk or the theme of the film discussing the funeral generally, and not the funeral firm or services of the speaker.

A talk that can be adapted for these appearances is found in Appendix II. "Too Personal to Be Private" is an excellent film to be used for programs of this sort.

Senior Citizens

Over 60% of the deaths in the United States are of people over 65 years of age. Many senior citizens resigned to their eventual death are interested in funerals because they have a concern and desire for a dignified funeral for themselves. They also want to know about costs.

Most people in these upper ages belong to clubs in or outside of segregated centers. They appreciate a program on funeral and burials. The following outline of a talk was used successfully before Senior Citizens' groups in the New England area:

1. Appreciation for their request to have a speaker.
2. Why the speaker chose the funeral field as a vocation.
3. Publicity pertaining to funeral service over the past few years.
4. The need for understanding funeral practices, and the responsibility of the next of kin.
5. Funeral procedures determined by ethnic background, customs and religion. (No such thing as a uniform funeral service; each funeral is unique to the person being buried.)
6. Therapy of grief.
   a. Facing reality of death
   b. Need for expression
   c. Community support
7. Duties and counselling of the funeral director and the services he renders.
8. Structure of funeral costs.
9. Benefits available.

Youth

Youth are interested in the funeral for one of two specific reasons, or a combination of both. They want information on the funeral as a custom and as a service that they eventually may be involved in arranging. Or they may be considering funeral service as their life's work.

Youth as a group are intelligent, educated, searching and quick to express an opinion or ask a question. They take nothing for granted and will not agree to something just because it was done or said before. They also are grateful for knowledge and advice. They cannot be overpowered by a presentation. Nor do they want to be coddled up to. And they are sensitive to the needs and feelings of others, especially the death of a contemporary.

Anyone appearing before a group of youths should be prepared, pointed, frank and stand his ground unless proven wrong. And he should listen to what some youth may feel is the other side of the story.

In any kind of presentation before young people things should be said or done with which they can identify, or which relates to someone or something they know and appreciate.

Appendix III is the text of a talk prepared for youth. It can be used in whole or in part.

The manuscript for a public-information–vocational-guidance talk for career days, job fairs and similar occasions is in Appendix VI.

As to films, young people like "The Last Full Measure of Devotion" because it goes into the funerals of Presidents Lincoln, Franklin D. Roosevelt and John F. Kennedy. They also identify well with the children in "Too Personal to Be Private" and they get the message of both movies.

Millions of youth who may never hear a speech or see a film on the funeral will read about it in fulfillment of an assignment or a desire. That is why books on death, grief, bereavement and the funeral should be in every library in the country and it is an obligation of each funeral director to help bring this about. A list of recommended packets makes up Appendix VII.

Conclusion

At the very beginning of this chapter reference was made to the subject of death being taboo. While the taboo is being removed to some extent, the process of this removal is creating uneasiness in some, especially when a funeral functionary such as a funeral director is involved.

Panel discussions and speeches on the funeral generally begin with some of the audience having a "show me" attitude, some being morbidly curious, and others almost defiant. Of course, a segment of most groups will approach the presentation in a positive manner.

If the message is interesting, as it can be, and if the speaker is sincere, as he must be, most of the audience drops its questioning or "anti" attitude. They become absorbed in what they hear or see. They may not agree with everything, but they will be grateful for the information.

The same kind of reaction often accompanies funeral service literature. Many who have gotten it are at first skeptical. But after scanning, interest builds. Evidence of this response extends beyond reports from individuals. It carries into libraries and is reflected in the wide use of many of the source books referred to previously in this chapter.

The removal of the taboo on the subject of death should be concurrent with the recognition of the values of the funeral. Funeral directors have a big stake in this recognition and they should help establish or reinforce it whatever the particular need might be in the area they serve.

In addition to the other material in this chapter which should be helpful, during the past 15 years some statements basic to the funeral have been made. Funeral directors should know, understand and use these as part of their public information programs, especially the following:

- Death is too personal a matter to be left a private event.
- The casket is not the funeral and the funeral is not the casket.
- Joy expressed is joy increased; grief expressed is grief diminished.
- The funeral is a RITE for the dead and a RIGHT for the living.
- The funeral usually is the only ceremony to which none is invited but all may come.

- During a funeral love is given and not expected in return, as the sorrows of one become the sorrows of all.
- A funeral service is not something bought at wholesale and sold at retail.
- The funeral is a gift both given and received by the deceased and those who survive.
- The funeral can be an experience of value as it meets the needs of those who mourn.
- There is one funeral per person. Unless it is adequate those who survive could suffer.
- The funeral meets spiritual needs for those who are able to participate in it.
- The funeral not only is a declaration that a death has occurred, it also is testimony that a life has been lived.

10

CLERGY AND FUNERAL
DIRECTOR RELATIONS

Edgar N. Jackson
and
Robert C. Slater

Introduction

In our culture at the time of death funeral directors and clergymen are usually brought together in their respective roles in ministering to the needs of the bereaved. Because of the nature of these roles there is opportunity for professional cooperation that can effectively meet the needs of the mourners. Without such cooperation there can be tension, conflict and misunderstanding which is mutually disconcerting to those who serve, and possibly damaging to the quality of service given to those in need. It is therefore important to consider the bounds of these respective roles and the possibilities for wise and useful cooperation.

It is axiomatic that at times of emotional crises those who are distressed will be highly sensitive. They will be responsive to kind and understanding service. They will also be easily hurt and even angered by anything that appears to be unaware of their feelings or inconsiderate of them. Those who work with the emotionally sensitive therefore need to be doubly careful not to give cause for offense. They also can respond to the opportunity that is afforded to meet the needs of people at a time when they are most sensitive, most appreciative and also most vulnerable.

Because the event of death brings man face to face with the ultimate problem of his existence, the termination of it, he has almost always been inclined to try to cope with it in a religious context. Nearly every culture has surrounded death with meaningful ritualized activities that helped to verify the strength of the community at the same time that they recognized the special needs of those who suffer loss. In most cultures

138

these rites and rituals have been supervised and conducted by the religious leaders of the community.

Until recently these ceremonials have been created out of the folk ways of the people in response to unconsciously perceived needs. More recently they have been held up for examination and usually have been found to be well designed for meeting the deeper needs that are experienced in times of emotional crisis even though they may not be as easily explained on purely rational grounds. Emotions are usually below or beyond the range of rational control for they have their own validity and have to be judged on the basis of that larger human need. Grief is essentially an emotion; therefore it must be looked at in the light of what it is.

While most religious practices are designed not to violate reason, it is generally recognized that the needs of religion emerge from the deep reservoirs of emotion that dominate human experience. The quest for meaning in the face of the apparently meaningless, the need for strength in the presence of weakness, the desire for sustaining faith in the presence of doubt, and for hope amidst the apparently hopeless circumstances of life—these are the core considerations of religion. In the presence of death the shattered hopes, damaged faith, generalized weakness and the need for adequate meaning tend to put the religious community in a place for strategic and significant service to the bereaved.

The role of the funeral director has emerged from comparable needs in an increasingly specialized culture. In more primitive societies the bodies of the dead and the needs of the bereaved are cared for by specially designated individuals or groups. Sometimes these were committees of the parish. It was their function to prepare the dead for burial at the same time that they tried to ease the pains of the bereft. In rural Colonial America these procedures were quite simple and burial was usually carried out as a neighborly act by those who were compassionate friends or close relatives.

In our specialized culture what was originally done by neighbors and relatives has been delegated to those who by training and the possession of special equipment are better prepared to do it. However, the persistent emotional needs of the bereaved still remain the major concern of both the funeral director and the pastor, for it is the people who survive who have feelings and can suffer the emotional backlash of unwisely handled bereavement.

Psychological Needs

The psychological study of the needs of the bereaved has been advanced rapidly in recent years through specialized research and extended study. It is quite clear that in the light of these new insights the pastor and the funeral director need to understand each other's roles and cooperate for the benefit of those they serve.

Three important psychological needs should be met by the funeral. First, there should be group support. Second, there should be immediate and effective repair to the damaged personality of the bereaved. And third, there should be provided an effective atmosphere in which the emotions may be expressed and worked through.

Studies of the emotional impact of grief show that the person is most vulnerable at the time of death. In fact, Goeffrey Gorer says in his *Death, Grief and Mourning* that, aside from early infancy, the person who has suffered acute loss is more emotionally exposed than at any other time of life. He is in need of emotional support. He needs friends and relatives to stand by him, understand his feelings, and accept them as valid. The accepted feeling can more readily be expressed while the rejected feeling is the one that is publicly denied and actively repressed. Medical studies show that it is the repressed feeling that finds a detour into the form of behavior we call illness, while it is the healthy feeling that is poured out, worked through and resolved.

Group Support

Group support can be most readily given when people can use familiar, psychologically sound and readily available ways for working through their feelings. Here traditional practice has a special value for people know what it means and quickly and easily use it because it is for them the common language of the emotions. They can express their feelings, even those that are too deep to be put into words, by doing things whose meaning is readily understood. In this way the supportive group fulfills its function and the acutely deprived are communicated with in ways both they and the community understand.

Repair of Damaged Personality

The second psychological need is the repair of the damage to the self-image and the body-image. The mechanics of the grief process are built about the investment of emotion in another and the necessity of retrieving the part of the self that is so invested when death comes. Studies of the phantom-limb phenomenon, and the adoption process give us some clues as to the emotional process involved. The longer the relationship exists the deeper is apt to be the bereavement. And the more acute and tragic the severance the more threat there appears to be to the injured self. The need then is to find the ways by which the self can confirm its integrity and gain the strength to engage in the important but often painful task of withdrawal.

It has been found that the supportive community in the act of accepting the reality of death helps the acutely bereaved to come to terms with the emotional meaning of the event. But it is also apparent that the meaning of the event should be communicated to all of the levels of consciousness. We must recognize the varied and powerful impulses toward denial. Just as the body feels the pain in the amputated limb after it is gone, and the mother feels her identity to the baby she has placed for adoption without ever seeing it, so the bereaved person wants to live on in the deceased even though it is psychologically unsound and emotionally unhealthy to do so.

Perhaps the one most important function of the act of viewing the remains is this confrontation of the emotional fact that one is so anxious to deny. Seeing the dead body seems to break through the defenses more effectively and more completely than any other part of the funeral process. The clearly lifeless body in the symbolic setting of the casket penetrates the defenses that employ denial and brings the relief which comes when the self affirms its selfhood. In effect the person says to himself, "Now I see that he is dead and I am still alive." It is at this point that the denial is defeated, the strength of the self affirmed, and the mourning process begins. Because the mourning process takes great emotional strength, persons often use a variety of ways to avoid doing the hard work. But ultimately it must be done to preserve the integrity of being, and the sooner it is done the better it is for the health of the person. Clerics and funeral directors alike must know this and counsel those they serve accordingly.

Emotional Release

The other significant need is the focus for the emotions at the physical level for it is here that the impact of death is necessarily faced. The study of effigy illuminates the emotional processes that are employed. We tend to think of effigy in essentially negative terms as a device for expressing hostile, hateful and destructive emotions. We speak of "burning in effigy" or "hanging in effigy." However, there is a positive side to this for it is healthier for all concerned to hang a person in effigy than to lynch him in fact, or to burn him in effigy rather than assassinate him in fact. But even the emotions need not be negative, for the most common form of effigy, the Crucifix, is viewed as a symbol of redemptive love and a basis for eternal life.

Anthropological studies have revealed that the death effigy has long been in use as a substitute for the body of the dead person. In primitive tribes, in traditional English practices and in major forms of art, the effigy has been employed to make it possible for the bereaved to have a channel through which they could express their valid feelings. In England the King would be buried and the populace would express their grief for weeks around his effigy. Wealthy persons spent large sums of money while they were alive to supervise the creating of their effigy, and often preferred that their effigy be placed in Westminister Abbey rather than their dead body. The reason for this was quite simple. They had no effective way of preserving the body for the period of time that was necessary for the working through of grief, so they did the only thing they could, and that was to prepare a substitute body. Because of the emotional needs of the populace the effigy actually became more important than the body itself.

In a recent study Frank Willett of Oxford University found that "St. John Hope seems to believe that these English figures were devised because the corruption of the body made its exposure unwholesome." But the significance of the effigy was such that in time it became the focal point for the expression of grief. Again Willett observes, "Thenceforth in France the effigy became increasingly important until at the funeral of Francois I in 1547 the body went first in the procession, scarcely noticed, while the effigy not only had the place of honor at the rear, but acquired something of a triumphal aspect."

With the passing of time the value of the effigy as a focal point for expressing grief became not only a matter for the royal family and the wealthy, but its usefulness was effused throughout society. "This diffusion of the practice through the ranks of society below the king demonstrated a lessening awareness of the original ideas which the two figures symbolized." So it was no longer a device to say, "The king is dead, long live the king," but rather became the method people generally used to work through powerful emotions that surrounded the event of death.

In more recent years, through the advancement of techniques for preparing the body and effective embalming procedures, two important purposes have been served. The needs of the common people for a likeness toward which they can focus their emotional processes as the basis for healthful withdrawal is now available through the skill of the funeral director and embalmer. This serves the psychological needs for an effigy, a likeness, to realistically sharpen up the process of affirming reality and engaging in the emotional work of mourning. The embalmer makes possible the most exact form of effigy, for the body in death, properly prepared, is the real physical substance toward which emotion was directed in life. It is the effigy in function psychologically at the same time that it is the dead body in actuality. At this point the psychological value of embalming is most explicit.

But a second matter of importance here is that the processes of embalming now available to everyone make the beneficial nature of the effigy universally available. Instead of being the sole privilege of the royal family, the wealthy or famous, it is now an expression of the democratic process at work in death as in life. The funeral of any man can now be provided in good taste and dignity, and well within the means of everyone. And instead of the necessity for the quick disposition of the body with the accompanying limitation of the psychologically healthy processes of confrontation, viewing and the creative processes of confronting the effigy, the time can be extended safely for the three to four days necessary for the start of the process of the wise mourning activity.

It becomes quite clear that the skills of the licensed funeral functionary supplement the ministrations of the pastor in providing most wisely for the needs of the bereaved. Where there is wise and appreciative cooperation, all benefit from the process. Where there is misunderstanding and senseless competition, all tend to suffer the unfortunate consequences.

Clergy– Funeral-Director Cooperation

As early as 1954 programs were established where clergy and funeral director could meet and share their concerns and ideas relative to the value of the funeral and its related experiences. Some of these meetings gave evidence of mutual appreciation and respect. Some of them revealed a lack of communication, a restraint on shared information and insight, and a suspicion that could affect the cooperative relationship that could exist. The misgivings are not one-sided, for some funeral directors are apprehensive about the attitudes of the clergymen and some clergymen feel threatened by the role and status of the funeral director.

Suspicions, Threats, Apprehensions

It would seem wise to look at some of these suspicions, threats and apprehensions as basic to better communication and cooperation. Part of the problem emerges at the point where there is confusion as to the boundaries of the role played by the other. The average pastor cherishes the relationship he has with his people as their friend and spiritual guide. He wants to be close to them in their times of acute need. If he finds that a funeral director has been called and has worked with the family in making most of the arrangements for the services at time of death, he feels left out, separated from his people, and naturally the funeral director seems to be the one toward whom the pastor's misgivings could be directed. Alternately, when the pastor intrudes upon the domain where the funeral director thinks he has special responsibility, there is apt to be misunderstanding and resentment. These unfortunate breakdowns in communication do not need to exist and can be easily overcome.

One of the first opportunities that the funeral director and pastor have to work together is when the pastor comes to the parish for the first time. It would be advisable if the funeral director and pastor could meet each other before their respective services were needed by a family in the grief situation. This would give each of them an opportunity to discuss their feelings and reactions with each other as well as to share insights that each might have as to the particular needs of people in that parish or community. It is apparent that the pastor would usually welcome suggestions and information from the funeral director as to customs and procedures that existed prior to his arrival in the parish. It would be advantageous for the pastor to share with the funeral director the insights that he might bring to the parish from other experiences and situations in which he has served. It would be important at this time to identify each of their respective roles in order that confusion, anxiety and misunderstanding would not present itself at the time a family was being served.

Sometimes in order to try to resolve the role relationship with its apparent conflicts, some pastors would eliminate the funeral director entirely and set up a procedure in their parish where the funeral director does nothing but dispose of the dead body and the pastor presides at a special service often called a "memorial service" with no body present and no funeral director in evidence. Although this drastic method may reduce the possible role conflict, it does so at the expense of the people who are most important, the bereaved, for it denies them the basic elements of sound mourning practice. Paul Irion has perceptively said that the "memorial" type service puts together in one package all we have learned to be psychologically unsound and tries to give it religious blessing.

Perhaps the positive approach to the problem of role relationship is found when each party finds a large enough meaning in the ceremonials surrounding death to make it easy to subject his own part to the important total. Recent research has moved in that direction. Yet it is evident that there is a cultural lag at this point for neither the funeral director nor the pastor seems to be generally aware of the importance of the funeral for the people it serves, nor of the importance of his role in the total process.

Psychosomatic medical research has made it clear that much of the human behavior we call disease is an organic response to emotional crises. When a crises like that produced by the death of an emotionally important person takes place, and becomes chronic, the body chemistry is disturbed for long periods of time, thus limiting the body's built-in disease control system. If pastors and funeral directors sensed the importance of their mission to the bereaved, it could reduce the unwisely handled emotions and thus become an important factor in both physical and mental health.

Psychological research shows that despair which leads to major personality changes, emotional illness and partial or total suicide is often related to the loss of meaning for life through the death of an important person in the emotional life of the bereaved. When feelings can be acted out, thoughts can be talked out, and social needs be met through healthful ceremonials, an important first step is taken toward the restoration of true wholeness of being.

Sociological research shows that the larger community is more involved in the death of its members than at first appears. The ramifications of death economically, socially and spiritually are such that the community needs to reaffirm its faith in itself as a viable institution. So even the cemetery speaks of the vitality of life in the face of death, and a well-kept cemetery carries on a constant dialogue with those who pass by it, saying in effect that the community is not afraid of death but has come to terms with it in maturity and not in fear, in security and not in disorganization.

When the pastor and the funeral director sense the importance of the funeral and its varied meanings in the lives of the people they serve, there will be little time or place for working out conflict of feelings, for the important goals will engage all of their energy and skill.

Much of the misunderstanding regarding funerals and their importance to individuals and the community grows from a lack of communications. Confused ideas of what is done, why it is done, what it costs, and why it is important cause irresponsible action. There is no better way for the problems to be resolved than for all involved to sit down in advance of the emotional crisis to talk about the important questions involved, share information, and explore the importance of and reasons for active cooperation.

One of the best ways to do this is to look at some of the questions that are most often raised when funeral directors and pastors sit down together to talk. In hundreds of sessions with thousands of pastors and funeral directors the following subjects were most often raised for discussion. While there are no final answers because of the variations of local practice and tradition, there are some general points where understanding can be improved.

Funeral Costs

This is a point where misunderstanding quite often emerges. The reasons are quite apparent. The pastor has no financial investment in the funeral. He is sensitive to the overall cost that comes at the time of death and attributes this cost to the necessity of the funeral director's making a living through the services he provides. The funeral director, on the other hand, is sensitive about the matter of cost for he must make a living in order to continue to provide the services that are important to the community and its members when they need them. Generally speaking, no one wants a person to die so that he will need a funeral or the services of the funeral director. But specifically speaking, when they want them they want them immediately, usually without limitation as to quality and quantity.

The costs involved in a funeral are dealt with at length elsewhere in this book. It is not our purpose to deal with that subject except to say that a funeral director by explaining his pricing method and the total cost of the funeral to an arranging family will avoid some of the present-day criticism voiced through some clergymen.

The honorarium is one area of cost causing concern for some clergy. Most pastors have a professional attitude and feel that pastoral services can neither be bought nor sold, so they prefer that the honorarium be handled in a way that makes it a church matter and be treated more as a contribution than an honorarium or gratuity for services.

The funeral director needs to be and usually is aware of the pastor's wishes in this regard. If the arranging family holds membership in the church from which the pastor will officiate, oftentimes the suggestion is made that the matter of an honorarium be left to a personal arrangement between the family and the pastor. In the event that the pastor is not related to the family through church membership the funeral director will suggest that an honorarium be given and will arrange for its presentation if the family so desires. Where the funeral home is responsible for the presentation of the honorarium it will usually be in the form of a funeral-home check and treated as a cash advance on behalf of the family. This then assures the family of the appropriate action being taken by the funeral home and also serves as a matter of record for tax and audit purposes. In any event it is important for the funeral director and pastor to have a clear understanding as to the desires and practices so that unfortunate circumstances and misunderstandings may be avoided.

Place of Funeral

The location for the actual funeral service itself is often a matter of concern to the family. Today the choice usually rests between having the service in the church where the deceased was a member, or in the funeral home where special facilities are available. With an increasing number of persons having no church affiliation or membership, the choice is usually limited to the funeral home itself.

Early tradition in this country made the individual home the center for the family ceremonials. Most funerals were at home in a built-in ceremonial room called the parlor. Times and architecture have changed, and these changes have to be taken into account.

For many the church is the fitting and proper place for the funeral of anyone whose life has been centered about the confession and profession of his faith. However, it is quite obvious that for many church architects this was not a consideration. Many churches were built with steep and winding stairways which make it almost impossible to move a casket in or out.

The funeral home has emerged as a reasonable and sensible answer to changing architecture and changing times. Usually it is centrally located, clearly marked and has adequate parking space. When people come from a distance and by car these are important considerations.

However, there are some conditions that are more ideal than others and these should be sought in both church and funeral home. People should have freedom of choice as to what best suits their own emotional needs and family circumstances. They should also have available to them facilities that can serve the purpose of wise funeral practice. This would mean that there should be a clearly manifest supportive relationship between the acutely bereaved and the rest of the community. In some funeral homes that are adaptations of former dwellings families are separated from the rest of the group. It would seem wise wherever possible that the family and the rest of the community be together.

In many instances both the church and the funeral home serve a useful purpose. For visitation the funeral home provides facilities ideally designed for the purpose. They do this with freedom from the housekeeping chores that would be doubly burdensome at such a time. In the dignified and useful setting of the funeral home many of the aspects of grief work can be done, for here it is that reality can be confirmed and useful communication take place. And when this part of the funeral process is completed it is possible to proceed to the church for the final religious service. When we recognize the significance of the process, both community resources can be used to fuller advantage.

Type of Service

Questions are often raised as to the type of service that is most valid and useful for those who are bereaved. In the book *The Christian Funeral* this matter is explored in length. Here it is probably sufficient to say that the funeral can and should be a service that is primarily concerned with meeting the emotional and spiritual needs of those who mourn.

The funeral should never be treated lightly or conducted in a perfunctory manner. Each funeral is unique for it is a service designed to meet the needs of individuals at the time of a specific event in their personal histories. Therefore, it is important for the officiant to explore with the bereaved as to their own thoughts and feelings. In the light of these he can then adapt what he has to say and the traditional practices of his religious group to the needs of the mourning community.

While funeral services need not be long they should never be insignificant. As life is personal so the funeral should be personalized. This may be done through the selections of the readings, the content of the prayer, or the focus of the declaration of faith that is the central part of any service. This statement of faith need not be a sermon, or as long as a sermon, but it should be a definite effort to speak to the specific needs of the moment in the light of the basic tenets of the faith and the resources of the historic and scriptural tradition.

It should be clearly understood that the pastor and funeral director work together to make the service a well-coordinated and dignified event, but the lines of communication should be so well established that in working together neither intrudes upon the area of the other's primary responsibility. The pastor should be consulted in all aspects of the service that take place within the church or the funeral home so that they are in accord with his tradition and practice. Similarly the pastor seeks to make it comfortable and convenient for the funeral director to do those things that are the normal part of the physical arrangements. This would be true of the committal service as well as the services in church or funeral home.

A Visit with the Clergymen with Whom You Serve

Understanding avoids problems generated by misunderstanding. Understanding builds cooperation and trust. A good way for a funeral director to know what the thoughts are of the clergymen with whom he serves—or will be serving—is to ask for them. A proven method of "touching all bases" in such a conference and recording the cleric's wishes is to use one of the forms reproduced in Appendices VIII and IX.

The forms and their use as prepared or as they can be adapted are clear by a reading of them. One is suggested for the Protestant ministers and a different one for the Catholic priests. It is felt those of the Jewish tradition have well-defined procedures which are understood and have few variations. Therefore, no form has been suggested.

Specific Religious Disciplines

Judaism

Jewish tradition with its roots deep in ancient practices has undergone some major changes. The funeral services for the late Prime Minister of Israel, Levi Eshkol, make it clear that burial before sundown has given way to the more modern practices of viewing, embalming and lying in state. What has been true of a national leader can well become a matter of common practice.

However, certain basic concerns in Jewish funeral practices continue to be important. One is the encouragement to express valid feelings. Another is the emphasis on well-defined modes for doing mourning work over an extended period of time, and yet another is the emphasis on religion and tradition in working to resolve grief. Because much of our Christian practice grows out of the Jewish tradition, it is important for us to observe how they have preserved the best of the past and adapted it to the new resources for wise funeral procedure that our culture makes available.

Roman Catholicism

These days of change leave few if any areas untouched. Evidence of this fact is found in the present reworking, rethinking and reevaluation of the Funeral Rite by the Roman Catholic Church in the United States.

Following the Vatican Council two dioceses in the United States were given permission to experiment with the Catholic Funeral Rite, namely, the archdiocese of St. Louis and the archdiocese of Atlanta. After a period of about one year, the archdiocese of Chicago, because of an extensive parish education program, became interested in the funeral rite as well. With special permission they pursued suggestions for change and have developed an "Experimental Funeral Rite" which is being adopted by many dioceses throughout the United States. The new rite has been approved and is in the process of being fully authorized.

It is encouraging to note that the new rite is based fundamentally upon the premise that the needs of the people involved must be met and those things which they do must be meaningful and significant in meeting those needs.

The new rite divides the funeral into three basic areas. The visitation or wake, the funeral mass, and the interment. The emphasis for the visitation or wake is directed towards human sorrow, and the scripture readings, prayers and hymns are chosen with this fact in mind. The funeral service emphasis during the Mass is on Atonement relating it to baptism, with death becoming the ultimate reunion with God. The interment through its liturgy, readings and prayers directs one's thoughts to the Resurrection of the body. A film entitled "Of Life and Death" portrays visually this new service. It is available through the NFDA headquarters office.

Wherever the rite has been introduced the diocese has insisted that proper study be given to the rite by both pastors and funeral directors before it is used in any church. The evaluation following a funeral service that has used the rite is a cooperative venture between the parish priest, the funeral director, and the family involved.

The changes made throughout the rite give added significance and value to meeting the needs of the bereaved.

Other Major Religious Faiths

Other major religious faiths especially those related to the Eastern Orthodox Church have individual funeral practices all of which are filled with rich and traditional ceremony. Funeral directors will find that these customs and traditions although they may seem strange in this culture take on special meaning for the individuals involved. It is important that every funeral director familiarize himself with these rites and rituals by close cooperation and communication with the religious officiant that is involved in such rites. In almost every instance the pastors involved are more than willing to cooperate in order that complete and thorough understanding can exist between the pastor and the funeral director as together they meet the needs of the families they serve.

Humanist and Contemporary Services

Funeral directors are receiving more requests for ceremonies that cannot be considered either religious or traditional in the commonly accepted definitions of these terms.

The humanist or secular service is requested by those who do not profess a religious faith. They want a ceremony consisting of poetry, philosophical readings and literature of a non-religious content. The officiant will usually be a lawyer, judge, educator, public official, or in some instances the funeral functionary. However, the funeral director should carefully consider such a request in view of his professional role and avoid the impression that he is serving a religious role as well.

The contemporary service may or may not have a religious context. It will differ primarily from the standpoint of the number of participants, music and order of service. There may be several participants, particularly from the peer group of the departed, who will share in reading the eulogy or the music. The music may be very contemporary and produced by instruments not normally associated with funerals, e.g., guitars, zither, banjo or others. The order of service may be very flexible and even unstructured or free flowing as in the Quaker tradition.

The funeral director should carefully explain that the value of the funeral ceremony need not be compromised or mitigated even though a humanist or other non-traditional service is requested or planned.

Paul Irion has told funeral directors, "Don't you ever deny the psychological value of a funeral ceremony to a family just because they may desire a non-religious funeral." This is sound advice not only for the funeral director but also for the family he is serving.

Other Important Considerations

Value of Ceremony

There has been a tendency on the part of some in recent years to try to reduce the number and significance of the ceremonial events that take place at the time of death.

Some of this has been done by funeral directors who have reduced or eliminated the visitations or the committal services, or who have not spoken positively to families thinking this is what they should have. Some has been done by clergymen who would shorten both the number and length of services and in some instances eliminate viewing and the presence of the closed casket at the service.

This invites a consideration of the meaning and function of the funeral process. The events that are a part of the funeral practice are designed to meet the deep emotional and often unconscious needs of those who have to work through these feelings. Research in this matter indicates that the more there are of such pertinent rites and ceremonies, the more opportunity is afforded for healthful grief work. It seems quite clear from these studies that the more numerous and meaningful the events that can channel the powerful emotions, the better for the persons who are emotionally involved.

So in reality it is not a matter of too little or too much, but rather how well the variety of events can be filled with significance for the bereaved. It would seem reasonable that skill would be employed to enlarge and enrich the number of ceremonial events so that the benefits would be enlarged rather than curtailed. To implement wisely the insight of the students of human behavior we should be employing our resources to enrich and improve funeral practices rather than to reduce or curtail them.

Pastoral Care

It is important to realize that wise funeral practice is one of the essentials of pastoral care. But pastoral care may well move in both directions for the bereaved. It can aid in preparation for emotional crises and it can help in resolving them.

Preparation for emotional crises would vary as events vary. Some of the most difficult emotional experiences are those that come with tragic suddenness and no warning. Here the shock is great just because the event intrudes so ruthlessly on life. The value of every funeral is seen here, for each funeral is part of the preparation that must be made for coping with acute deprivation.

But just as each funeral gives the community a chance to give some anticipatory consideration to the nature of mortality, so also each funeral provides an opportunity for doing some of the unfinished work of mourning. The pastor as the custodian of some of these rites and rituals needs to know how important they may be for the persons who use them to resolve their emotional crises, for often these persons are inaccessible to counselling.

The understanding pastor, the one who acts as if he understands the emotions of his people, will often have persons come to him for pastoral counselling. Here he can help them talk out the variety of feelings and concerns that center about the experience of death. These matters for dialogue may include personal feelings such as loneliness, despair, and a feeling that life is becoming meaningless. They may include the more theological interests such as the nature of God, the meaning of guilt and the problems of punishment. The pastor who is close to his people, willing to let them talk and able to listen without judgment or preaching in response, may be a useful instrument in working through the complex feelings that accompany the experience of the death of one dearly loved and deeply mourned.

The understanding pastor not only welcomes the counselee and wisely administers the ceremonials entrusted to him, but he also seeks to build into the total educational and worship life of his parish those insights and practices that make the parish a supportive community that is not afraid of death, but accepts it with spiritual insight and ministers to the needs of the bereaved members. When this is done the climate for expressing strong feelings is provided and the processes of repression give way to the processes of wise and useful expression. Then the church and its ministry work together to help the bereaved move into the future strengthened by the experience rather than broken by it.

Children and the Funeral

Questions are quite often raised about participation of children in funerals. These also include queries as to whether children should be told of tragic events or should rather be shielded from them.

There are some basic principles that should be kept in mind in working with children. Children are human beings. They have a strong capacity for feeling. They can experience grief. Their grief may be different from that of the adult, but it may be quite as intense and may have important impact upon the life of the child. So it is important that the child's needs be approached with understanding and insight.

It is difficult to lie to children. They have built-in lie detectors. They may be confused about events, but they tend to be aware of the emotional meaning of the events. Children fit new experience into the accumulated understanding they have acquired. They may know little of space or time and so can know little of death as a personal event in the life of another. But they can be deeply aware of its impact on their own world of limited experience. If a young child loses a parent it is important that the child be surrounded by love and care so that it will not suffer too deeply of acute deprivation. Older children have similar but expanding needs. They need information and facts to build into their understanding. These facts may be elicited by the questions they ask. These questions should normally be answered, but not over-answered, for over-answering may be a sign of adult anxiety and children are sensitive to anxiety.

Children have a ready capacity for engaging in family events so the rites and rituals surrounding death should not be foreign to them. They would be able to adapt them to their own level of understanding, and would probably be more able to adjust to the events by being included than by being excluded. If the child has usually been a part of family activity, it would be damaging to exclude him when an important event like a funeral takes place.

But most of all children should be treated with consideration and concern. Each child is different from every other, and what happens to him in time of emotional crisis should be observed with insight by the adults who share his life. He may act out his grief by withdrawal, or by angry and destructive behavior. Each communicates his feelings of difficulty in coping with life and its new experience. Punishment may compound the problem that understanding would relieve. Usually punishment indicates that those around the child have not gotten the message acted out in his behavior.

In time of emotional crises it is most important to pay attention to what the child is trying to say in all the varied ways he communicates his feelings.

The funeral director will usually have considerable experience in working with children and should be looked upon as a resource person, not only for guidance but participation in including the child in the arrangements, the visitation and the funeral service itself.

Some Concluding Thoughts

Many persons wonder about the impact of our fast-moving culture with its many changes as they may bear on funeral service. It is inevitable that in any changing culture the major institutions will feel the impact of change. This has certainly been true of the church, our educational institutions, and even our political institutions. Changes in communication and mobility are bound to affect the way people think and act.

Funeral service has gone through many changes down through history. Basically funeral service exists to meet two needs, the emotional needs of the bereaved, and the need for disposing of dead human bodies with dignity and within the prescribed legal and health standards of the community. In England the coroner was the agent of the crown to see that basic law was observed. In our early colonial life primitive conditions and scattered communities made it necessary for men to improvise. But in the tradition of most civilized people burial took place in a special place, a God's acre. As churches were built, burial grounds surrounded the church and the burial committees of the parish supervised the care for the dead. With time a specialized function developed and a functionary served the needs of the parish. Whatever he was called, his role remained largely that of assisting the parish in arranging for funerals and providing the services and equipment that was necessary.

With modern times that role has continued much the same although the specialization has become more highly developed and the equipment has become more extensive. The funeral director provides specialized skills and considerable equipment to aid both the parish and the people in meeting the needs that are acute in time of death. Some of the needs have changed with our changing culture, but the basic requirements remain the same. The important thing for our day is to see that the changes that take place are such that the basic needs of people are met more adequately and that the increased insight that we are gaining into the importance of wise grief management are incorporated into the practices people employ in meeting their emotional needs. This means that those, pastor and funeral director, who understand these needs and who help to meet them should work together to guarantee that the changes that take place are wise and good, rather than unwise and impoverishing to the needs of people. We are learning so much about people and their needs that it would be unfortunate if this understanding were not incorporated into the way we do things. Therefore, it is doubly important for pastors and funeral directors to work together to increase understanding and wise practice, for in a sense they are the custodians of the common welfare of the community. When they cooperate with understanding and good will, those they serve will surely benefit.

11

THE LAW AND A
FUNERAL SERVICE PRACTICE

Thomas H. Clark

The customs and procedures involving funerals and burials of earliest times were not based on material considerations. They were based on superstition and/or religious beliefs as seen by the High Priest or by the King or Temporal Ruler. Later during the early Christian era, rights of burial, and the rights of those entrusted or charged therewith were determined, in a large degree, by Papal decrees issued in Rome and became a part of Canon Law. When judges, lawyers and other state officials became Christians, the state law took on the robes of the Canon Law and Canon and Civil Law became one in substance and one in fact.

The one (Canon and Civil) Law continued until the British enacted the English Burial Acts of 1855 which acts were to change burial practices, rights and obligations, taking into consideration the then existing Canon Law, Civil Law and State Law. The English Civil Law was quite different from the Roman Civil Law and became the "Common" Law. The acts provided, among other things, for court jurisdiction over the burial of the dead and authorized private and group burial arrangements. The Act of 1855 was the legal seed which germinated into funeral service law of today.

General Aspects of the Law of the Funeral and Burial

At first, common law was only recognized in most of the states because of the states reluctance to permit any ecclesiastical control over our way of life. Trying to give justice under all conditions, the United States turned to the "temporal" courts which later became known as courts of equity in much the same vein as we know them today. As a result, services and ceremonies for, and the final disposition of the dead in the United States are regulated by the secular law as interpreted by our Courts of Equity. The Courts of Equity in appearance do not differ from our regular courts but simply are courts whose judges take the intangible into consideration rather than following the fine line of the law. From the 17th century into the 20th laws have been enacted up-dating and sometimes superseding the common law. Today the common law is becoming of less and less importance.

The law concerning funerals and interment is evidence that man has desired to bury his dead decently and with ceremony and that society recognizes the deep-seated feelings most survivors have for the departed whose body once contained an immortal soul. This is indicated by the specifics covering type and place of burial of the dead to protect the interest of the public who make up our society and by the rights, powers and obligations in the law in respect to the decedent himself and his next of kin. The legal basis of such rights, powers and obligations is found in the police powers of the individual states, rather than in any constitutional or statutory powers of the Federal Government, and the police powers of a state find their basis in what is best for the public welfare or public interest. The public interest in proper burial rights, powers and obligations is an established legal fact. Thus the law recognizes that a decedent should receive and is entitled to a decent burial, or at least a burial which is not offensive to society's sensitivities. The court will, in the public interest, see to it that mankind's obligation to bury its dead which is a real legal obligation, is fulfilled and that where involved the public health is protected.

Rights of the Decedent

The common law of the old world and the law in the United States, prior to existing statutes, did not create in a decedent any rights concerning his own burial but left the selection of the type of funeral and place of the burial to those surviving. A request made, while living, regardless of how formal, had no legal basis and would be considered only at the discretion of those whose duty it was to bury the decedent. Today, however, statues in most states give the decedent the right to select the type of funeral and place of burial so long as his wishes are explicit and are not violative of the sensitivities or sensibilities of his next of kin and/or society. The principal reason for those new statutes is the legal right of the decedent during life to arrange for a decent burial and since the right cannot be exercised after death by the decedent himself, some means had to be adopted to permit him to do this during his lifetime even though he will never know whether his wishes have been fulfilled. In contrast to the old canon law, and common law, today a man's body is subject to some quasi-property rights and a living person now has such property rights in his own body as to permit him to set forth, sometimes for implementation by his survivors, the donation of his entire body or parts thereof, and/or a type of funeral he desires and the place in which he wants his remains interred. The form of the decedent's actions and the way in which he makes his wishes known usually need not be in any special form and they may be either written or oral. Obviously the more formal, the better the courts can interpret them.

In 1968 a Uniform Anatomical Gift Act was proposed to the states. By the end of 1970, the District of Columbia and all states but Massachusetts and Nebraska passed the measure in some form. This law gives the decedent the right to donate his entire body or parts of his body. In instances of the gift of the entire body, the availability of the body for a funeral prior to delivery to the donee medical institution is subject to the authorization of said donee in most of the states.

Where the gift is of a part of the body, the law usually provides that the part is to be removed without unnecessary mutilation after which custody of the "remainder of the body vests in the surviving spouse, next of kin or other persons under obligation to dispose of the body." All anatomical gift laws require the gift when by the decedent to be made through a written instrument of some sort such as a will or "donee card," and most states require at least two witnesses to the gift.

It is essential for all in the practice of funeral service to know the details of the Uniform Anatomical Gift Law and of the pre-need trust statute in their state if there be such statute(s).

Rights of Survivors

Society has the responsibility to bury its dead. To be effective this responsibility must rest as a duty in someone or something. As to the funeral and interment, that "someone" is in the person or persons of the survivors, whether of the blood or otherwise. Their degree of closeness to the decedent based on all the salient facts will determine exactly with whom the duty or obligation of a "decent" funeral and/or burial lies. It is logical that the duties involved carry concomitant rights with them.

There is no property right in a dead body in a commercial sense, but there is a quasi-property right therein vested in the nearest relatives of the decedent to enable the surviving next of kin to carry out their duties to bury their dead unless the decedent has legally provided for disposition of his body. The quasi-property right acknowledgement includes the right to possession and custody of the body for funeral and committal purposes, and includes the right for the next of kin to select the type of funeral for the decedent they desire, and also the right of the next of kin to choose the place where the body will be interred, and also includes the right not to have the interred remains disturbed, and also the right to sue in damages for a violation of any of these rights.

The most fundamental of such rights is the possession and control of the body for purpose of the funeral and interment as defined or acknowledged in their broadest terms. The rights of those whose duty it is to provide for a funeral and interment includes the right to possession of the body in order to choose the type of funeral and place of burial, except where the law gives one or more of these rights to the decedent and where he has so exercised such rights.

The person having charge of the body cannot be considered the owner of it; he holds it only as a trust obligation for the benefit of those who may, because of family relationship or personal friendship, have an interest in the decedent's remains. The rights of the survivors, as will be discussed later, in deciding the format of the funeral, including the place of burial, does not necessarily create on those survivors the obligation to pay for the funeral and/or the interment.

Where a decedent has not donated his body and/or failed to specify a format of his funeral, or for some aesthetic or legal reason his wishes are not followed by his survivors and he is survived by a spouse with whom he was living, the surviving spouse shall have the right of choosing the type of funeral to be provided for the deceased spouse and the place of interment.

The right can be waived. As an example, if a surviving husband has the right to the custody of the body of his deceased wife for burial because they shared the same household and, as a consequence the husband has the right to select the type and place of burial, but makes no demand for custody for such purpose or makes no attempt to select a funeral, he is said to have waived his rights of selection.

If the decedent is not living with his wife and no children are surviving, the wife unless divorced, has the right of selection. A divorced wife has no right and merely becomes a volunteer and may subject herself to the demands of the next of kin and/or the financial responsibility of paying for the entire funeral.

If there are children surviving and the decedent and his wife are living apart, the child with whom the decedent was living at the time of his decease shall have the right of selection. If the decedent left no wife and was not living with any particular child at the time of his decease, the children jointly have the right of selecting the type of funeral and place of burial.

Where no spouse and no children are surviving the right of selection of the funeral shall generally be determined by the statutes of descent and distribution of the state in which the decedent resided at the time of his death, keeping in mind that the court sitting in equity may vary the line of right of selection from that set forth in such statute depending on the pertinent facts. The statute in such cases is merely a guide. The statute of descent and distribution is that statute which sets up the line of inheritance for the estate of a decedent who has left no valid last will and testament.

Regardless of who has the right of selection, this right is always subject to propriety and to the sensitivities of the decedent, if he were living, and to the sensitivities of his other survivors and the public generally. Thus, one who has the right or privilege of selection has a sacred trust and must act in good faith, without malice and with due regard for that which is prudent.

Personal Representative

The right of selection, if the decedent has not expressed a selection, vests in the surviving spouse and next of kin. The question arises as to what happens if they do not exercise this right since the decedent, irrespective of his next of kin's action, is entitled to a decent burial. The law generally puts the duty of providing and selecting a funeral on the executor or administrator (personal representative—fiduciary) either (i) to fulfill the selection made by the decedent prior to death, or (ii) to fill the void left when the related survivors or close friends do not act. The duty to select and provide a funeral is not to be confused with the obligation to pay for the funeral, to be discussed later.

Type of Burial

Most Americans believe they have the right to expect a proper disposition of their remains. Early American law based this right with the corresponding obligation on custom and beliefs together with a growing emphasis on public health.

Proper disposition has sometimes been referred to as "decent Christian burial." The phraseology "decent Christian burial" has no religious connotations but merely a moral connotation based on the customs and traditions of the people in ethnic groups of this country. The emphasis in the phraseology which now most times is "decent burial" is on the word "decent" which means in terms of law that which is ordinary, that which is morally and customarily right concerning the station in life, religious beliefs and ethnic background of the decedent.

The law rightly takes into consideration the customs, usages and considerations of the various people of this country and transforms these customs into the decedent having a legal right to a decent burial. But such right is not possible unless there is a duty imposed on one's survivors that is legally recognized and enforceable. Therefore, the laws and regulations of the various states put a duty on the survivors or personal representatives (executors or administrators) not merely to provide a burial, but to provide a decent burial.

In determining what is a decent burial one must look at all of the facts concerning the place and time of the decedent's death and the condition of the body at the time of death and the circumstances under which death occurred. One must also look at the religious, ethnic and economic background and circumstances of the decedent and his survivors. Being entitled to a decent burial also entitles one to a burial within a reasonable time.

Enforcement of Rights

Where there is an obligation, that obligation to be binding and effective must be capable of enforcement. There are two means of enforcement. One, a criminal procedure, that is, enforcement filed in behalf of the general public through a governmental authority. Two, suit for damages by those who feel that their rights have been violated by others. Suit by one or more of the next of kin for a violation by another of the decedent's right to a decent burial must involve a violation of a legal duty, not just a breach of sensitivities, unless the desire for a special type funeral has been conveyed to the performer of the funeral services by those having right of selection, and those desires were not carried out as agreed.

The public recognition and acceptance of a decedent's right to a decent burial, and numerous other factors such as public health and welfare, have given rise to certain laws. Laws which require a death certificate signed by a physician, medical examiner or coroner, which require a burial permit before burial, which grant to law enforcement officials the right to delay burial until after full examination of the remains in order to determine if a law has been violated are in effect in all states. Similarly, laws give rules for the location and operation of cemeteries.

The right to select the type and place of burial often carries with it the legal right to attend the funeral and/or witness the interment of the body. Common decency and custom strongly suggest that a person who has the right of selection should permit the relatives and friends of the decedent to call at the funeral home (or other place where the body is in state) and/or to be present at the funeral for the purpose of paying their respects if at all possible. However, this is a matter of social propriety rather than a legal right. Thus, relatives other than the one entitled to select the type of funeral and place of burial have no legal right to visitation or to be at the funeral, or to attend the committal service. A husband who makes no demands to use his right to select his wife's funeral can be excluded from participating in funeral ceremonies if they take place on the premises of a third party who undertook the duty or obligation of providing the wife with a decent burial. The husband has waived his right by his actions.

Interference with the right which a person has to the solace of burying the body of his loved one is an actionable wrong. Examples of such actionable wrongs are: multilation of the body after death; unduly disturbing the body; withholding the body from one entitled to possession and custody for burial purposes; withholding of the body from an agent of one entitled to possession or custody such as a funeral director; unauthorized acts (embalming) in preparing the body for burial; and for negligence involving improper burial, damage to body by mud and water by failure properly to close and inter the casket, and substitution of a cheaper casket for the one selected. In addition, a funeral director who has taken charge of a dead body may be held liable in damages to the next of kin in case he directly or indirectly is a party to an unauthorized autopsy. If a coroner or other duly authorized medical officer has authority to perform an autopsy, a funeral director is not liable for his acts in cooperation with the coroner.

Damages

As we have noted, our courts of equity settle controversies concerning the burial of our dead. So too the courts of equity enforce rights concerning burial through criminal actions filed by the governmental authority or, as in a vast majority of instances, enforce through a suit for damages. In most cases only nominal damages can be recovered by the kin of a dead person for the disturbance of his remains. The opinions in these cases say that damages are incapable of measurement. However, an increasing number of courts recognize that substantial damage is recoverable by those who have their right of burial interfered with; for an indignity to the remains; or for unlawfully withholding the body from the relative entitled thereto for the purpose of reimbursement from the estate unless he was a volunteer, a meddler, or the expenses are held to be unreasonable.

The circumstances involved in the aggrievement to the body could aggravate or mitigate the amount of damages. If the injury is wanton or malicious, the result of gross negligence, or a reckless disregard of the rights of others which amounts to an intentional violation of those rights, exemplary damages may be awarded. (Exemplary damages are those damages or penalties which are not calculated on loss but are calculated as to be a penalty for the damage caused to the complainant.) Although there is a split in various court jurisdictions, a majority of the courts support the view that a complainant who has the right of burial is entitled to recover for the mental anguish caused him by the willful or wanton mutilation, dissection, unauthorized autopsy, wrongful detention or breach of faith by the person caring for the body as to the body. In all cases the jury in setting damages may take into consideration the feelings of the complainant.

Expenses of the Funeral

There is an old saying in law which in substance means that where there is a right, there is an accompanying obligation or duty. So it is with burial, the obligation in this instance is the obligation to pay burial expenses. There is a presumption that funeral expenses are incurred on the credit of the estate of the decedent and therefore the primary responsibility in most cases rests upon the decedent's estate, that is, the estate acting through the executor, administrator or other fiduciary. Although funeral expenses are not debts of the decedent, and are not strictly speaking expenses of administration, they are classified as debts of the estate and a person paying for funeral expenses, if not primarily liable therefor, may be entitled to reimbursement from the estate unless he was a volunteer, a meddler, or the expenses are held to be unreasonable.

The responsibility for such fiduciary to pay the decedent's funeral expenses is not an individual one; it is one he accepts only in his position as such fiduciary. His personal obligation will depend on his legal obligation to provide a funeral for the deceased because of his relationship to the deceased. The mere request that funeral services be furnished will not bind the person so requesting personally since primarily the estate of the decedent is liable for funeral expenses and the law will not imply liability on the part of another from a request alone. If under the facts the funeral director relied on the credit and ability to pay of the person requesting the funeral service, that person will be liable to the extent that the estate cannot or refuses to pay.

The obligation of the fiduciary is limited only to the payment of reasonable burial expenses. What is reasonable depends on the size of the estate, on the ability of the estate to pay such expenses, and on the assets of the beneficiaries of the estate and who the beneficiaries are. What is reasonable—by defining the words "decent burial"— also depends upon the religious, economic and ethnic background of the decedent. Where an executor is vested by a will with authority to expend for funeral expenses such amount as he deems proper, the exercise of his discretion will not be reviewed by a court in the absence of a showing that he arbitrarily and improperly determined the amount to be expended for funeral expenses. The primary obligation of the estate to pay the funeral bill exists even though the fiduciary did not select the funeral provided, inasmuch as the obligation to pay for such expenses does not in all instances coincide with that of the right of selection.

The recognition of the estate's primary responsibility to pay reasonable expenses is shown in laws found in most states which permit the reasonable burial expenses to be a *preferred claim* against the estate, at least to a stipulated amount. Some legislatures have considered at least $300 to $700 as a reasonable bill for funeral and burial expenses as to the preference in paying those expenses out of the estate. Of course, larger sums are allowed as part of and depending on the size of the estate.

If the funeral bill is not paid by the estate and it is reasonable in amount, those persons who received the assets of the estate received such assets subject to the liability of the funeral bill.

As in many situations in law, there are exceptions to this general rule. A minor child's estate is not liable for the funeral bill of its parent if there is a financially responsible surviving parent, or if there are enough assets in the estate of the deceased parent. A child under 21 years of age has the right to depend on his father for necessity, even in death, and though the minor child's estate would be quite large the father still, if he survives, has the obligation to pay for funeral services. The same is true if the father is deceased and his estate is still being administered. Though it has been said that a child is not liable for the funeral bill of a parent, where there are no assets of the deceased parent or a surviving parent with assets, under some unusual circumstances where the assets of the child permit, the child's estate would be liable for the "reasonable" funeral and burial expenses.

Where an individual who does not have the right of selection of the funeral contracts for a funeral for a decedent, the estate of the decedent and those legally having the right of selection are relieved from any responsibility for the payment of the funeral bill and the so-called volunteer has the complete responsibility.

The question today arises as to the responsibility concerning funeral bills where the funeral has been prearranged and/or prefinanced by the decedent prior to his death. The general rule is that the estate is liable for a prearranged funeral to the extent that it has not been paid for in advance.

Where the decedent leaves no estate the person or persons having the right of selection and duty of burial have the obligation to pay the expenses of the funeral, unless contracted for by one not having the duty of burial whom we referred to as being a volunteer. Where those having the right of selection and duty of burial are a class and consist of more than one individual (more than one child), the child who has actually selected the funeral based on contract law has the obligation to pay the entire funeral bill. This child then has the legal right of contribution from the other members of the class—from his brothers and sisters—for the "reasonable" funeral expenses. Where no person came forward to accept the responsibility and liability of burial and there is no estate, and the decedent has not prepaid his funeral, the state or county in most states will provide for the burial of the decedent as an indigent, the cost of which is usually set by such governmental authority and accepted as a public service by the funeral directors.

The determining factors in considering what is a reasonable funeral bill are the items which make up that bill. The following list thereof gives most items which may be included in a funeral bill individually or collectively and which are by necessity and under the law allowable expenses. The total amount of them will determine who is to pay for them.

   a. *Expenses for care of the body*
      Embalming, clothing, casket
   b. *Services of funeral director*
      Professional services of funeral director
      Use of facilities of the funeral home
      Transportation of body from place of death
      Transportation of body from funeral home and/or church to place of burial
   c. *Other merchandise*
      Vault
      Flowers
      Urn

       d. Cash advancements
         Opening and closing grave
         Newspaper notices
         Religious service honorarium
         Forwarding expenses, auto, rail, air
      e. Cemetery and memorial charges
         Cemetery lot or mausoleum space
         Cost of Cremation
         Monument or marker

Funeral Service Licensees and Licenses

Historical Background

Historically the care, preparation and burial of the dead was entrusted to a variety of individuals and/or groups. Today the care and preparation of the dead for burial is entrusted to funeral service licensees such as funeral directors, embalmers, morticians and undertakers.

For many years the only funeral service licensee was the embalmer. His particular function was to disinfect and further prepare the body for the funeral and burial. His work was done within the framework of the law by which he was licensed and the rules and regulations thereto. Most times his licensing board was the state board of health, or a committee responsible to such board. He sold caskets and provided livery. But his primary duty involved the dead body and "undertaking" means to help the family with accouterments for a "wake" at home and a service at home or at church.

Shortly after World War I the funeral home came into existence. It was a remodeled residence or a portion of a building perhaps housing a furniture business, or a specially built one-purpose building.

The embalmer found himself dividing his effort between caring for the body and serving the survivors. He became a "director" of a series of events which involved duties not covered by the laws by which he became an embalmer. So funeral director laws were passed to meet that need.

Inasmuch as 70 to 75% of all licensed funeral directors must also be embalmers to practice in their communities, some states passed laws covering both the funeral director's and the embalmer's license laws.

The National Funeral Directors Association recommends such a single license law. It feels that a license for the practice of funeral service should be established in all states for persons engaged in the care and/or disposition of the human dead and/or in the practice of disinfecting and preparing by embalming or otherwise the human dead for the funeral service, transportation, burial or cremation, and/or in the practice of helping to meet the emotions and dispositions of the bereaved, and/or in the practice of funeral directing or embalming as presently known, whether under these titles or designations or otherwise. It shall also mean a person who makes arrangements for funeral services and/or who sells supplies to the public, or who makes financial arrangements for the rendering of such services and/or the sale of such supplies.

Until the time when most states have such a law the following facts prevail.

A funeral director is a person who engages in the vocation and profession of providing facilities for the care of dead human bodies, who helps conduct funeral services, and who, thereafter, sees to the burial of such deceased and provides for the needs of the survivors during the period of and immediately after the funeral. The work of the funeral director in most instances starts at the time of death and continues until committal has been completed and the needs of the survivors met. Although there has been a difference of opinion in various states, the funeral director is generally considered a businessman or quasi-professional and not a member of the pure arts or professions even though statutes have referred to both funeral directing and embalming as a "business or profession," not specifically placing them in or excluding them from either category.

A funeral home or funeral establishment or mortuary is generally understood to be a place for the preparation of human bodies for the purpose of burial or other disposition, together with a place for the period of the funeral, including visitation prior to the funeral service itself which is followed by final disposition of the remains. A funeral home or mortuary is not a public or semi-public building.

An embalmer as such does not perform the same functions as generally performed by a funeral director. His particular function is to prepare the remains by embalming— the art of disinfecting dead bodies and thereby slowing the process of decay. The embalmer also does restorative work to the face and hands. Legally speaking, embalming is not generally required for burial. However, it is required when sending remains over state lines or out of the United States and it is required by many common carriers prior to shipment. Some states require embalming if burial is not completed within a stated number of hours and/or if death was due to certain diseases.

The function of a funeral director and embalmer may be performed by the same person, or by separate individuals, depending on the license requirements of the state in which that individual practices and depending on the license or licenses held by the practitioner. In those states which have a single license law a practitioner can perform functions of both a funeral director and an embalmer. In states which have dual license laws, that is, one license for a funeral director and one license for an embalmer, the licensee may obtain either or both of these licenses if he is qualified and therefore restrict or extend his services by the licenses he obtains. An embalmer does not have to be a funeral director. But in some states, some or all of the requirements for an embalmer are the same or similar to those for a funeral director.

The Granting and Responsibility of Licenses

The business or profession of operating a mortuary, funeral home, funeral establishment and/or the practice of funeral directing and embalming are of a public or quasi-public nature closely related to the health, safety and general welfare of a community. Therefore under the police power of the state these may be subjected to reasonable regulation and control by state statutes or municipal regulations. Because of the public welfare the courts have generally recognized the propriety of legislation regulating the exercise of the vocations and professions of funeral directing and embalming.

States and cities have governmental power to create and act through administrative agencies. This power has been applied in cases dealing with the regulation of funeral directors and embalmers. This enables the legislature to set the scope and boundaries of the purpose which it attempts to obtain by the passage of regulatory legislation, and to have an authority to see to the enforcement and proper supervision thereto in order to achieve its legislative aims.

The enabling legislation must have some certainty, that is, guidelines within which its administrative agency must operate legally and effectively. An enabling statute which creates a state agency, such as the state board of funeral directors and embalmers, may give and usually does give the agency the power to make rules and regulations to implement and further the legislation.

The acts of such agencies will be sustained unless there was an unlawful delegation of legislative power to such agency, or unless the agencies acted in an arbitrary, capricious or unreasonable manner, or unless the agency's rules or regulations were not within the confines and aims as set forth in enabling statute.

The state board of funeral directors and embalmers usually consists of from five to nine members who are authorized to conduct examinations and see to it that applicants meet the qualifications of licensure as set forth in the enabling statute. Once the practitioner has obtained his license the state board should police his actions under that license in accordance with the law and moral business conduct. Appointment to the state board is made by the Governor, sometimes upon the advisory recommendation of a funeral directors association, and the membership of such agencies may be limited to persons engaged in the profession of funeral directing and embalming, though there seems to be an increasing interest shown by law makers and by some of the interested public to have at least one non-licensee as a public member of the board.

The state board must comply with the procedural requirements of the administrative procedures act, if any, of the state. The administrative procedures act is a uniform act creating a procedure for the securing of rights of practitioners and providing for a method through which their complaints against the state board, or the state board's complaints against the practitioners, can be resolved.

The statutes which create the governmental agency must, of course, provide, as must all statutes, for due process of law. Judicial review of administrative actions in most cases is a matter of constitutional necessity. A statute regulating funeral directors and embalmers amply provides due process of law if it establishes standards of conduct, provides for an open, free and fair hearing before a properly constituted administrative agency after timely notice, and thereafter provides for speedy and adequate judicial determination of the rights of the persons regulated.

It is established legally that the care of dead human bodies and the disposition of them by burial or otherwise is so closely related to the health and general welfare of a community that the business or profession of caring for and disposing of such bodies may be regulated by license and special regulations under the police power of the state, and that persons engaging in the funeral directing or embalming business or profession be licensed and that they pay a reasonable fee for that license. All the states have laws requiring licenses for those engaged as funeral directors and/or embalmers.

Revocation of License

Laws and rules regulating those licensed in funeral service usually authorize the revocation or suspension of licenses by administrative boards for sufficient reason. This is a corollary of the right to regulate in the first instance. A license is not a property right or a contract and, therefore, may be suspended or revoked upon sufficient cause even though the licensee has expended money and relied upon its issuance. An administrative agency may be empowered to revoke or suspend a license for causes deemed sufficient in the judgment of the board. The actions of the board and the grounds for revocation must apply to all licensees in the same manner and be reasonable. A large measure of discretion must necessarily be left to the administrative agency in charge of enforcement of a statute to decide what constitutes "misconduct." Assuming that a state board has statutory authorization to propagate rules relating to revocation of licenses of funeral directors or embalmers, it is incumbent on the board so to particularize the rules that a licensee is not left in doubt as to what will constitute grounds for revocation.

There are many specific grounds for which a funeral director's and/or embalmer's license can be revoked. This would also apply to the license of a funeral service practitioner where the licensing statute creates but one license. Some of the specific grounds for revocation are:

1. Conviction of a crime involving moral turpitude.
2. Conviction of a felony.
3. Unprofessional conduct which includes:
   a. Misrepresentation or fraud in the conduct of the funeral service profession.
   b. False or misleading advertising as the holder of a license for the practice of funeral service; advertising or using the name of an unlicensed person in connection with that of any funeral establishment.
   c. Solicitation of dead human bodies by the licensee, his agents, assistants or employees, whether such solicitation occurs after death or while death is impending, providing, that this shall not be deemed to prohibit general advertising.
   d. Employment by the licensee of persons known as "cappers," or "steerers," or "solicitors," or other such persons to obtain the services of a holder of a license for the practice of funeral service.
   e. Employment directly or indirectly of any apprentice, agent, assistant, employee, or other person, on part or full time, or on commission, for the purpose of calling upon individuals or institutions by whose influence dead human bodies may be turned over to a particular funeral establishment.
   f. The direct or indirect payment or offer of payment of a commission by the licensee, his agents, assistants, or employees for the purpose of securing business.
   g. Gross immorality.
   h. Aiding or abetting an unlicensed person to practice within the funeral service profession.
   i. Using profane, indecent or obscene language in the presence of a dead human body, or within the immediate hearing of the family or relatives of a deceased whose body has not yet been interred or otherwise disposed of.
   j. Solicitation or acceptance by a licensee of any commission or bonus or rebate in consideration of recommending or causing a dead human body to be disposed of in any crematory, mausoleum or cemetery.

k. Using any casket or part of a casket which has previously been used as a receptacle for, or in connection with, the burial or other disposition of a dead human body.

l. Violation of any of the provisions of the licensing act.

m. Violation of any state law or municipal or county ordinance or regulation affecting the handling, custody, care or transportation of dead human bodies.

n. Fraud or misrepresentation in obtaining or renewing a license.

o. Refusing promptly to surrender the custody of a dead human body upon the express order of the person lawfully entitled to the custody thereof.

p. Failure to secure permit for removal or burial of dead human body prior to interment or disposal.

q. Knowingly making any false statement on a certificate of death.

r. Solicitation of a request before need to provide funeral services or funeral merchandise at a price less than that available to others at time of need.

s. Employment of others for the solicitation of a request to provide funeral services or funeral merchandise at a price less than that available to others at time of need.

t. Accepting a request to provide funeral services or funeral merchandise at a price less than that available to others at time of need.

u. Participating in a contract to fulfill a promise which has for its purpose the providing of a funeral service at a cost that is less than that for which that funeral is available to the general public.

v. Participating in a contract to fulfill a promise which has for its purpose the providing of funeral merchandise at a cost that is less than that for which that merchandise is available to the general public.

w. Violation of any statute of any state having to do with the prearrangement and/or prefinancing of a funeral.

x. Using another's license.

Other Laws and Regulations Affecting Funeral Service

Zoning and Branch Establishments

Local governments generally have the power properly to regulate and restrict the location of different types of enterprises and professions. This is commonly referred to as zoning powers. The right to have zoning powers includes the right of the governmental authority to regulate and restrict the location of funeral homes. Such enactments are under the police power of the governmental authority and these powers permit legislation which would prohibit the locating of a funeral home in a purely residential area, and whether funeral service is a business or a profession is not important or significant for this purpose since the zoning regulatory power covers both businesses and professions. Therefore, when the existence of a funeral home violates a valid zoning ordinance, the existence of the funeral home may be enjoined by a governmental authority or by a private action. While each case must be decided on its own facts and the surrounding circumstances, certain basic tenets as to zoning are evident. They are enumerated in Chapter 14.

Laws prohibiting the granting of branch licenses to funeral establishments not having them on the effective date of the statute, or providing that such a license shall terminate with the licensee, have been upheld and a requirement that a branch establishment of a funeral director be conducted under the charge of a licensed manager has been held to be reasonable. The regulations concerning branch establishments generally follow the same regulations as apply to funeral homes owned by a corporation which have to be under the supervision and management of a designated licensed person.

Minimum Wage Laws and Others
Affecting Employers and Employees

There is a federal and some state wage and hour laws. The federal law stipulates the minimum hourly rate of pay that is to be paid an individual who is employed in a non-retail activity regardless of its size as it affects interstate commerce. An example of such non-retail activities would be burial insurance and ambulance service. If employed in a retail activity, and a funeral home is such an activity, the employee is covered and is to be paid the minimum hourly rate of pay if such retail activity (funeral home) grosses $250,000 or more per year. Therefore, generally speaking, those funeral-home establishments grossing less than $250,000 per year will not be covered or affected by the wage and hour law unless an employee is particularly engaged in a non-retail activity, such as ambulance service. For those funeral homes that are covered by the act, the employee must be paid time and a half for all hours worked in excess of 40 in any one work week based on not less than the minimum hourly rate of pay. If paid more than the minimum hourly rate of pay, the time and a half must be based on the average hourly rate paid to the employee. This law is very exacting and has many facets and it should be studied in detail by those who work for or own an establishment doing more than $250,000 gross a year, or become involved in a non-retail activity. For those in funeral service it should be pointed out that insurance is a non-retail activity and the handling of insurance by employees of a funeral home will, in all probability, subject the funeral home to the terms and obligations of the wage and hour law.

Although hearse and ambulance drivers of a particular funeral home might be covered by the wage and hour provisions, such drivers who regularly drive on trips which are a continuation of an *interstate* journey are exempt from the overtime provision of the law, but are not exempt from the minimum wage provisions. Thus, where there is establishment coverage there might be overtime exemption for certain drivers on certain trips. Where there is not establishment coverage, the drivers who spend less than 20% of their time driving ambulances are still exempt; those driving ambulances more than 20% of the time are covered and might be entitled to the overtime exemption.

The federal wage and hour law also contains a child labor provision which makes 16 years of age the minimum age for employment. However, for those persons driving or being a helper on a funeral car or ambulance, the minimum permissible age is 18 years and the employer is charged with compliance, regardless of representations by the employee.

The law also contains provision that any employer who employs 25 or more persons may not discriminate against any employee who is between the ages of 40 and 65 because of his or her age.

The same law specifies that the employer must keep certain records showing compliance or non-compliance with provisions of the law. Although no special format is required, at least the following should be available for up to a three year period:

1. Name of employee in full.
2. Home address, including zip code.
3. Date of birth, if under 19.
4. Sex and occupation.
5. Time of day and date of week on which the employee's work week begins.
6. Regular hourly rate of pay in any work week in which overtime premium is due; basis of wage payment (such as "$2 hr.", "$16 day", "$80 wk. plus extras where they exist).
7. Daily and weekly hours of work.
8. Total daily or weekly straight-time earnings.
9. Total overtime compensation for the work week.
10. Total additions to or deductions from wages paid each pay period.
11. Total wages paid each pay period.
12. Date of payment and the pay period covered by payment.

In addition special information is required where uncommon pay arrangements exist or where board, lodging, or other facilities are furnished by the employer.

If the funeral establishment is covered, or if not and one or more of its employees has individual coverage, a poster obtainable from the wage and hour division of the United States Department of Labor should be displayed, which sets forth the employees' entitlements.

There is also a Federal Wage Garnishment law which limits the amount that can be obtained by a creditor by attaching (garnisheeing) an employee's wages. Most states have their own garnishment laws. The state law will prevail if it puts a greater limitation on the amount of wages which can be attached and if that state has applied for and received a U.S. Department of Labor ruling that the state law applies.

Most of the businesses which affect interstate commerce are controlled by the National Labor Relations Board Act, which act sets up the rights and obligations of both the employees and the employer concerning bargaining, contract rights and other rights of the individuals. To date, most of the funeral homes of the country are not affected by this labor act; however, those large corporations dealing in funeral service which extensively operate between various states (interstate) would be covered by the act and the rights and privileges of the employees affected thereby.

Miscellaneous

In addition to the kinds of regulations heretofore discussed, various other types of regulations may be enacted or promulgated in the public interest. These other matters connected with funeral service include the giving of a bond in a reasonable amount to secure the performance by a funeral director of his duties; regulations providing for the inspection of the premises in which the profession of a funeral director is conducted or where embalming is practiced; and the imposition of a statutory duty to compile certain statistics concerning persons who die and the filing of death certificates and/or burial permits. In much the same vein there are court decisions which indicate that a funeral director does not have an insurable interest in an individual whose funeral the funeral director might handle, and as a consequence a funeral director cannot be a direct beneficiary of a life insurance policy.

The conduct of a funeral can be affected by a regulation or ordinance concerning funeral processions. In some states and/or in some local municipalities funeral processions are given the right-of-way except as to emergency vehicles, providing that certain requirements such as keeping a close formation, the display of headlights, the display of funeral flags and the like are met.

There now is a Consumer Protection Act, commonly referred to as the Truth in Lending Act. For those in funeral service who extend credit for payment of a funeral bill, or who charge interest for delayed payment of a bill, or who grant discounts for early payment of a bill, or who advertise any of the foregoing, this law becomes important and its terms must be adhered to. Like the provisions of the wage and hour law, the truth in lending provisions are quite complicated and intricate. Every owner or manager of a funeral establishment should become familiar with this act. Chapter 5 includes detailed information thereon in the discussion of business aspects of a funeral service practice.

Some Liabilities of a Funeral Service Practice

Each person has a legal duty to care for the rights of others and not act in violation thereof. Any individual who has a legal duty to observe the rights of others and violates that duty is liable for the damage caused by such violation. Failure to care for the rights of others may be both active and passive. So it is with funeral directors and dead bodies and funeral directors and the survivors of the decedent.

A funeral service licensee is charged with the effects of impropriety imposed upon the dead bodies entrusted to his care and the mental pain and anguish that these acts may bring about. Because of the foregoing, the law imposes upon a funeral director and embalmer the obligation to properly care for a dead body and treat the survivors of a deceased fairly. The duty and obligation is imposed regardless of the contractual obligations involved. So too a funeral director who has taken charge of a body and agreed to perform funeral services and to provide funeral merchandise, assumes the ordinary obligation of performance required of his profession and calling and is charged with the responsibility to use ordinary skill and due care under the circumstances, and is liable for failure to do so whether such failure is brought about by acts of omission or commission. The funeral director having assumed this obligation cannot shift the burden to one of his agents, because he is liable for the negligence or wrongful act of such agent.

The proprietor or operator of a funeral home owes to invitees on his premises the same duty owed generally by land owners to invitees. He has the duty of exercising reasonable care to keep the premises in reasonably safe condition for the intended use and he will be held liable for the failure to do so where such failure is the approximate cause of an injury to an invitee who is not himself chargeable with contributory negligence or with having assumed the risk.

In the case of funeral homes in particular an invitee is a person who might reasonably be expected to visit the funeral home for the purpose of discussing future funeral arrangements either for himself, or for another, or a person who might reasonably be expected to come to see the remains of a deceased relative or friend. The reasonable care required of a funeral home owner is somewhat in excess of the amount of reasonable care imposed upon others in the ordinary business functions such as a retail store, because it can be assumed that an invitee is apt to be emotionally disturbed when visiting the funeral home. Perhaps the most common situation involves a fall on exterior premises made slippery by ice, snow or rain and recovery has been permitted in such case.

The funeral home furnishes at the request of the relatives and friends transportation to and from the place where the service is held, if not in the funeral home, and to the cemetery. Sometimes transportation is desired to the funeral home or to go to some other location to select the funeral merchandise to be used in connection with the funeral. Injuries are sometimes sustained by persons being transported. In the event of injury the funeral home is ordinarily liable even if the funeral director was not, in fact, the operator or controller of the vehicle in which the survivor was injured. The funeral director contracts to provide funeral services, one of which is transportation, and the law infers from this contractual obligation an additional obligation to transport the bereaved survivors in safety, much as the bus company agrees to transport its passengers in safety for a stipulated sum. For those who are injured and are not among the bereaved survivors who had any contractual obligation with the funeral director, liability of the funeral director depends on whom the vehicle belonged to and who had control of the driver of the vehicle, if in fact the vehicle was not owned by or driven by the funeral director. If the vehicle was owned by or driven by the funeral director, the funeral director is liable for negligence which causes injury to those attending a funeral. Where the funeral director has hired outside livery (automobiles rented from automobile or limousine rental company) and where the driver is employed directly by this livery company, the question of the liability of the funeral director evolves around the question of who had control over the driver at the time that the injury was sustained. The facts of each case must therefore determine the liability on the part of the funeral director.

The funeral director is the agent of the person who hires him to perform services and as a result has the rights delegated to him by the person who hired him including the right of custody of the body and the right to exclude objectionable people from participating in or being at the funeral services. The funeral director has no greater rights than does the person who hired him to perform the services and the funeral director may be liable with the employer for improper interference with the rights of others.

Estate and Gift Taxes

A funeral service licensee who has or acquires an ownership interest in the funeral home with which he is associated must be cognizant of how such interest is affected by Gift Tax Laws and Estate Tax Laws. The licensee should plan ahead to the time when his ownership interest will by his voluntary act during life, or by inheritance on his death, pass to others. Since taxes of significant amounts can be involved, licensees should be made aware at least as to the broad principles involved.

Estate Taxes

Estate taxes, like income taxes, are graduated taxes. That is, the percentage of tax increases as the size of the estate increases. Therefore, in determining the amount of the estate taxes one should first determine the size of his estate, that is, the assets which will be inuring to the benefit of others upon his death. Included in such assets would be life insurance owned by the decedent regardless of beneficiary and the full value of jointly owned property.

Once the amount of the taxable assets has been determined, the estate tax can be determined by arriving at the net taxable estate. The net taxable estate where an individual dies leaving *no spouse* is the amount of the total taxable assets less the sum of (i) $60,000, (ii) cost of administration, and (iii) debts of the decedent.

Where the decedent is *survived by a spouse* the net taxable estate is an amount equal to the taxable assets less the sum of (i) the amount inherited by the spouse, not to exceed one-half of the taxable assets, (ii) $60,000, (iii) cost of administration, and (iv) debts of the decedent. A simple chart based on these statements is as follows:

Amount of Estate Less Cost of Administration and Debts*	Spouse Receiving One-Half	Spouse Receiving One-Third	No Spouse
$ 75,000	$ 0	$ 0	$ 1,050
105,000	0	500	5,900
150,000	1,050	4,800	17,900
240,000	9,500	20,700	44,700

* This does not include a deduction for the $60,000 exemption.

Gift Taxes

People are living longer and as a result more owner-licensees are retiring from funeral service and leaving the management of their funeral home or mortuary to other licensees. Many times the retiring licensee desires the successor licensee to have some ownership interest in the firm to go along with his management duties. Where outright sales are not the desired means of transfer, the usual way to transfer said ownership interest is by gift. This is especially true in the event that the successor licensee is a child, relative, or a valued employee. If the gift is during one's lifetime, it is affected by the gift tax. If the gift takes effect at time of death, it is affected by the estate tax.

The donor (retiring licensee) must take the following into consideration in determining if he desires to make such a gift:

1. Does donor desire to have control over or use of the item given?

2. Does donor desire the donee (receiver of the gift) to have control over or use of the gift?

3. The taxability of the amounts of gifts in excess of $3,000 for the year per donee—$6,000 if spouse joined in gift, even though not spouse's property.

4. The amount of gifts, if any, in previous years in excess of the $3,000 or $6,000 per year per donee as applicable are excluded from tax. Amounts in excess thereof in each year, unless included in the exemption referred to in Item 5, are taxable.

5. Donor in his lifetime may give $30,000 tax free in excess of the $3,000-$6,000 per year set out in Item 3. If donor is married at time of gift, the spouse may again join in with an additional exemption of $30,000 subject to the same limitations.

6. The amount of gifts in excess of the $3,000–$6,000 in any one year not applied to the $30,000–$60,000 exemption in Item 5 or in excess thereof, are taxable.

7. The ability of one's estate to pay estate taxes and the amount thereof. Many owner-licensees die owning all or part of their establishment. Often the value thereof is the major part of their estate (that which they owned and/or was taxable at their death) and the other assets and insurance might not be enough to pay estate taxes.

8. The amount of tax payable by reason of the taxable gifts, if any, set forth in Items 3, 4, 5 and 6.

9. That a Gift Tax return should be filed.

10. Donee's tax consequences on his sale or gift of the item given. A short schedule of the amounts of gift taxes is as follows:

Taxable Gifts	Amount of Tax
$10,000.	$ 375.
30,000.	2,250.
50,000.	5,250.
100,000.	15,525.

Many purposes may arise for the making of a gift. Such purpose will generally make the gift tax applicable, rather than the estate tax, unless it can be shown that the real purpose of the gift was to avoid estate taxes, or unless the gift was made within three years of the date of death, in which event it will be incumbent upon the estate of the donor to prove that the gift was not in contemplation of death.

When property is given, the value at the time of the gift is used in determining the tax, not the cost of the item given in the hands of the donor. However, on a sale by the donee (the person receiving the gift item), his cost basis will be the cost to the donor and not the value at the time the gift is made, plus the tax on the gift.

Forms to Assist Survivors and to Avoid Unnecessary Funeral Director Liability

Autopsy Consent

The number of requests for an autopsy or a post mortem examination of a body is steadily increasing. Three of the reasons for this are: (1) more deaths in medical or semi-medical institutions; (2) more emphasis on an increased percentage of autopsies for such medical institutions; and, (3) expanded prerequisites for certain conditions of hospitalization or the payment of hospitalization and/or death benefits.

There are times by law when a body can be autopsied pursuant to governmental authority without the consent of the next of kin—when there is a question as to what caused death. But most times it is legally sound that a consent must be secured. And, most individuals or institutions making the request will have a consent form to be completed with the post mortem examination to be held in a place other than in the preparation room of a funeral home.

However, there still are autopsies performed in funeral homes. (Or some tissue or a sample of blood may be taken from a body there.) Unless a law enforcement agency is making the request that this be done, the funeral director should not permit it in his establishment without a signed consent to do so. Also, a funeral director should not release the body to other than a government official without a consent being signed. If a consent has not been signed the following form may be used to get the consent. This form also may prove helpful to some families who wish an autopsy and would appreciate a proper consent form to sign.

N. F. D. A. Form 3

_____
                                City   Date

The undersigned relative (or friend, if no relative see footnote) of_____
                                                                    Name of Deceased

of_____ who died at_____
              Address   Place of Death

_____ on the_____ day of_____ 19____
     County   State

hereby gives permission for a post mortem examination of the body of said deceased, at, the_____

_____ and the taking of such samples for
              Hospital or Mortuary

tests as are deemed advisable. It is understood that prior to such post mortem examination, the family funeral

director shall be consulted with respect to the arterial injection of a non-hardening embalming fluid.

Name_____   _____
                                                        Relationship to Deceased

Address _____

Witness:

_____

_____

NOTE: The word friend in this case, to be interpreted as including
the person or organization paying the burial expenses.

N.F.D.A. Form 3

Embalming Report

There has been litigation because of alleged improper embalming. Sometimes this stems from a situation where the funeral and burial take place in the community where death occurred. Other times it results from the allegation that a remains was not properly prepared before it was forwarded for the funeral and/or burial elsewhere. Certainly a lawsuit and the possibility of paying damages are to be avoided. But more important, there are the sensitivities of the survivors.

The use of the following embalming report for all bodies prepared for casketing and/or forwarding is recommended for two reasons.

First, the necessity of completing the report acts as a disciplined way of checking what was done and knowing what is still to be done.

Second, a completed form could provide valuable evidence against a claim that the embalming was improper or indicated gross negligence. (See NFDA Form 2.)

Authorization to Transport Remains

Early in 1969 it was estimated that well over 100,000 human remains were shipped by air in 1968 in the planes of major passenger airlines or cargo lines. There still are thousands sent each year by rail although that number is decreasing. Annually there are thousands of instances of "over the road" transporting of bodies by hearses and other automotive vehicles. Finally, there are a growing number of bodies being transported in small planes some of which are owned by funeral directors.

NFDA Form 5 should be completed for each instance of the forwarding of a body for other than a "local" funeral and/or burial. (See page 175.)

Forms for Use where Body Kept Other Than in a Funeral Home

There are places where a funeral Mass is said at night in a Catholic Church or where a funeral service is conducted in a church of another denomination and the body kept in the church until the morning when it is taken to the cemetery for the committal and/or interment.

There are also instances where the body is taken to a public place other than a church for the visitation period or the funeral and left overnight.

The risk of having something happen to that body and/or casket in these cases is clear. Fire, vandalism and desecration are all possibilities about which the next of kin and the minister or other responsible person must be aware and against which the funeral director should be protected.

The use of Forms 7a and 7b will do this diplomatically and legally (page 176).

Conclusion

The law as it affects funeral service practices and those licensed therein does not vary generally from the laws covering the operation of most other businesses or professions insofar as such laws vary or are non-existent in the states. Furthermore, both federal and state laws are subject to interpretations and decisions by administrative bodies and courts of law in various jurisdictions. These sometimes differ as to a similar set of circumstances under the same or similar statute or rule. Then too, the "law" set forth in a decision today sometimes barely resembles what the "law" was a few years ago. This chapter, studied with this in mind, should prove basically helpful. However, a lawyer's advice often will be necessary regarding a specific set of facts.

NFDA Form 2

EMBALMING REPORT

Date................................Case No..................................Funeral Record No...................................

History and Description:

Name of deceased..Address..

Place of death.................................. Date ....19.... Time......................... { AM } PM

Age............Sex.........Color or Race................Height.................Approximate Weight..............

Beard { Long............ Short............ }Moustache ....Eyes..............Teeth..............Hair..............

Scars, Birth Marks, Moles, Warts, Tattoo—Describe: ....

....

Cause of Death...How ascertained................................

Medical Attendant or Coronor..Address ....

Received at funeral home: Date... 19........Time............. { AM } PM

Condition of Body Before Embalming:

Normal............clean............dirty............evidence of disease............emaciation............evidence of surgery............

evidence of external wounds............eruptions............dropsical............post-mortem pigmentation............skin-

slip............gas............tumors............ulcerations............mutilations............purge (type)............rigor mortis............

Autopsy (type)............Authorized by..Performed by............................

Remarks: ....

What tests of death were made?...

Embalming:

Elapsed time between death and start of embalming:..

Arteries used for injection ....

Veins used for drainage ....

Auxiliary drainage methods used..

Method of injection: Hand pump...................Gravity...................Pressure Machine...................

Fluid used: A...................B...................C...................
(Trade name   pre-injection   arterial   cavity
and index)

Fluid Dilution: (Ounces to two quarts)

1st bottle..................... 2nd bottle..................... 3rd bottle................ 4th bottle................

5th bottle..................... 6th bottle..................... 7th bottle................ 8th bottle................

Cavity fluids: (ounces injected undiluted)..

Other cavity treatment .... Treatment.....................................

Parts receiving poor circulation ....and treatment................

Restorative art treatment..Authorized by................................

Cosmetics used ....

Length of time required to complete operation...

Note: Place additional remarks or sketches on reverse side.

Condition of Body After Embalming:

Condition of body at completion of operation ....

Condition of body at time of funeral ....

Special post-embalming treatment required...

N.F.D.A. Form 2

Place of { burial..
          { cremation.. Date.......................19.......
          { entombment...........................

Body shipped to ....Date ....Arrive ....

Body embalmed for ....Address ....

Record of personal effects including jewelry, clothing, money, papers, etc. received with body ....

....

Disposition of personal effects ....

....

Record of personal effects, jewelry, etc., placed on body for burial...

....

Signature of Embalmer ....Apprentice..

Anatomical Sketch

Front View   Back View

Additional comments regarding special aspects of case: ....

....

....

....

N.F.D.A. Form 2 (continued)

N.F.D.A. Form 5

AUTHORIZATION TO TRANSPORT REMAINS

....
City   State

....
Date

To.. :
      (Name of Funeral Home)

This is your authority to carry out our request and remove and transport the remains of the late

....

from..to..

via..
      (Name rail, air or other transport line)

Having full power and authority to grant this authorization, I hereby agree to hold the above named funeral home harmless, and to indemnify it or its assigns from any and all claims, demands, or damages which may be made or declared against said funeral home or its assigns, by reason of removal and transportation of said remains as above requested.

....
               (Next of kin)

....
      (Witness)

N.F.D.A. Form 5

N.F.D.A. Form 1

ASSIGNMENT OF PROCEEDS OF INSURANCE

For and in consideration of the sum of one dollar ($1.00) and for services rendered by ....
....Funeral Directors, for and in connection with the

burial of ...., I hereby assign, set over and transfer to the said
...., Funeral Directors, the sum of ....
.... dollars ($..............................) of the proceeds of that certain

Policy Number .... in the ....
Insurance Company, which may be or is due me from the said company as beneficiary of said policy, or to
which I may otherwise be entitled under the terms of said policy.

I hereby instruct, authorize and direct the said ....
Insurance Company to pay over to the said ....
Funeral Directors the sum of .... dollars ($..............................) out
of said proceeds upon presentation and release by the said ....
of this assignment and a duly receipted funeral bill for the burial of the said ....
...., and the payment of the said sum of ....
dollars ($..............................) by the said .... Insurance Company,
which shall be a release and certificate for the said amount so due me out of said proceeds.

              Signed..
              Address..

STATE OF ...., ... COUNTY, SS:
Personally appeared before me, a Notary Public in and for said .... County,
.............................., the above mentioned .... who, first being
duly sworn, says that the above facts are true to the best of .... knowledge and belief, and says that the
execution of the above assignment is .... voluntary act and deed, being under no restraint whatever.

Dated..   ....Notary Public.

N.F.D.A. Form 1

NFDA Form 7a

RELEASE OF NEXT OF KIN
And/Or Legal Custodian

The undersigned represents that he is a next of kin and/or legal custodian of the

body of_____ and as such next of kin and/or legal custodian
                    (Deceased)

hereby requests that_____
                                              (Funeral Home)

deliver the body and its casket to_____
                                    A.M.
on or before _____ P.M. on _____
                                              (Date)

The undersigned in behalf of himself/herself, the next of kin, the heirs at law and

the estate of said_____ hereby agrees to hold
                              (Deceased)

the said_____ harmless from any liability or loss
                    (Funeral Home)

incurred by said funeral home by reason of delivering to and/or leaving the casket and/or

body at such designated place.

                                    _____
                                        (Next of Kin and/or Legal Custodian)

Date: _____

N.F.D.A. Form 7a

NFDA Form 7b

GUARANTEE BY CHURCH
Or Other Designated Place

The _____
                        (Church — or Other Designated Place)
hereby acknowledges receiving the casket and body of
                                                                        A.M.
_____ at _____ P.M.
                    (Deceased)

on_____ and hereby agrees to hold
              (Date)

_____
                                    (Funeral Home)
harmless from any liability or loss sustained by said Funeral Home, which loss is incurred
by reason of said body and casket being at the undersigned church or other designated
place. The period of this guarantee is from the time the body and casket is left at the
church or other designated place until it has been called for and removed by a representative of the Funeral Home.

                                    _____
                                        (Church or Other Designated Place)

                                    By_____
                                        (Representative of Church or Other Designated Place)

Date:_____

N.F.D.A. Form 7b

12

THE PREARRANGING AND PREFINANCING OF FUNERALS

Thomas H. Clark
and
Howard C. Raether

A Brief Background

In the chapter "The Law and a Funeral Service Practice" reference is made to changes in the law to permit an individual during his lifetime to take steps to get the kind of funeral he desires and to determine the method and place of final disposition of his body.

There have been developments toward this new concept for many years, but it has been only since the end of World War II that a significant impact of the move was felt. It was not until 1952 that the National Funeral Directors Association felt the situation warranted a policy statement which concluded with the recommendation which has led to laws controlling and regulating prefinanced funeral contracts being enacted in a large majority of the states.

The Sociology of Life and Death

The funerals for most people are selected at the time of death. Unless one knows when, where and under what circumstances he is going to die, it is difficult for him to prearrange his own funeral, either alone or with a member of his family, and feel that it will be as planned.

There are few people who are sure things won't change sufficiently to upset pre-arranged plans. And in cases when they are changed and are different, problems are often created instead of being solved.

A national study showed that in 1967 less *than 1%* of all funerals conducted, except in the Pacific and Mountain regions, were prearranged. It also revealed that *from 25% to 33%* (depending on the region) of the funerals conducted in 1967 that were prearranged were changed by the survivors. However, *about 50%* of funeral directors said at that time that prearrangements were on the increase.

Why?

There are those who feel, as is pointed out elsewhere herein, that our society is changing from a family culture to a generation culture. Families are being separated by age, by distance, by knowledge and by philosophy.

Sometimes an elder member, especially if living alone, wants to make sure he or she gets the kind of funeral he desires. Often a surviving spouse will make arrangements for the same kind of funeral that was just conducted for the husband or wife.

Sometimes differences in a family are such that segments thereof feel they have to protect themselves against each other as to funeral arrangements and costs.

Sometimes cost is the primary reason for the prearrangement and prefinancing. There are those who want a moderate to expensive service and who want to be sure they get it. Often prearranging is done in an attempt to keep costs down, to indicate to the family or other survivors that they should not go "overboard" in the pre-arranger's opinion.

Finally, there are those who prearrange and prefinance their own funeral because they want a specific type of service involving a particular church and/or clergyman and/or funeral director and/or any one of many other reasons trivial to some but important to the person doing the prearranging.

Prearrangements are a part of just about every funeral director's files and practice. They must be recognized as an aspect of present-day funeral service, and important facets of the overall picture must be understood.

Psychological Aspects

Some who have studied death, grief and bereavement say that following death there is a therapy in doing things and in having responsibilities. When most of the details of a funeral have been worked out and perhaps paid for by the deceased, this could leave the survivors with little to do in the actual at-need planning and decision making.

Equally important, survivors and the community may want to do some last thing or things in honor and/or respect and/or in recognition of the deceased. There may be the feeling this shouldn't or can't be done when the person has made his own arrangements. Or, there may be some things that the deceased has arranged which might affect the sensibilities of a survivor, or survivors, and bother them for years, but they won't suggest a change lest they "offend" the departed and his memory.

The Promotions of the Fifties

The idea of the prearranged or prefinanced funeral was not first conceived in the early fifties, but it was then that it became the basis for promotions to sell the idea of prearranging and prefinancing funerals.

Some of these promotions were built around package deals covering the funeral service, funeral merchandise, flowers, burial vault, cemetery lot, opening and closing of the grave, and the grave marker.

Sales crews were trained and often blanketed an area pushing door bells and at times offering an item of merchandise free to get into the door to make their presentation.

In this presentation the alleged high cost of dying, peace of mind, and a special purchase price of the prearranged service and merchandise were usually stressed.

These developments led to two separate actions which although not related complemented each other.

The Association of Better Business Bureaus, now the Council of Better Business Bureaus, came out with three publications on the subject in seven years. In the same period many states enacted laws to control the prearranging and prefinancing of funerals.

The ABBBI publications are:

1. *Facts Every Family Should Know About Funerals and Interments.* Some paragraphs were devoted to package deals therein.
2. *Questions You Should Ask About Cemetery Lot Promotions.* Since many promotions—pre-need and otherwise—were cemetery initiated, this leaflet was prepared.
3. *Facts You Should Know. . .Questions You Should Ask. . .The Prearrangement and Prefinancing of Funerals.*

All three of these publications are kept current and their widespread distribution continues.

Because the last-mentioned booklet is pertinent to this chapter, the following excerpts from it are quoted:

> In recent years a growing number of individuals, firms and groups have sought to stimulate public interest in prearranged, prefinanced funeral plans. Among them have been sales organizations and promoters outside the funeral profession who seek to interpose themselves as third parties in the traditional personal and confidential relationship between the funeral director and the survivors of the deceased. Grievous disappointments and severe financial losses have resulted from some unsound promotional schemes foisted on a credulous public by armies of high-pressure salesmen.

*   *   *

> Sometimes, belief that a funeral has been fully prearranged and paid for can create a false sense of security for survivors.

*   *   *

> The simplest way to prearrange a funeral is to leave written instructions for those who will make the arrangements. If advance payments are involved under a contract which does not permit the individual to alter the prearrangements to meet changing circumstances, the possibilities. . .can lead to serious problems. What assurance do you have that the funds deposited will be intact when the time for their disbursement arrives or that they will be available to you if you want them? Who will receive the interest on your money during the many years which may intervene between the date of deposit and the date of death? Will such interest revert to you? Will you be better off by depositing the money in your own bank where you will get the benefit of all interest earned? You also are free to withdraw your funds in an emergency.

*   *   *

Savings claims and promises of "bargain" rates are stressed in selling many of these promotional plans. Weigh carefully any representation that a "plan" will give you adequate services for less than you can obtain them from other funeral directors against the fact that the sales commissions and costs must be added to the cost of the funeral under the plan.

The material in these excerpts pinpoints the problem for many of the public.

The State Pre-Need Trust Laws

The questions which the Association of Better Business Bureaus was asking in its booklet on prefinanced funerals were often asked across the country during the fifties and sixties as many states considered legislation to regulate and control the contracts as to such funerals. The chart which is Appendix X gives the names of all the states within the continental limits of the United States. It shows the majority of them with a statute which in some way regulates these contracts. It also gives the basics of each state's statute.

The breakdown of state laws and/or opinions shows, as the Better Business Bureaus point out, that most of these statutes require that all money, or a major share of all monies, paid in advance for funeral merchandise or services, and accruing interest thereon, must be deposited in trust with an approved financial institution until the need for disbursement arises. In most of these states monies paid in advance for burial vaults must also be entrusted and there have been opinions of attorney generals and of state supreme courts upholding this requirement. In some states amounts paid for markers and mausoleum space sold in advance of death must also be placed in trust.

A West Virginia statute was held to be unconstitutional and a new law passed since. The constitutionality of the Arkansas, Idaho, Iowa, Illinois, Kansas, Utah and Texas statutes has been upheld by the supreme courts of those states.

Some promoting prefinanced funerals object to putting in trust or reserve 100% of monies paid in advance for funeral merchandise and services. In the Illinois case one of the suggestions made was that a lesser amount be deposited. The supreme court of the state in its decision points out that the plaintiff cemetery entered the "prearrangement business by choice" and that its procedures invite "regulation of a stringent nature." The matter was appealed to the Supreme Court of the United States which refused to consider the case.

Some Present-day Thoughts
About Prearranged and Prefinanced Funerals

In the previously referred to Illinois decision the supreme court of that state said:

In the long interval between full receipt of the purchase price and contract performance the opportunities for fraud are great and risk of insolvency, with consequent inability to perform, apparent.

It is doubtful whether anyone has or will doubt the validity of this statement. And in many areas there has been a slackening of pre-need promotion activity. The economics of the situation has much to do with this for reasons funeral directors know.

The Plan with the Special Price

ABBBI queries a $795 funeral being sold in advance for $595. In its brochure an arrangement is cited "between one sales organization and 'participating' funeral homes (in which) the latter are required to represent that a designated funeral, available to customers of the 'plan' at the 'reduced price' of $595, is 'regularly' priced at $795. The actual price to the company selling the plan is only $420."

The BBB asks, "Do you believe that a funeral home can afford to sell services and merchandise honestly priced at $795 for little more than half that amount and still make a profit?"

Supposing that there was no sales organization, could a funeral home with a plan of providing a $795 service for $595 come out ahead with that amount?

If this is in a state where the interest on the monies paid in advance cannot accrue to the benefit of the funeral firm, the amount paid will not increase. Even in those states where the interest can accrue, as earned, to the benefit of the funeral firm, unless the entire amount, or a sizable portion of it, is held for a long period of time, the increment is not large enough to close the gap between the "before-need" and "at-need" figures if both are realistic.

Another factor of importance is the annual increased cost of providing the service. This is especially true if the components of the funeral and a particular casket are spelled out. Few things have gone down in price or remained stable in a number of years. Therefore every cost increase decreases the actual amount available for the funeral.

Finally, if the pre-need contract was solicited by a salesman, it is estimated that 15 to 30% of the total contract price will be used to absorb sales and administration costs.

Income for Federal Tax Purposes

When a funeral is prefinanced, if the firm to whom that money is paid has constructive, permissive or actual use of the money, the money is taxable as income by the federal government for the year in which the money was received. This is true whether the amount is a partial payment or the entire prepaid price of the service.

What to Do

This chapter shows that many states have enacted laws controlling and/or regulating the contracts made in advance of need for funeral services and/or merchandise. This coupled with significant variations in the pre-need laws and the divergent opinions which exist among funeral directors warrants the following recommendations:

1. Pre-need contracts and their solication *are* fraught with the danger of fraud and funeral directors should avoid any contract or plan which could harm their clientele or their service or place in the community.

2. Those who wish to prearrange their own funeral or one for someone for whom they have responsibility should be able to do so.

3. When a funeral is prearranged and monies are paid in advance of need for funeral services and/or merchandise including burial vaults, *all* such monies should be deposited in a trust fund with the person or persons prearranging having the control thereof to be entitled to the earnings therefrom. Furthermore such prearranger shall have the right to terminate the contract at any time without forfeiture of any of the funds which have been paid or earnings accrued.

4. Where a contract is entered into it should be in accordance with the laws of the state in which the prearrangement is made. Some state funeral directors associations have prepared contract forms. If there is no pre-need law and/or if no form is available—the suggested wording for one is at the conclusion of this chapter. In all such contracts the funeral director should bind himself only to the kind of funeral and merchandise which will be available at the time of need for the face amount of the contract.

5. Funeral directors should carefully consider the potential negative effects and cost of allowing a third party to step between themselves and their firm and the family through the representations of a third party soliciting a pre-need program or plan which will be serviced by the funeral home when the person for whom the service was prearranged dies.

6. No funeral business should be purchased which has the liability of providing funerals which have been prefinanced in whole or in part until the purchaser of the business is sure the monies paid in advance are on hand for the funerals which will have to be provided.

It is not the intent of the writers of this chapter to discourage individuals and families from discussing funerals and perhaps making tentative plans for a funeral or funerals. This is encouraged especially when there is a family or close friends and they share in the discussion. Death is not as commonplace as it once was. Millions of people in the country today have never experienced a death and funeral of someone close to them. They don't know what is involved and they should.

There is a big difference between tentative arrangements considering survivors and formal agreements which might disregard and adversely affect the sensibilities of those who will mourn.

Where there is no family or its members are disinterested or feel specific prearrangement is good, a formal agreement in line with the following contract suggestion will not only be proper but may also be helpful.

*   *   *

THIS AGREEMENT made and entered into this____day of_____ 19____,by and between_____,party of the first part, hereinafter sometimes referred to as "Funeral Director," and_____,party of the second part, sometimes hereinafter referred to as "Buyer."

WITNESSETH:

WHEREAS, party of the second part desires and hereby requests to enter into a contract to provide for payment for funeral merchandise and/or services in advance of death, which merchandise and /or services are to be delivered and performed subsequent to the death of _____ _____, herinafter referred to as Beneficiary as follows:

Professional services and casket

_____

_____

_____

NOW, THEREFORE, in consideration of the mutual promises, it is hereby agreed as follows:

1. Funeral Director will supply to Beneficiary out of the funds deposited by Buyer the services and/or merchandise as set forth above for the sum of $_____, payable as follows:

_____

_____

_____

2. Said funds as aforesaid shall be placed with _____ hereinafter sometimes referred to as "Trustee" within ten days after receipt thereof. In the event, upon the death of Beneficiary, said funds are inadequate to provide for the services above described, then the funds shall be used by the Funeral Director to provide professional services and/or merchandise of a type as nearly similar as may be purchased with said funds at the time of Beneficiary's death.

3. Upon the death of Beneficiary, the said funds shall be released by the Trustee forthwith to the Funeral Director upon receipt of a certified copy of certificate of death or other evidence of death satisfactory to said Trustee and where required by State Law, an affidavit by the Funeral Director that the funeral services and/or merchandise which has been contracted for have been so provided and that the cost was not less than the amount on deposit. Any amount on deposit not required to pay for funeral services and/or funeral merchandise shall be returned on request to the Buyer if living, or if not living to the estate of the beneficiary.

4. Said funds shall remain on deposit with the Trustee and shall remain intact as a fund until the death of the Beneficiary, or until withdrawal by Buyer as hereinafter provided; and said funds may be withdrawn only for the full amount thereof and not in part, and said withdrawals must comply with the rules and regulations of said Trustee; provided, however, that the Buyer may, at any time upon complying with the rules and regulations of the Trustee, withdraw the funds deposited to date with the Trustee pursuant to this contract. In the event of withdrawal the Buyer shall notify the Funeral Director within twenty-four hours prior to such withdrawal, and in the event the withdrawal is completed, the Funeral Director shall be relieved from any of the obligations contained in this agreement.

5. It is mutually agreed that the said Trustee is only the repository of said funds and is not liable for the fulfillment of the contract by the Funeral Director, and upon payment over to said Funeral Director of the said funds, or repayment to Buyer, the Trustee's liability shall terminate.

6. Interest earnings which may accrue on said funeral fund shall be added to and become part of said fund.

7. Upon the death of Buyer, in the event the said funds shall exceed the amount required to provide services set forth above, any surplus shall be paid over to Beneficiary's estate (or) to _____, by the Funeral Director.

8. This Agreement shall be binding upon the heirs, administrators, executors and assigns of the parties hereto.

IN WITNESS WHEREOF the parties hereto have caused this Agreement to be executed the day and year first above written.

In the presence of:

_____
(Funeral Director)

_____

_____
(Buyer)

_____

We consent to this agreement
and the acceptance of these funds:

_____

by_____
(Title)

Dated_____ 19 _____

13

MERGERS, ACQUISITIONS AND
MULTI-UNIT ORGANIZATIONS

Thomas H. Clark
and
Howard C. Raether

Late in 1969 the U.S. Department of Commerce decided to include an "outlook" on funeral service in its *1970 Industrial Outlook*. This was done presumably because of the interest in funeral home mergers and acquisitions and some publicly held funeral service corporations. The acquisition fever had spread to funeral service even to the point of some conglomerates expressing an interest in funeral service companies operating either horizontally or vertically.

Funeral homes which are a part of a multi-unit operation are not new, especially in some of the larger cities and on the West Coast. Previously most such operations were "local" to benefit "pooling" or "floating" facilities, equipment and personnel, and often some centralized buying, warehousing and servicing.

Most of these are intra-state and within a comparatively limited area. The exceptions are an interstate operation established to serve the same basic clientele. An example of this would be a New York based funeral home which also has a funeral home or homes in Florida.

During 1970 there was increased activity and publicity at the national level regarding some interstate operations being built through the acquisition method. Most times the "news" was misleading because it told of funeral homes being merged. There was some of this on a local basis. But usually the firms were being acquired by outright purchase.

Early in 1968 we started a lengthy and thorough study of mergers and acquisitions generally, and specifically of those in funeral service.

185

The studies found, as reported often by either or both of us, that in many mergers and acquisitions few, if any, of the benefits are apparent on the surface. In the opinion of some authorities this is the case in funeral service. Many funeral service acquisitions cannot be explained because of obvious deficiencies in integrating the production of the so-called marketing facilities of the firms involved. In fact, in funeral service the overall "market" is limited to the number of deaths and the specific market area being served.

A merger market has developed in business. This means that financial analysts and investors are often interested in firms that are seeking to acquire or that are seeking to be acquired as a response to basic problems facing their firms or to satisfy needs for expansion and growth. In some instances mergers are helpful to the firms involved and the improvement is reflected in the price of the firm's stock. In many other instances mergers are of little help in solving the firm's problems and sometimes merely compound the problems. Consequently, financial analysts increasingly recognize that, while mergers may be desirable in some situations, they are no panacea to the firm's problems and in some cases may cause more problems than they solve.

Another reason for merger activity is that in many cases it replaces proxy fights as methods for affecting changes in corporate control. This applies to larger, more broadly owned firms than those generally found in funeral service.

There are two main reasons which make an owner of a business or a professional service firm, including a funeral firm, desirous of having his or its operation acquired or having it merged into another organization. One is the need for some resources more readily accessible to larger enterprises. These might include ready access to capital for expansion of facilities, management recruitment and development and assistance in financial budgeting and planning. A second reason is management secession or estate problems. Perhaps there would be no one whom the owner would want to carry on his business, or an owner might feel his estate needs liquid funds for payment of such obligations as estate taxes.

One of the basic principles leading to a merger or acquisition is that increased volume will result from the same or less overhead and increased capital investment will result in producing the product or service at a lower cost to the public, thus building a more profitable business. It argues for more economical operations because it reduces the amount of capital investment and overhead per "sales" dollar.

Funeral service has not been regarded as such an example, up to this point at least. Surveys indicate that where services, facilities, and merchandise are offered and provided on a comparable basis the cost of providing the funeral service on a unit basis is about the same and the owner's compensation and/or profit is also comparable. The validity of this statement is attested to by the fact that in those firms which have been acquired to date, funeral prices usually remained the same or were raised by the new owners. If savings are possible by centralized operation and/or management expertise, those savings apparently are dissipated by the cost of the central office including officials' salaries, which cost is actually non-productive as to "on the scene" rendering of what has been a highly personalized service.

We do not imply that there are no uneconomical funeral service operations. Nor can it be said that there are not some economies which could be effected in funeral homes by joint or pooled use of facilities, equipment and manpower, or by central management involving administration, purchasing, warehousing, bookkeeping and the like. But providing the funeral as it has been known for the last half century presents a unique situation which might be difficult if not impossible to overcome if the facets of the funeral which help make it an experience of value are to be continued.

Mass production procedures are not generally applicable to individualized, personalized, care taking services of such a nature that they often cannot be pre-scheduled as to time or place. There have been instances where families have felt that a merger or acquisition would bring "Mass Mortuary" policies and procedures. There have been reports of shifts in loyalty from families that had called the funeral home previous to its acquisition. This undoubtedly is why some who have been acquired insist that they have merged to make it seem they still own a major part of the firm and have a real voice in its management.

On the other hand some acquiring organizations maintain their size and management allow them to serve better, even on a personal basis. Regardless, there undoubtedly are communities, mostly in large metropolitan areas, where a segment of the population is not interested in personalized service or in facets of the funeral which make it most meaningful to those who mourn. This segment might not object if a large multi-unit organization with distant and absentee ownership economizes by eliminating some of the things that help make the funeral an experience of value for others. They might not care if the organization acquiring the funeral home that has or might serve them would merge or be acquired by another group which has gains in profits as a publicized purpose.

Observations and Advice

Beyond the general observations as to primary demand for the funeral and the selective demand for the funeral director or firm there are some observations that must be made for those thinking of being acquired, or selling to a firm making acquisitions. Advice will be interspersed.

When a large funeral home is acquired it usually becomes a wholly owned subsidiary of the holding company and when the acquired funeral home is not too large, or where conditions in the area favor it, it may become part of one subsidiary of the holding company.

An interesting factor is the formula used to determine the price to be paid for any acquired funeral home. Some buyers look mostly to net earnings and the ratio of earnings to the expected purchase price, and to them the book value and cash flow are only miscellaneous items to be considered. Others employ no set formula, often putting weight on the book value and the cash flow of the organization to be acquired as well as the net earnings.

A well financed holding company in its early stages may purchase funeral homes for "cash." Some money is paid immediately with the balance in installments covered by commercial paper such as notes. If not well financed, installment payments and/or stock of the acquiring company have been used.

As companies become bigger they go from the simple use of "cash" in making acquisitions to a combination of cash, stock debentures, warrants, and warrants and convertible debentures. The combination is what seems to be the more sophisticated way of paying for acquisitions. As holding companies get size or substance they often try to list their stock on a national trading basis on the stock exchange, or trade it "over the counter" so that it can be easily bought or sold.

In funeral service acquiring firms seem to prefer buying on the installment basis if stock is not involved and prefer buying the business rather than the real estate. Generally they are willing to rent the premises for a reasonable number of years, roughly three to ten.

A funeral director contemplating being acquired and considering accepting an installment obligation for stock must give a hard look at the financial condition of the acquiring firm. The financial statement of the firm should be gone over in detail by a financial advisor who should not be involved in the transaction other than to receive a fee for examining the financial data. Thus the advisor's answer would not be weighted because it does not affect him.

In the process certainly one of the matters of concern would be the indebtedness often found in rapidly expanding companies. This is especially true where mergers and/or acquisitions have been the basis for expansion.

In evaluating the prospects of selling a firm it should be recognized that stock values may have substantial declines. Although stock values may increase, the seller should also be able to absorb, both financially and psychologically, the experience of having assets acquired over a lifetime drop to a fraction of their original value based upon the attitudes of stock market analysts and investors.

In recent years many tax advantages of stock option programs and other deferred payment plans have been changed or withdrawn by federal authorities. Thus it is important to receive thorough and specialized tax counsel before committing oneself to a complex compensation contract.

What have the prospective purchasers of funeral homes looked for? Generally the bigger the acquiring firm, the bigger the funeral home they prefer. They want a funeral home which has a history or potential of solid growth in an area or a community which itself has all indications of continued growth. They feel the funeral home should be located in an area which is not liable to depreciate within ten years after acquisition.

In some cases the acquiring firm may not insist on buying management, believing it is able and willing to supply its own management from training programs it has or is developing. Some apparently feel that in the larger funeral homes the present owner or manager is not as important now as he once was. This is especially true in metropolitan areas. Subsequently they think there need be no continuity of management to make the acquired firm profitable to the holding company. Usually this is not the case because of the personal aspect of funeral service. However, there could be instances where management will be affected eventually as it has in other fields where, despite announcements to the contrary, personnel changes are made often involving those in the top positions.

Most acquiring firms feel that it is advantageous to pool all of the material assets of one funeral home with another. These are generally referred to as "floating assets." So they seek to acquire more than one firm in one area.

Some acquiring firms do not believe in above average educational standards for funeral service personnel. Some do. Those who don't say that the education of licensees should be along technical lines with only the group supervisor and manager needing management abilities supplemented by formal education beyond high school.

Vertical holding companies in funeral service are a distinct probability; that is, adding cemeteries and/or manufacturing funeral merchandise as well as owning their own livery companies. The vertical expansion thus far has not generally extended into companies that manufacture caskets and other burial merchandise, supplies and equipment. One publicly owned group, however, has funeral homes, cemeteries, a vault company and a grave marker firm.

A tight money market somewhat reduces the seller's market and gives importance to the "liquid" buyer who has the financial ability to pay cash for the business or to make an investment in the business when it is acquired or both.

Large conglomerates and other firms which have been busy in the overall acquisition field, whether horizontal or vertical, were affected appreciably in 1970. The upward spiral could stop, if it hasn't already. In those situations where this spiraling has been artificial and not based on good business practices and sound financial arrangements, the conglomerates or holding companies will feel, more than anyone else, the adverse effects of stock market fluctuations and other business influences.

In conclusion, the question often asked is whether independent funeral firms can meet the competition of the group organizations which are often public stock corporations. Marketing expert Dr. Roger D. Blackwell of Ohio State University says they can. He adds that the independent firm can do as good if not a better job of being able to serve well if they have the right "tools." He suggests that cooperation and sharing with other independent firms could provide some of these "tools." The economist insists, however, that new emphasis must be placed on public relations activities and encourages continued research on consumer decision processes.

14

MODERN FUNERAL HOME PLANNING, DESIGNING, DECORATING AND LIGHTING

Paul E. Bollman

Thinking of Building a New Funeral Home

Does your practice require a branch? What about re-locating an already established firm? Are you opening an entirely "new" business?

A great many factors must be considered when thinking about or planning the construction of a new funeral home. Consideration must not only be given to the area in which it is to be built to serve the people of the community, but also to whether it is a "new business" in a "new location." Or is it a branch operation serving an expanding population from a pre-established general location? Or is it one of several branches (existing or projected) which will function in the outlying community?

Many firms, especially those with a sizable annual number of funerals, are planning branch operation(s). If the already established funeral home is located in the "downtown area," parking is possibly becoming a problem. People, both in the business and residential communities, are moving away from centrally located areas to the newer and multiplying suburbs. Funeral directors facing these conditions may be wise to think of a branch operation or a re-location of their establishment.

Locating a new funeral home properly requires a great deal of planning with experts in the architectural and constructional fields. Experts for some specialized projects are available. However, those who are knowledgeable as to funeral homes and their specific needs are very limited.

There is an established trend regarding the moving from such downtown locations to the "fringe areas"; first people start to leave, then the "shopping centers" spring up, then the churches go to serve the people and, finally, the funeral director must re-locate or add to his present accommodations by branch(es). Branch locations should be situated where they will be sufficient and even more than adequate to serve for possibly the next ten, twenty or more years. This is, of course, applicable to a completely new business as well.

Preliminary Planning

What are the determining factors in the selection of property? Some are: (1) the population now and projected over a given period of time; (2) the physical makeup of the area to be served; (3) the average per capita income; (4) the accessibility to the traffic flow now and anticipated; and (5) the city zoning codes which would govern construction and/or business.

When the property is considered it must conform to the need of the ratio of the property, the size of the land to the size of the building. Also a purchase arrangement must be possible which will serve the financial structure of the business.

All these factors are vital to preliminary planning. Some of them can be answered by accountants, some by real estate consultants, and some by a very careful study of the zoning laws where they exist.

In the overall planning, consideration should be given as to what is now the potential for the area to be served, and what it might be at a later date. This information is needed so that additional in-state rooms, another chapel, and additional office and storage space may be subsequently constructed if necessary.

Location

Regardless of whether the funeral home is to be built as a re-located funeral home, a branch, or an entirely new establishment, a great deal of study must be made to find the right location.

Freeways, cemetery locations, heavily trafficked streets, as well as right-of-way entrances and exits to the property should all be carefully studied. It is important to ascertain if there is enough property for off-street parking, and that the building itself might be so located on the selected property that the flow of traffic is not hindered for the many functions of the funeral home.

Funeral homes on well-traveled streets often are confronted with problems as to present and future traffic arteries. For example, if a new freeway is to be constructed, or perhaps an access made to an existing expressway, the funeral home could find itself in an undesirable situation.

Site location is one of the most important factors with which the prospective funeral home owner has to deal. A preliminary survey should determine whether the population of the vicinity is or will be large enough to support a funeral home. Is it a young community of growing families, or is it a community of older people? What are the public transportation facilities?

The accessibility of traffic flow is important. There are areas into which a funeral procession might not be permitted on a freeway, or some other major traffic artery before or after certain hours. If this is so the alternate routes must be located and planned to churches and to cemeteries.

When all the preliminary needs have been met before a piece of land is purchased it should be determined if the property conforms to the needs of a funeral home or morturary. A rule-of-thumb formula would be to purchase a piece of land *at least* four times as large as the number of square feet planned for the building. In other words, the ratio of the building size to the property is four to one. Beyond this, requirements may enter into this projected ratio to see what is necessary for off-street parking. In some areas the space required by ordinance is one car for each three or four people to be served at a given time.

Zoning

The site selected must be such that a funeral home can be built within the limits of the zoning ordinance where one exists, or reasonably free of the displeasure of the neighbors where there is no ordinance.

In 1965 the general counsel of the National Funeral Directors Association studied zoning laws and wrote about the practical aspects of them as they pertain to the operation of funeral homes. In summary, John F. Hellebush, writing for Clark, Robinson and Hellebush, said:

> While each case must be decided on its own facts and the surrounding circumstances, certain basic tenets would appear evident:
>
> 1. Zoning laws and ordinances passed by the various states and municipalities must be reasonable and must have a proper relation to the health, safety, morals and general welfare of the public.
>
> 2. If the zoning laws are reasonable and do have such a proper relation, courts are reluctant to second-guess the judgment of the legislative body of the municipality and will not upset the zoning structure.
>
> 3. Where there is no zoning ordinance in effect, the weight of authority would indicate that the operation of a funeral home in a residential neighborhood constitutes a nuisance in fact and is enjoinable as such. In this area of the law, however, the character of the neighborhood is a major consideration; is it predominantly residential, or is the neighborhood in question of a transitional nature, having lost its importance as a strictly residential area with the changing times, giving way to the use of the area for other than residential purposes? Here again, the facts and circumstances of each case play a vital and most important part.
>
> 4. Where a zoning ordinance is in effect and a funeral home is properly operated within the confines of that zone, it will be allowed to operate. This does not mean, however, that merely because it is operated in an area properly zoned for such use, that it will escape legal intervention if the funeral director operates his establishment in such a manner as to constitute a nuisance. But this basic principle of law is not peculiar to funeral homes or funeral directors; it is equally applicable to anyone's use of property. The law of equity will not permit anyone to use his property in such a way that reasonable minds can come to no other conclusion than that the manner of such use constitutes a nuisance.

Remember, in selecting a site, you want to build a funeral home, not start a lawsuit.

Architectural Planning

It is best to retain an architect before purchasing the real estate on which a funeral home will be built. His advice as to the final property selection can definitely be a constructional advantage, and it costs no more for his services as is pointed out later in this chapter.

Naturally it would be wise to have the services of an architect experienced in the planning and design of buildings for a funeral service practice. But there are very few such architects. Therefore most times your architect will be one who has not previously designed a funeral home. Additional time and effort must be spent by him and by you for research to understand this unique project. Even if this causes a delay such delay usually avoids mistakes based on an inadequate or improper knowledge.

An architect should never be chosen primarily on a friendship basis.

If the architect selected has built other funeral homes his general knowledge should be fitted to your specific needs.

If the architect has not had previous funeral home planning experience:

- You and he should look at as many funeral homes and/or the plans for them as possible. Benefit by the good features of each of the buildings. Try to learn the mistakes made and then avoid them.
- As you and he look at other funeral homes or mortuaries and/or study the plans for them, keep in mind the parcel of land you have purchased or have in mind. Do not try to force a particular plan into the size and location of the property on which you are going to build.
- At all times keep in mind the needs of the community you are going to serve and the amount of money you will have available for land and buildings, and the interest you think you can afford to pay to meet those needs.

Wishful thinking as to potential and the building of a funeral home for that "wished for" potential have caused problems for a number of funeral home owners. There is nothing more frustrating than operating an "overbuilt" funeral home. There is nothing more dangerous than the temptation to operate in the fringe or grey area to overcome some of the financial problems that accompany overbuilding.

Architectural Fees

Architect's fees vary over the United States depending upon the state in which the architect is registered. A fee schedule may be obtained from the American Institute of Architects (1735 New York Avenue, N.W., Washington, D.C. 20006), or from their local state office.

A funeral home is considered a special-purpose building, or a one-purpose building. Usually the standard fee is from 1 to 2 percent higher than the average fee charged for a "regular" building. This is because the average architect must spend a great deal of time in research before he can arrive at a workable preliminary floor plan.

For remodeling it is well to know that most architects will charge from 3 to 4 percent more than the average fee since a great deal of time is required in the supervision of tearing out part of a building as well as in the time spent to rebuild such a facility.

We have worked successfully for the past fifteen years with many different architects in some twenty-five states. In some instances we have worked with the same architect several times and this is, of course, an additional advantage.

Very few architects or firms are interested in specializing in the development of funeral home design and construction. At the present time we know of one firm which specializes in funeral homes or mortuaries. It is presently constructing and/or planning about thirty such buildings per year and continuing to expand. Such knowledge combined with expert treatment of decorating and lighting makes for a successfully executed plan of funeral home efficiency and beauty.

Further Planning

Two series of checks are recommended in determining the needs of a funeral home. I have reviewed the one as to site location.

The other is a "preliminary funeral home needs" list. With the completion of such information, the size and needs of the funeral home have become basic information. Both these "lists" will be referred to several times in this text as the information is pertinent to many areas of planning and construction.

When both of these are used by architects, upon further interviewing of the funeral home client, a determination of the requirements is outlined and even at such an early meeting a realistic budget may be projected depending on the size, needs and plans for the future.

Assume the site has been selected, the architect has been commissioned and he has assisted in the research and determination of the needs and code restrictions. It is time to proceed with the preliminary drawings.

Realize that the process of "preliminary drawings" might take from one to six months. These drawings must take into consideration such inside things as room sizes, service halls (locations and dimensions), chapels, and traffic flow. Regarding the outside, the plot-planning of the physical location on the property and the parking space in ratio to the size of the building itself are essential.

Before the outside elevation is completed these things should be worked out. Certainly the architect should know, and be advised in the beginning, just what the owner's preference might be as to outside elevation, i.e., design and style, such as contemporary, Georgian, colonial, traditional, or another, but this is not the order of first importance in the actual planning at this time.

After the preliminary plans and/or drawings and the elevation have been approved by the owner, the next step will be taken by the architect.

This will involve the structural, electrical and mechanical plans. Here again possibly two or three or more months will be involved depending upon how extensive is the individual project.

Costs

After the preliminary plans and elevation are completed the architect can give a more accurate estimate as to cost of construction. This will depend, of course, on the many factors of design, the building costs relative to the area (with which the architect should be completely familiar) and the materials.

Never go into such a project unaware of the potential expense. Costs vary widely and are established by the labor market as well as by the kind of and detail in the building desired.

The funeral director client should be kept advised at all times as to the cost of the project as it proceeds, in the event there is an increase in the first projection of costs and/or when the actual construction bids are submitted.

The architect in his advisory capacity should keep the funeral director from "building a memorial to himself," or what would actually be known as "overbuilding" for the area.

Here again is where an architect with experience in building funeral homes is a monetary as well as a functional advantage.

A small, well-designed building may be more functional to a funeral practice than a large one.

The average funeral home runs from 8,000 to 16,000 square feet. There are some very workable plans with as little as 4,000 square feet and some up to more than 28,000. This depends on the volume of business and the needs of the practice.

In the determination of the size and the cost of the building there are many factors to consider. To recap some of them: What number of services are expected to be conducted annually from this building? How many people are to be seated in the largest room or rooms for a service? Will this room or rooms be a chapel with pews or benches, or will it be a room or rooms in which the body or bodies will also lie in state? Will there be a family room and how big should it be? How many floral pieces would be expected on the average? Does the plan call for a room to be used by the clergyman? Is the music room to house an organ, or taped music facilities, or both?

Additionally, what about a family lounge? In what manner is the family to enter and leave the funeral home? Where is the parking to be? What about the loading area and should it be covered to protect against sun, rain, snow or wind?

Great care should be given in the positioning of the chapel, or room or rooms where the funeral service is to be held when not in church. This room or rooms should be close to a public entrance direct to and from the parking facilities.

Once the architect has made the preliminary drawings and floor plans he will have determined the size and area of each room with consideration having been given even to the size of the door openings so that caskets and casketed bodies may be moved and turned with ease.

In an efficiently functioning funeral home many things will be happening at the same time. While one service is being conducted a family may be coming in to make arrangements for another. Last minute flowers will be delivered, or loaded to be taken to the cemetery. A body or bodies will be viewed while in state. And routine business matters will be conducted in the offices.

Sometimes while in the last stages of planning, potential funeral home owners have been known to ask about adding a two- or three-bedroom apartment to the plans.

While this can be done it is a very expensive afterthought. If a funeral home is to include an apartment this should be a part of the original plans.

Interior of the Building

The planning, decorating and lighting of the funeral home is vitally important if it is to function to best advantage, and each room should be considered separately, keeping in mind the overall effect. This consideration will be made taking a family through the service of the funeral director, step by step.

The first steps into a funeral home should be into an entrance hall or foyer that is inviting and warm and will lend itself to adaptations and changes in decor at minimal cost.

Picture 1.

This entrance hall or foyer (Picture 1) is pleasing to the eye and comfortable to those who may want to visit briefly while entering or leaving. The decorations are those for the Christmas season.

The Arrangements Room

The service and counselling of a funeral director is very personal. Inasmuch as most deaths now occur in hospitals or nursing homes, or on highways or battlefields, often the first time the funeral director sees a family that has called him after a death has occurred is in his funeral home. His preliminary discussions with that family should be in what I choose to call an arrangements room.

This room should be big enough for four family members plus the funeral director to sit in comfortable chairs. If the family group is larger, folding chairs can be brought in. The room should be bright and not overdone. It may include a table for a lamp and perhaps an end table, but it *should not* include a desk. The funeral director should sit *with* the family when arrangements are being made. He should not be behind a desk looking down at them.

Picture 2.

This room (Picture 2) can serve both as an arrangements room and as a family lounge. Note the "togetherness" of the placement of chairs and the absence of a desk.

The Casket Selection Room

This room requires a large square footage in the building, depending upon the number of units to be displayed (14—18—25—30 or more) and this should be anticipated and planned for *prior* to the allocation of space for the room.

In planning the number of units consideration should be given as to the use of single or double racks, or both. Double racks provide space for caskets to be stored underneath and pulled out for display, thereby adding more "show space" to the floor space.

Picture 3.

This selection room (Picture 3) is very compact. Note the casket in the lower left-hand corner which is on a rack that allows the casket to be stored underneath when the room is not being used for selection purposes.

There are a number of new funeral homes that have approximately one-third of their caskets shown in a "double-deck" arrangement in their selection room. For the sake of a suggested plan assume that 27 caskets are in the up position and nine are concealed underneath.

There are funeral homes so designed that there is a lot of space available for casket display and selection purpose.

Picture 4.

This selection room (Picture 4) is spacious and well lighted. Today's building costs could bring into question this size room unless a one-floor plan allowed for a large area in the lower level as is the case here.

A most important factor in a casket selection room is to locate and properly size the doors. A poorly planned entrance or exit could possibly eliminate the display space for two or three caskets.

Doors should be located convenient to traffic flow and certainly should be built to the size of allowance for ease in entrance and exit, without marring either the casket or the door facings.

Selective, meticulous care should be given to the use of color and decor in the selection room. Solid color carpeting is recommended strongly and should be one to blend harmoniously with all caskets rather than detracting from the units displayed by some busy pattern. A preference is emerging for beiges, greyed-greens and subtle golds. Use as much care in the selection of fabric and color to drape the display trucks if such trucks are going to be used. Velvets are extremely well received, long-lasting and luxurious looking, especially when selected in an exact match to the carpet color.

In the choosing of the casket display trucks, when use of a double rack (truck) is proposed, all these should be planned to a mono-height for the best overall effect. For example, a 26-inch height is generally accepted, but more and more funeral homes are using a 30-inch level.

Let us assume that a double rack is to be used, where one casket is being stored underneath and is displayed at the 30-inch height. This would be the same height as a casket sitting on top of a vault. If a single truck is to be used in the same room then it, also, should be elevated to the same top height.

A general space recommendation is 70 square feet per casket display. By deciding upon the number of caskets to display before the room is built, it will total and approximate the number of square feet to be anticipated.

The decorating and space allotment is most important. Of equal importance is the lighting to be installed in the selection room.

The true color of the casket and the basic fabrics should be shown in the selection room to avoid any displeasure when moved from the room. This can be so easily and effectively accomplished by the general overall lighting plan, but it must be a specialized one to eliminate shadows or color distortion.

There are several different manners in which this room can be properly illuminated. The use of a luminous ceiling with 90 to 100 foot candles (depending upon the individual need) of light will do a very effective lighting job in the custom-designed sales room.

If the ceiling is too low to use a luminous ceiling then certain types of special fluorescent strips, either recessed or surface mounted, may be used to accomplish the overall effect of properly illuminated sales rooms. Deluxe cool white tubes will give the best true color finish of the casket, both exterior and interior.

In the selection room the wall finishes are a definite consideration, and the use of murals and/or patterned paper certainly is not recommended. Such wall treatment (as in the case of "busy carpet") could distract from the casket display. A neutral background, color-keyed to carpet and drapes, with the properly lighted ceiling, will show the caskets in their truest light.

Other Selection Rooms

All funeral homes sell vaults—concrete, metal or both. Some sell vaults of man-made materials. When feasible these vaults should be displayed either as complete vaults or cutaway models of them.

If possible, a separate room may be planned to display vaults and burial clothing, as well as baby caskets and vaults.

If a separate room is not possible, then displays of each of these items should be tastefully incorporated into the casket selection room.

"Visitations" or "In State" Rooms

There are two basic plans for a funeral home or mortuary. One is predicated on using one, two or three large rooms for the period of the "visitation" or "in state" period and also for the funeral service. While the body is in state the night or nights before the funeral, the room or rooms have large pieces of furniture with few folding chairs. Except for the members of the family and close friends few people stay long enough to sit down after paying their respects.

Picture 5.

This room (Picture 5) is "set up" with folding chairs for a funeral service. When there is a "visitation" or "wake" many of the folding chairs are removed and the more comfortable chairs and sofas put in. Also a lot of room is available for standing around and visiting.

The other plan is built around one large room generally called the "chapel." This room has pews or benches in it and it is used mostly for the funeral service when it is not held in a church.

Picture 6.

This (Picture 6) is a colonial style chapel.

This chapel (Picture 7) is modernistic or contemporary in style.

Chapels are seldom used to "lay out" a body for viewing purposes during the "wake," "in state" or "visitation" period. Instead there are a number of smaller rooms for such purposes.

Picture 7.

This (Picture 8) is a room used solely for visitation. It is an adjunct to the "chapel" or "funeral service room."

The more visitation rooms there are the greater the foyer or lobby and hall space has to be. A building with four to six visitation rooms will require a lobby of approximately half the size of those rooms. These rooms can be an overflow area for the chapel with general seating arranged in such a way that the traffic flow will not be hindered by an unusually large gathering of one or two families.

(Many funeral homes today plan a large "coffee room" accessible to the family and viewing area with a nearby location for restroom facilities for the use of the public.)

Behind the scene of what the public actually sees are service halls located behind these visitation rooms for the purpose of moving a body in or out, the placement and transportation of flowers from these rooms to the chapel, and for other purposes without the public area being disrupted or disturbed.

The lighting in the visitation rooms should be the same as in the chapel to which the body may be moved. The decor should be correlated as to carpets, drapes and wall finishes. It should be subtle and low-keyed in order to properly display the casket and flowers and the moods of the people there.

Flower lighting will be needed also and specially designed as to placement of caskets.

Picture 8.

The Chapel or Funeral Service Room

The decoration of the chapel or funeral service room requires special attention beyond its dimensions. Decor and color of wall finish and carpet color are most important. Careful consideration should be given to whether the walls will be textured, paneled, and/or masonry.

Individual parts of the walls are important because wall effects, such as flowers, might be used.

As far as most of the general public is concerned there are three focal points in the chapel: (1) The location of the casket setting which should involve a bier for the casket and the chapel or service room decor; (2) an arrangement for the convenient display of the flowers to their best advantage; and (3) the location and setting of the "pulpit," rostrum, or podium for the clergyman and other persons who might speak at a service.

The lighting of the casket should be custom designed. No glare nor harsh effect must be possible. The lighting of the flowers must be such as to bring out their true colors. The area in which the casketed bodies are placed should be sufficient in size so that flowers may be properly and tastefully arranged and not "stacked in."

The family portion of the chapel or funeral service room, or the adjacent family room, should have access to a focal point of its own so that the family may view the casketed body and see the flowers and have a direct line of vision to the minister. These people are of utmost importance to the service because it is primarily for them.

For many years family rooms were felt to be highly desirable since it enabled the family to be in the chapel or funeral service room, but yet separated from it for the sake of privacy. An increasing number of families want to sit with relatives and friends in the large room, not in the family room. But there still are many who want to use the family room with its louvres, separate toilet facilities and comfortable chairs. Therefore, a family room should be included. It should coordinate with the larger room and the lighting be controlled by a dimmer. If a louvre is not used then a translucent drape works out well between the family room and the area where the service is being held. This should be of such texture as not to obstruct the vision of the family members.

The lighting above the pulpit or podium should be adequate for reading and as subdued as necessary to avoid distraction. This must be custom designed for each individual chapel.

Location of the music room off the chapel should be at the vantage point of musician to minister in order to correlate the music to the proper funeral service. Lighting must be controlled so that adequate vision is available without being noticeable to the people in the chapel.

Furnishings in the chapel should remain in the same taste and low-keyed decor as the walls and carpet; it should be comfortable and upholstered to absorb noise as opposed to the wooden-bench type.

The Preparation Room

To plan the size of the preparation and casketing room a determination of the number of funerals and/or bodies to be handled by this establishment should be ascertained. Whether one, two or more tables are to be used will help decide the size. This is a functional operating room which should be brought to a fine point of efficiency, including special plumbing, lighting, venting, air-conditioning needs, and storage requirements.

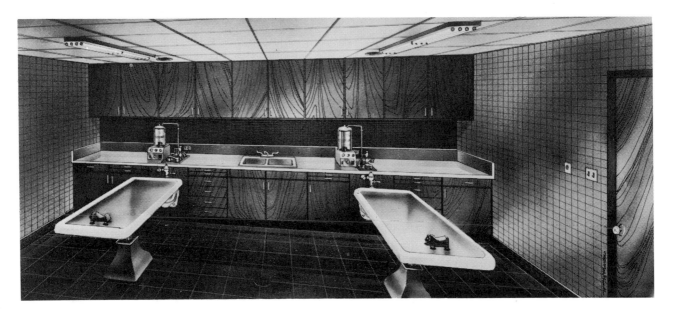

Picture 9.

A modern preparation room (Picture 9) is planned in size and efficiency based on the projected number of funerals anticipated. Lighting, positioning, equipment, all should be planned at the time of the building.

If a separate casketing room can be made available, then it should be adjacent to the preparation room and should function as an area for hair dressers as well as to dress and apply cosmetics to the body prior to casketing. Dressing rooms relieve the congestion in the preparation room in large-volume funeral homes.

Both the preparation room and the dressing room are areas in which special attention should be given as to proper lighting. Some multiple use may be effected in the preparation room if the body is also casketed there; the lighting over the embalming table must be suitable for the application of cosmetics. Certain fluorescent lighting fixtures in possibly four-foot or eight-foot tubes can be located directly above the table for good vision as well as to point up the true color in the restorative art work.

When a body is finally dressed and cosmetized it most times will be viewed in the funeral home and sometimes in the church. Proper lighting is essential for proper cosmetizing with these factors in mind.

Room for Clergy

The funeral is a religious rite for most people. When it is, a clergyman is involved sometimes during the visitation period and always during the funeral service. When the funeral service is at the funeral home the clergyman likes to have a place where he can change his clothes if necessary and make last-minute toilet and other preparations.

Most clergymen welcome the privacy of a separate room for this. There are times when this room is used also for consultation between the funeral director and the cleric, or between the minister, priest or rabbi and a member or members of the family. While a wash basin and toilet are convenient, they are not absolutely necessary. But a coat rack, mirror, a small table or desk, and a couple of chairs are essential. This room is most convenient if located near the pulpit or podium and near an entrance other than the main one to the funeral home.

Offices, Storage, Lounges, Dormitories and Service Areas

Consideration should be given to an employee dormitory, coffee room (or kitchenette possibly) for those who might be working nights. Also, if the funeral home is one that gives emergency ambulance service to the community, then adequate sleeping quarters should be anticipated for this need as well. The size of the employee area would depend upon the number of employees and the services rendered by the funeral home.

Flower receiving and handling should definitely be in a separate room with not only the vitally necessary outside accessibility, but in reasonable proximity to the visitation room as well as to the chapel or funeral service room for convenience of placing the floral remembrances in the proper locations. The size of this room depends upon the customs of the community as to sending flowers. And most importantly, the flower room must have the most effective air conditioning possible.

Storage space is essential to the planning of a funeral home. It should be preplanned to the best possible advantage. Many items stored in a funeral home of unusual size and bulk demand special attention. These include caskets not in the selection room, cemetery equipment, vaults, shipping boxes and other containers, items of storage such as chairs, church trucks, and the normal office supplies.

Garage space too must be considered and very carefully, taking into consideration how many automobiles and pieces of rolling stock need to be under cover. Also if there is to be a car port which is roofed but not closed in, the decision will have to be made whether it will be the width of one car or several. This involves the exterior plans but the architect needs to anticipate its square footage and take this into the overall construction costs.

General business offices should be functional in design and if it is necessary they be compact, they can still be so designed as to service a large office purpose. It is of the utmost importance that they have a direct outside entrance to avoid confusion with the families being served. Great care should be given to this consideration.

A men's lounge or smoking lounge is a must. It can either be inviting or it can be cold. Its use should determine its size and serviceability. The decorating theme should be warm and cheerful—never gaudy. Color should be used pleasantly and chairs should be grouped without an overcrowded appearance.

A ladies' lounge or rest room is not nearly as much used for congregating as is the men's lounge or smoking room. Yet it is an important room and it should be done in delicate colors with commodious if not luxurious furnishings.

Exterior—Landscaping and Lighting

The exterior of the building will depend upon the physical surroundings and the desires of the funeral home owner. Consideration must be given to the factors of outward appearance in the light of other buildings around it and/or the neighborhood in which it is being built. A few of the more popular designs in today's funeral homes are shown in Pictures 10 through 15. (The funeral home elevation pictures were made available by James H. Roberts, AIA Architects, Dallas, Texas.)

The landscaping of the grounds will enhance the design of the building to a great extent and should be carefully planned. In many funeral homes being built today the use of a garden entrance (especially the family entrance) is well received, and much care should be taken in the selection of the flora to be placed in such an area. A landscape engineer will know of the climate limitations and the soil which would determine the extent of plantings. Fountains and garden-type lighting add to the grounds.

Lighting of parking lots should be adequate but subtle to the point of not distracting from the exterior beauty of the landscaping and lighting.

Many firms identify themselves with a particular sign. This should be away from the building and properly lighted. It should be large enough to be seen, but not so large as to distract. A properly designed sign harmonizing with the structure theme should be placed where the most traffic will be able to see and identify the institution.

There are so many vast areas of planning and building of a new funeral home and we have tried to present in some detail some of the essential considerations for this.

The individual location, the amount of business established or projected, the personal tastes of the funeral home owner as well as the demands and customs of the community itself are among things of prime importance.

A "plan" that has been successfully used in one area will not, necessarily, be a success in another.

Careful and professional guidance is the best standard to use in the building of a new funeral home just as careful and professional guidance to a family by funeral personnel is the best standard of a funeral service.

Picture 10. A "contemporary" with pre-stressed concrete building material and a flat-decked roof.

Picture 11. Georgian—an ever-popular design and particularly pertinent to some geographical areas.

Picture 12. Gabled-modern colonial combines the flat deck with additional gabled areas to emphasize the colonial design.

Picture 13. Mansard flat-deck roof in multi-levels. Raising of the French mansard roof brings the French modern theme into focus.

Picture 14. Mansard roof wrap-around emphasizes the total French look.

Picture 15. The Raised Chapel modified by use of a mansard on a flat deck is a successful combination of modern and thematic.

15

CONTINUING PROFESSIONAL GROWTH THROUGH RECENTLY ACQUIRED KNOWLEDGE

Robert C. Slater

The eminent Harvard sociologist, Talcott Parsons, said "No one can take the place of the funeral director." To those in funeral service this becomes at first reading a wonderful compliment, but on second reading it takes on the aspect of a tremendous challenge; a challenge that demands a never ceasing effort on the part of each individual funeral director to make sure he is as adequately prepared as possible to fulfill the role that Dr. Parsons says no one else can fulfill. The answer to this challenge is continual professional growth and academic learning.

Compared to their accepted status in a community the general overall level of formal educational preparation for the funeral director is less than that of any other professional servant. He must compensate for this by taking advantage of every opportunity available to funeral directors, but only the major ones to which highest priority should be assigned will be discussed here.

Formal Academic Training

Many funeral homes are located in areas where colleges and universities are to be found. No one should overlook the opportunity to complete formal academic requirements for basic degrees or for advanced degrees. If one is not interested in completing requirements for a degree surely the completion of specific courses can be beneficial—particularly courses in the humanities, psychology, sociology, anthropology and economics. Many times a specific course will give much applicable knowledge and will also serve as a motivator for further course work.

Extension courses are usually readily available through either late afternoon or evening courses as well as by correspondence. The course areas mentioned above are often included in such offerings.

Special seminars offered by colleges and universities should also be considered. They usually deal in specific areas such as public relations, communications, efficient reading, and others. These offer growth in specific skills or techniques.

Many times colleges of funeral service education offer one- or two-day seminars, or have new curriculums developed since the individual funeral director last attended such a school, or will offer special post-graduate courses.

Community Resources

Many communities offer either special courses such as Dale Carnegie, or special organizations such as Toastmasters, both of which can be used to increase and sharpen personal skills and techniques.

Professional Association Opportunities

There is an ever increasing availability of seminars and workshops for funeral service personnel. These seminars sponsored by local, district, state and national associations offer one of the finest, most readily available and least expensive opportunities of all. They are planned by competent professional persons, adapted to the needs of current funeral service practice, and often staffed or taught by practicing funeral directors who have successfully used the techniques or procedures being taught or discussed.

One opportunity for professional growth that should not be overlooked is participation in professional activities at every level. Not only does the experience from participating in these activities create new learning experiences, but often the additional source material and releases from national and state association offices provide much information not available to the general funeral service profession.

Reading Opportunities

A leading pastoral psychologist who also serves as a funeral service consultant states, "The foremost weakness of funeral directors is their reluctance to read literature pertinent to their care-taking responsibility." Funeral directors have presented more books as gifts to other professionals than any other single group, but many of them have not read the books they give despite their relevance to funeral service. In the last decade the amount of literature that has been written and published is more than the total amount published previously. There are licensees who feel that unless a book or article is written by a funeral director and published by the funeral directors association it will have no value to them. To the contrary such funeral association-oriented literature is extremely limited. But literature coming from the diciplines of psychology, psychiatry, nursing, theology and sociology is filled with research and insight relative to death, grief, mourning and bereavement, much of which directly or indirectly involves or implies the value and significance of funerals. To benefit from these publications and new insights a funeral director must be observant and alert to such material. He also can rely on his professional association to review these articles and books and then procure those that can best serve to meet his needs.

The funeral director especially sensitive to the importance of such material purchases books and articles in sufficient quantity so that all of his staff may read them. Following a period of time for such reading to be accomplished he makes the book or article the subject of a staff meeting. He also requires some books to be studied to the point that his staff can be tested as to their comprehension of the material.

Another source of such learning is current news articles and periodicals. Often a news item or magazine article contains material that supports the significance and value of the funeral and its ceremonial function. Prime examples of this are the articles or news items surrounding the funerals of notable persons, such as the Kennedys, General Eisenhower and others, funerals following tragic accidents such as mine disasters, and funerals where individuals by their actions or deeds support the premise of sound grief therapy. Funeral directors who can become sensitive to such articles can often use them in counselling with families who might not understand or question the value of a funeral. Those who do have gained not only new insights but have added to their professional growth.

Professional Meetings and Professional Conferences

All professional associations at both the state and national level have made great strides in the educational content of their annual or other stated meetings. They have discovered that a growing segment of their membership is no longer interested in attending convention sessions purely for fellowship or social activities. Instead they expect not only to participate in the ongoing concern of the profession, but to receive educational exposure to current, new and projected ideas. Learning and personal professional growth thrives in such an atmosphere.

Interprofessional Conferences

There is an increasing number of inter-disciplinary opportunities becoming available. As clergymen develop studies on liturgical and ceremonial procedure, as sociologists devote seminars in the care of the aging, and as the health sciences deal with death and dying, the funeral director will find an ever increasing interest in these studies because of their interrelationship to funeral service. Not only can a funeral director gain personal knowledge to his benefit, but his community and clientele will gain added respect for him because of his willingness to expose himself to new learning experiences and his consequent knowledge of an important subject few lay persons would study by themselves.

Post-Funeral Evaluations

Although a staff conference to evaluate a funeral service may not at first glance appear to be a learning situation it perhaps is such in the truest sense of the word. Medicine and law have long maintained the practice of case analysis and review. The funeral director, his staff, the clergy officiant and other professionals who have been involved can learn much from such post-funeral evaluation. Not only is it a learning experience but it is a typical procedure of a care-taking profession. Any knowledge gained accrues to the benefit of families who in the future experience similar problems.

Total Participation

All of the above opportunities should be available to all persons practicing in funeral service. All too often an attitude develops that seminars and conferences are for the owners or top personnel only. Many times it is the other staff members who can benefit the most. The attitude of an owner who does not permit periodic staff participation in such learning experiences is self-defeating. Staff personnel who are permitted to participate bring back a compound dividend. Not only are they better prepared to serve, but they are also proud of the fact that they have been permitted to attend, and reflect such pride and gratitude in their attitude of renewed interest and desire. Allowing such participation is in the truest sense a fringe benefit for both the employee and the employer.

Summary

Unlike law, dentistry and medicine there are few newsworthy breakthroughs in funeral service. Like religion, there are values and importance in rites, rituals and ceremonials in working through the deep emotions of grief, and the body of knowledge in this regard is so recent that immediate action to assimilate and put into practice such knowledge is imperative if funeral service is to be the care-taking service that no one else can perform other than a funeral director.

Funeral directors must grow in and with this knowledge for the funeral to persevere and for there to be a continued need for funeral functionaries. Funeral directors must know what they do which is helpful to people and why. They must continue to learn new business practices and procedures, but they must realize the continuation of a profession dependent upon a custom is contingent upon the continuation of that custom. The custom upon which funeral service is based will continue only as long as those values inherent in the custom speak to and fulfill the needs of those for whom the custom is functional.

16

THE FUNERAL AND THE FUNERAL
DIRECTOR: A CONTEMPORARY ANALYSIS*

Robert Fulton

Burial of the dead is an ancient practice among men. From pre-Biblical times to the present, man has responded to the death of his fellow man with solemnity and ceremony. The event of death has evoked not only a religious awe in men, but also its threat to the survival of community life has engendered fear, just as its disruption of family life has aroused sorrow.

The vehicle through which these reactions to death have been expressed has been the funeral. The funeral traditionally has served as a religious rite; as a ceremony acknowledging a death; as an occasion to reassure and to reestablish the social group; as a commemoration of a life; and as a ritual of disposal.

In the past few years criticism of funeral practices in the United States has been both strident and extensive. The funeral has been charged with being pagan in origin and ostentatious in practice, while the funeral director has been characterized as one who exploits the dead at the expense of the living.

For a decade, the writer has conducted three nationwide surveys dealing with the issues surrounding mortality in America. The most recent survey, and the one to be discussed here, was a study of funerary behavior across the United States. The survey provided an opportunity to study the manner as well as to measure the extent and variation of funeral rites in the country as Americans respond to new social values and challenge old cultural traditions.

*A revised version of the paper, "The Funeral and the Funeral Director: A Contemporary Analysis," presented at the Eighty-Sixth Annual Convention of the National Funeral Directors Association, Atlantic City, New Jersey, October 22–26, 1967.

The first study, conducted in 1959, surveyed the attitudes of clergymen toward funerals and funeral directors in the United States.[1] The study showed that clerical criticism of the funeral director and of funeral practices was both widespread and intensive in nature. Among the different reasons the clergy gave for their critical appraisal of funerary behavior, two stand out. One, the funeral director was charged with dramatizing the presence of the body while ignoring spiritual matters; and, two, the funeral director was accused of taking undue advantage of the bereaved. A third factor should be noted which was left largely unstated but was nevertheless implicit in the clergy's criticism. It was that the funeral director makes his services available to people of different faiths, and relates all funerals past and present. By such a relative attitude toward this religious rite he appears to leave himself open to the charge of paganism.

Specifically, the study showed that the Protestant clergyman, more so than his Catholic colleague, was troubled by contemporary funeral rites and practices, and by the emerging role of the funeral director in connection with these rites and practices. Inasmuch as the religious service for Protestants is most often held in the "chapel" of the funeral home, the relative change of function of the Protestant clergyman vis-a-vis the funeral director, is troubling for many clerics, both professionally as well as personally.

These factors, as well as others, have led some members of the clergy to charge the contemporary funeral with paganism and to view the expense associated with it as conspicuous waste. Such concern has also led to the active promotion of what is called the "simplified" funeral; to the advocacy of cremation; and to the recommendation that monies spent on funerals be diverted to scientific research and public charities.

The second study, conducted in 1962, surveyed the attitudes of the American public toward death, funerals, and funeral directors.[2] Included in the study was a cross-section of those persons who were members of the funeral reform or memorial society movement. The survey showed, as with the earlier clergy study, that negative and critical attitudes toward contemporary funeral rites and practices were held by some segments of the public. The survey showed, however, that these attitudes were not shared equally by the public, but rather that criticism of the contemporary funeral varies by geographical region as well as by religious affiliation, education, occupation, and income.

It was found that the majority of the American public surveyed was favorably disposed toward present-day funeral practices and toward the funeral director. The majority of respondents also viewed the funeral as providing a meaningful emotional experience for the survivors. More than half of the respondents, moreover, viewed the funeral director as a professional person, or as one who combined a professional service with a business function.

Members of the memorial societies surveyed expressed views strongly divergent from those of the general public. They believed the funeral director was primarily a businessman offering no professional service whatsoever to the public. In addition, the

---

[1] Robert Fulton, "The Clergyman and the Funeral Director: A Study in Role Conflict," *Social Forces,* 39 (1961), pp. 317-323.

[2] Robert Fulton, *The Sacred and the Secular: Attitudes of the American Public Toward Death* (Milwaukee: Bulfin Printers, 1963), 23 pp.

majority of them expressed an unfavorable opinion of both funerals and funeral directors. Further, the majority of these respondents did not believe that the purposes of the funeral were, in fact, served by the funeral ceremony. Only one out of four of the memorial society respondents believed that the funeral served the emotional needs of the family in any way, while 16 percent reported they perceived the traditional funeral as performing no useful function whatsoever.

Of interest, however, is the demographic profile of the memorial group. The study showed that the members of the memorial society group reported educational attainments significantly higher than the other participants, as well as the highest percentage of professional occupations, and an average annual income twice that of the typical American family. On the other hand, they reported the lowest percentage of traditional religious affiliation. As one would expect, moreover, the memorial society members were the foremost by a great margin in advocating cremation; the donation of the body to scientific research; and the avoidance of the ritual and ceremony of the funeral.

As a whole, the second study showed that favorable responses toward funerals and funeral directors varied with religious affiliation. Religious affiliation, or its absence, was the pivotal factor around which the various attitudes expressed in the study revolved. Simply stated, Catholics most often reported being favorably disposed toward the funeral and the funeral director, followed by Protestants, Jews, non-affiliated respondents, and Unitarians. The order was reversed with respect to the expression of critical attitudes. The Unitarians were the most critical followed by the non-affiliated, Jews, Protestants, and finally Catholics. Regionally, the most favorable attitudes toward the funeral and the funeral director were expressed by residents from central sections of the country while the least favorable views were expressed by respondents residing along the Atlantic and Pacific coasts.

The third study, conducted in 1967, sought to determine the character of contemporary funeral practices in the United States. A questionnaire was prepared and mailed to the entire 1967 membership of the National Funeral Directors Association. In addition, questionnaires were also sent to the membership of the Jewish Funeral Directors Association. In all, 14,144 questionnaires were mailed with 3474 being returned.

The analysis of the questionnaires provided a thumbnail sketch of what might be called the "modal" funeral director. It was a profile "drawn" by the funeral director himself on the basis of the most commonly reported replies to the different items on the questionnaire

A word of caution: the sketch must be understood in terms of those funeral directors who took the time and effort to participate in the study. The question must be asked; how representative were the responses? This is rather difficult to say. The combined membership of the NFDA and the JFDA is slightly more than 14,000. There are estimated to be, however, more than 23,000 funeral establishments in the United States. This is like comparing grapes and raisins, but in the absence of more reliable data, there is no other alternative. The sample represented one out of four funeral directors of the total number polled, and approximately one out of 6.5 funeral establishments across the country. In terms of volume of funerals per year, moreover, information exterior to the study indicates that there are funeral establishments that conduct more than 2,000 funerals per year, whereas, that was the largest single volume reported in the study. What can be said, then, about the survey and its representativeness? A closer look at the sample provides an answer.

Of the slightly more than 14,000 members of the NFDA and the JFDA who were mailed the questionnaire, nearly three and a half thousand responded. This represents a response of nearly 25 percent. It also represents a little over 15 percent of the estimated number of funeral homes in the United States.

The average funeral home in the United States in 1967 conducted 80 to 85 funerals per year while the average NFDA member conducted over 100 funerals. The average number of funerals conducted by the respondents of the questionnaire on the other hand was reported to be 106 per year, or above the average for funeral establishments in this country as a whole. The study, therefore, was not based on responses of what might be termed the "small volume" funeral director (although many of those were indeed included), but rather on responses from "average volume" or "above-average volume" funeral directors. An analysis of the respondents by census region, moreover, showed that the respondents represented from 17 percent (New England) to 32 percent (Mountain) of the NFDA members and from 10 percent (East South Central) to 23 percent (Mountain) of the total number of funeral homes in the region. The average number of funerals, by region, for all funeral homes ranged from 54 funerals (West North Central) to 226 (Pacific). In every region, the average number of funerals reported by our respondents was above the average number for all funeral directors in their respective regions.

As mentioned above, our respondents accounted for 15 percent of the total funeral homes, but reported handling 20 percent of the total deaths. In each area, the percentage of total deaths handled by the respondents was higher than the percent they represented of the total funeral homes. Our respondents, in other words, conducted a greater number of funerals than would otherwise be expected.

These facts permit us, it would appear, to place a high degree of confidence in the representativeness and reliability of the sample. The respondents of this study were neither the very small volume funeral director, not were they disproportionately representative of the large multi-unit establishment. Their replies, moreover, were based on the fact that they are responsible for one out of every five funerals conducted in this country.

Demographic and Service Characteristics Of the "Modal" American Funeral Director

From a purely statistical point of view the "modal" funeral director can be described as follows:

> He operates one establishment.
> He owns the establishment himself.
> His firm has been in existence approximately 42 years.
> He functions out of a converted residence.
> He serves in an area of 2,500 to 25,000 people.

He conducts 106 funerals a year.

In 1966 he had no charity funerals, but he did conduct between 1 and 5 percent welfare funerals.

At least nine out of ten funerals he conducts have a public viewing, a public service, and a public committal.

He has noticed no particular change in the type of funeral service requested over the past ten years.

At least eight out of ten families he serves are Protestant.

He serves no predominant ethnic or racial group.

At least 65 percent of his removals are from hospitals, with the remainder divided more or less evenly between private residences and nursing homes.

Less than 5 percent of his funerals in 1966 were prearranged.

Of the prearrangements he has, less than 5 percent are prefinanced.

If he has occasion to prefinance a funeral, he does so by a trust agreement.

He is not affiliated with any prearrangement group or plan.

The prearranged funerals he had in 1966 were, in 74 percent of the cases, conducted as originally contracted. When changes were made, the change involved in 50 percent of the cases the selection of a more expensive funeral than originally contracted.

He feels prearranged funerals are on a slight increase, or about the same as they have been until now.

He reports that the number of adults paying their last respects while a body lies in state is showing a slight increase, but the number of adults who actually attend a funeral is decreasing.

He has noticed no change in the number of children who attend funeral functions.

He has noticed, however, a definite increase in the number of persons who are pre-purchasing or pre-selecting a cemetery plot.

The time and effort spent by a family member or friends for a funeral is about the same, he reports, but the amount of money expended has been increasing. This is not out of line, he cautions, with the general overall increase in the cost of living.

In the majority of cases, he has noticed no change in attitude on the part of the clergy, but there are singular instances of clergymen (usually young ones) whom he describes as dictatorial, or distant and uncooperative. In general, however, the clergy in his area are not like this.

He notices even less change in attitude on the part of the families he serves, but mentions the fact that more families are requesting a simple, brief service than in years past. (If anything, he comments, the recent adverse publicity has helped rather than hurt his relationship with the family, for according to him, they appear better informed.)

Finally, he advertises his services, but usually by name only. He shuns price advertising. Although he may decide to mention his facilities in his advertisements, he may just as often donate advertising space to more worthwhile causes.

What has been described is a "statistical man." It is essentially a static and highly abstract view of the present-day funeral director and of contemporary funeral practices. It is important, therefore, to look beyond this initial statistical construct of respondents in order to get an overview of the funeral as well as to see where, and how, and in what degree, changes have and are taking place. A regional analysis of the replies of the respondents on the significant items of the questionnaire, will bring more sharply into focus features and details of the study previously obscured.

Major Regional Comparisons

Funeral service has followed the general pattern of growth and westward development of this country. While funeral firms cover a span of existence from one year to 200 years, the average age of funeral establishments decreases generally from East to West.

In New England, for instance, where respondents reported the fewest number of new establishments of all the census regions, almost a quarter of the funeral directors reported that their establishments have been in existence since before the turn of the century. The respondents of the West South Central states, the Mountain and Pacific states reported funeral establishments of that period only 10 percent of the time.

While the funeral directors who participated in this survey characteristically owned their own establishments, the variation by census region in manner of ownership (i.e., individual proprietorship, partnership, or corporate ownership) is quite marked. Individual ownership ranges from a high of 64.7 percent for the Middle Atlantic Region, to a low of 37 percent for both the South Atlantic Region and the Pacific Region. Partnerships range from 28.1 percent of the cases in the East South Central states to 10.7 percent of the New England states; the Pacific Region leads in corporate ownerships. This type of firm is specified in almost half its reported cases (48.7 percent). This compares with the lowest reported figure of 22.3 percent for the Middle Atlantic Region.

Although the greater proportion of funeral directors reported individual proprietorship of just one funeral establishment, a regional analysis shows considerable variation in that proportion. New England, West South Central, and West North Central funeral directors reported multiple establishments for almost one funeral director out of four. This compares to the Middle Atlantic states where the ratio of multiple to single establishments is one out of nine.

The West North Central Region also reported the greatest number of funeral homes serving areas under 2,500 population (20.8 percent). This compares with the Pacific Region which reported no area served with that size population. Over one-fourth (28.5 percent) of the Pacific respondents indicated they serve population areas of 100,000 or more. While the majority of funeral directors reported serving areas between 2,500 and 25,000 population, the range regionally, nevertheless, is considerable: from 41.7 percent in the New England Region to 70.9 percent in the Mountain states. The range in percentage is equally pronounced for population areas between 25,000 and 100,000. It varies from 38.9 percent in the New England region to 8.9 percent in the West North Central states.

Again, as with the other data just considered, the initial report on the average number of funerals per year in no way conveys the actual distribution of funerals. While it was reported that the average number of funerals conducted by the "modal" funeral director was 106, the regional variation from this figure ranges from an average of 81 for the West North Central states to a high of 226 for the Pacific states. It is worth noting that while more than 70 percent of the respondents from the Pacific Region reported conducting more than 100 funerals per year, less than 30 percent of the respondents from the Middle Atlantic, East North Central, and West North Central Regions conducted more than 100 funerals in 1966.

Nearly half (46 percent) of the Pacific Region funeral directors and approximately 33 percent of the New England, the West South Central, and the Mountain Region funeral directors provide charity or welfare funerals. Approximately 25 percent of the Middle Atlantic, the South Atlantic, and the East South Central Region funeral directors also reported providing charity funerals. The figure is less than 20 percent for those from the East North Central and West North Central Region.

In each area, very few, if any, respondents arranged charity funerals more than 10 percent of the time, although 12 (or 1.5 percent) of the Middle Atlantic Region funeral directors report funerals of this type more often than this.

In the South Atlantic, East South Central, and West South Central Regions a welfare service in which a stipulated allowance is received is conducted only by a minority of funeral directors. In the other six regions of the country, however, the majority report arranging this type of service up to 10 percent of the time. In the Pacific and New England Regions such services are reported being furnished even more often than this.

The regional variation in the different types of funerals conducted by American funeral directors again belies the statistical average given for the country as a whole. The traditional funeral service, i.e., a funeral in which a public viewing, a public service, and a public committal service are held, is found most consistently and in the greatest number of cases in the central regions of this country and diminishes in frequency as one moves toward either the East or West coasts. From a high of 45.7 percent of the funeral directors in the West North Central Region who reported that the traditional funeral is the only type that is requested, only 18.9 percent of the respondents of the New England states and a scant 3.7 percent of the Pacific Region funeral directors reported conducting traditional funerals exclusively. Put somewhat differently, traditional funerals are conducted 80 percent or more of the time by nine out of ten of the funeral directors from the four central regions of the country, by seven out of ten funeral directors from New England and the Middle Atlantic states, but by only five out of ten Pacific Region funeral directors.

Variations of the traditional funeral are conducted all across the country albeit far less frequently than the traditional funeral and with greater regional variation. For instance, funeral services in which there is a public service but a private viewing will be found to occur more frequently in the extreme eastern and western parts of the country than in the central and south central regions.

A funeral service consisting of a private viewing with a private service also follows the national pattern of being in little evidence in the central regions of the country while more frequently observed along the periphery. Fewer than 10 percent of the respondents reported any funeral services of this type.

Funerals consisting of a public service but no viewing or a private service and no viewing continue the pattern just described. In general, it can be reported that they are reported as occurring less than 10 percent of the time by a minority of the respondents from the central regions who conduct them at all while between a third and a half of the respondents from the eastern and pacific regions report conducting funerals of this type at least 10 percent of the time.

The regional pattern of funerary behavior asserts itself again with the service that consists of an immediate disposal or donation of the body with or without a memorial service following. The responses to this item repeat the fanning-out effect previously noted. What is to be remarked upon is the degree of difference reported. While only 5 percent of the respondents of the West North Central region reported funerals of this nature, some of the time (and in the majority of those cases less than 5 percent of the time) 61 percent of the respondents from the Pacific states reported arranging services of this type.

The question of which type of funeral has increased or decreased over the past five years leads to the observation that any change occurring with regard to the type of funeral is greater on the east and west coasts than it is anywhere else in the country. For instance, 17.9 percent of the Pacific Region respondents indicated that the greatest increase experienced was for the service that omitted the public committal. A similar percentage of these respondents noted that donation of the body to medical science also had increased over the past five years. The New England region respondents reported the greatest increase for the funeral service that omitted public viewing. Middle Atlantic respondents noted that funeral services without the body being viewed showed the greatest increase in that part of the country. Finally, the Pacific respondents reported that of all the funerals described, the traditional funeral had decreased the most in the past five years.

With the question of change over the past ten years, the pattern remains much the same. An increase is indicated for funerals in which there is private viewing, no visitation, no committal service, or a donation to a medical school with or without a memorial service. The number of funeral directors reporting or citing a decrease in the traditional funeral increases as one moves out across the country toward either coast. From a low of 6.5 percent of the respondents from the West North Central Region, the figure reaches 8.9 percent in the New England Region, while it rises to almost one third (30.5 percent) of the respondents from the Pacific states.

The general religious pattern of this country denominationally as well as geographically can be seen in the replies of the respondents. The Protestant denominations dominate our statistics and, as we know from external sources, find their greatest numerical strength in the central regions of this country. This is reflected in our findings. Sixty percent or more of the funeral directors of the central regions of this country reported that at least 80 percent of the families they served were Protestant.

However, in the New England Region we find that the dense Catholic population is reflected in the statistic that 43.8 percent of the funeral directors report a Catholic affiliation for their families 80 percent or more of the time.

In the New England and Middle Atlantic areas, moreover, as would be expected given the pattern of Jewish residency in the United States, 4.1 percent and 3.2 percent of the funeral directors reported conducting Jewish funerals exclusively. Less than 25 percent of all American funeral directors conduct funerals for Jewish families and among the non-Jewish funeral directors in this group, generally less than 10 percent of the funerals they conduct are for Jewish families.

The percentage of respondents who conducted funerals for families reporting no religious affiliation ranges from a low of 10.1 percent in the New England area to 54.7 percent in the Pacific area. Most of these respondents indicated, however, that non-religious services were requested less than 10 percent of the time. The Pacific Region respondents, on the other hand, reported serving such families 10 percent or more of the time. In fact, it is worth noting for an understanding of contemporary funeral trends that 4 percent of the Pacific respondents reported such requests more than 50 percent of the time.

Funeral directors from all regions reported overwhelmingly that they serve no predominant ethnic or racial group. In only one instance, the New England Region, is a group (namely the Irish) singled out by more than 10 percent of the respondents. As would be expected, Scandinavians are mentioned in the West North Central Region by 9.5 percent of the respondents, as are Germans (8.9 percent). The English are cited as the predominant group served in 6.6 percent of the cases in the South Atlantic Region; the French 8.3 percent in New England; and Jews 4.1 percent and 3.9 percent in New England and Middle Atlantic Regions respectively. Given the nature of the racial dichotomy that has prevailed in this country, it is to be expected that service to black citizens is rarely cited.[3] Only the respondents from the Middle Atlantic Region indicated service to the black community more than 1 percent of the time (1.6 percent).

The removal of a body from a hospital is now the common experience of funeral directors the country over. More than 70 percent of all respondents reported that they remove bodies from hospitals at least one half the time. While there is a slight tendency for funeral directors in the South Atlantic Region and the East South Central Region still to remove bodies in the majority of cases from the home, the pattern of where people now go to die in the United States appears evident. Several points are of interest here. Funeral directors from the Mountain and Pacific Regions reported the lowest percentage of home removals. The Pacific Region funeral directors, moreover, reported the lowest percentage of hospital removals over the 50 percent mark. This statistic may be the result of the emergence of the nursing home as an alternative place to die because 4.2 percent of the Pacific states funeral directors reported that they conducted removals from nursing homes more than 50 percent of the time.

Pacific Region funeral directors reported the largest percentage of prearranged funerals conducted in 1966. Eighty-six percent of the funeral directors from this region reported such funerals for that year. Only in the Mountain Region and the Pacific Region, however, did more than one out of every ten respondents report having had funerals of this type at least 10 percent of the time. For the two regions the figures are 18.9 percent and 24.1 percent respectively.

---

[3]While black funeral directors hold membership in the National Funeral Directors Association, the overwhelming majority belong to the National Funeral Directors and Morticians Association. The membership of that association was not included in this survey.

The prefinancing of prearranged funerals follows the regional pattern of prearrangement just described. That is, one third to one half of the funeral directors in all of the regions with the exception of the Pacific states reported that their prearranged funerals are not prefinanced at all. In the Pacific Region more prearranged funerals were also prefinanced and only 16 percent of the respondents reported having no prefinanced funerals. One out of two respondents from the Pacific Region, the Mountain states, and the West North Central Region report that approximately a third of their prearranged funerals are prefinanced.

In each of the census regions across the country the predominant method of prefinancing a funeral is the trust or escrow account. Only in the Pacific Region does insurance account for more than 10 percent of the funeral director's method of prefinancing. In this region 26 percent of the funeral directors reported using this method. Another 24 percent of the Pacific Region funeral directors use multiple methods of prefinancing, whereas very few (less than 5 percent) from any of the other regions use more than one method of prefinancing.

Nearly 40 percent of the Pacific Region funeral directors indicated some affiliation with a prearrangement group or plan. This is almost two and a half times greater than the number that reported an affiliation from the West South Central and Mountain Regions and almost 40 times greater than the New England area where less than 1 percent of the funeral directors reported such affiliation. For the remainder of the census areas, group or plan affiliation was reported in less than 10 percent of the cases.

In analyzing the question "What kind of plan?", it should be noted that less than 8 percent of the respondents designated a specific plan. With that limitation it is of interest to observe that the percentage of funeral directors reporting any kind of plan at all is considerably below 10 percent with the exception of the Pacific Region where more than 35 percent of the respondents checked funeral insurance as the kind of plan they are most closely affiliated with.

Most (two thirds to three fourths) of the funeral directors who conducted prearranged and/or prefinanced funerals in 1966 reported that these funerals were conducted as contracted. For the Pacific Region funeral director, however, the percentages of such funerals conducted as contracted was little more than half (57 percent). The significance of these figures is enhanced, moreover, when it is noted that 93 percent of the funeral directors from the Pacific Region are involved in such prearrangements compared to two thirds or less of the funeral directors from the other eight census regions. The more prearranged funerals contracted for, in other words, the less likely that they will be conducted as planned.

A disproportionately large percentage of prearranged funerals in the Pacific Region compared to the other areas of the country were not conducted as originally planned because the family called another funeral director. This occurred in over 25 percent of the cases.

On the other hand, prearranged funerals were not carried out as originally planned in the majority of census regions because the family decided to spend *more* money. Fifty percent or more of the funeral directors listed this item as the reason for change in the plans. Interestingly, no more than 1 percent of the funeral directors from any one region reported a family spending less than was originally planned.

A change in details accounted for one third of the plan changes for most of the census regions with the exception of the Pacific Region where change in funeral details accounted for almost 50 percent of the reasons given.

A plurality of funeral directors (from 33 percent to almost 50 percent) in eight of the nine census regions felt that prearranged funerals are on the increase. In the Pacific Region, where the increase is apparently being felt the most, more than 67 percent of the funeral directors felt that this was true on the basis of their experience.

With respect to funeral attendance, something of a paradox can be observed. In most of the regions half or more of the respondents stated that they believe funeral attendance is decreasing, but two thirds of the Mountain and Pacific Region respondents felt that funeral attendance is either remaining the same or is on the increase. Further analysis will be required to explain this unexpected finding.

Nearly half of the funeral directors in each region felt that children's attendance at funerals was remaining constant. For the other half of the respondents there are differences in perception that do not appear to follow any pattern of response heretofore described. The funeral directors of three regions perceived increased attendance. They were the New England, East North Central, and West North Central Regions. The respondents of the other six regions, on the other hand, perceived a decrease in attendance to some degree or other. The most notable was the West South Central Region where of those who perceived a change, four out of five felt that fewer children now attend funerals.

Between one half and three fourths of the respondents from the nine different census regions believed that the pre-purchase or pre-selection of cemetery plots or crypts was on the increase. A very few felt that they were decreasing (6 percent). The strongest indications for this first view were seen in the South Atlantic, East South Central, and West South Central Regions where more than three out of four respondents reporting expressed the view that such arrangements are on the increase.

With respect to the amount of time spent on the contemporary funeral, half to two thirds of all of the respondents from the nine census regions were in agreement that there was no change in the amount of time a family spends on a funeral. For the remaining one third to half of the respondents, it should be noted that in each of the nine census regions, most believed that the amount of time given over to the funeral was decreasing rather than increasing.

Briefly, it can be noted that the responses to the query "effort spent" duplicated, for the most part, the overall percentages as well as the direction of the findings regarding "time spent."

One half to three fourths of the respondents from all nine areas reported that they believe that money spent on the contemporary funeral is increasing. In no instance did more than 15 percent of the respondents in any census region express any view to the contrary.

With the exception of the respondents from the Pacific Region (56 percent of whom reported a change in attitude), appreciably more than a majority of funeral directors reported that they found no change in the clergy's attitude toward the religious aspects of the funeral. Such a finding is of interest particularly in the light of the criticism heard these past few years from clerical quarters. However, the funeral directors report that the clergy are concerned about, and may insist upon, the following: (1) a closed casket; (2) the funeral service in the church; (3) a memorial type service; (4) an inexpensive and unostentatious service; and, (5) a brief, simple service.

On the other side of the coin, some funeral directors reported that the clergy they are acquainted with are helpful, express a positive attitude toward the survivors, and are both considerate and concerned. At the same time, however, it was also reported that some clergymen are distant and unconcerned and are dictatorial toward both the funeral director and the family of the deceased.

Again, with the exception of the Pacific Region replies, change in family attitudes was reported in approximately one out of three cases. With the Pacific Region respondents, however, the ratio comes much closer to one out of two funeral directors who indicated a change in family attitude of some nature or other.

The comments and remarks of the funeral directors who responded to this question are many and varied. They include such comments as "families today are better educated about funerals and are more knowledgeable," "they are less religious," "they request brief services," "there are fewer emotional displays by families," "they are suspicious of over-charging," "they want memorial services," as well as such comments as "they are grateful to the funeral director," and "they are buying better merchandise." As with the previous question, there are one or two items that are of particular interest. First, across all regions there is a good proportion of funeral directors who reported that families want briefer services. The percentages range from a high of 14.6 percent in the South Atlantic Region to 3.1 percent in the Mountain Region. Second, the comment "less religious" is shown in the responses of the Mountain and Pacific Regions more markedly than in any of the other regions (6.3 percent and 8.4 percent respectively). Third, "less emotional display by family" appears across most of the regions as does the comment "object to clergy, call funeral director first." In both of these items the Pacific Region replies showed the highest percentages (3.1 percent and 4.2 percent respectively).

Approximately 75–90 percent of all funeral homes across the country advertise. Interestingly, and this may be a reflection of length of time of establishment in the community, the New England and Middle Atlantic census regions are at the lowest end of this range, while the Pacific Region is at the highest. On the average, a little more than four out of ten funeral directors use just one kind of advertising and as has been seen from the earlier "modal" profile, it is the name or symbol of the funeral establishment only that is employed. Of interest also is the fact that the percentage of funeral directors who price-advertise is less than 2 percent of the total reporting.

These regional comparisions give only a rough approximation at best of what is typical or characteristic of funeral service across the country. In no way do they take into account what is occasional, unusual, or unique in the character of a particular funeral or a specific funeral establishment. Moreover, if what is said and written is true, funeral service, like many other vocations and professions, experiences as well as reflects a difference in the character or size of its setting. In addition to the differences we have observed regionally an analysis of funeral service by size of local area should show differences obscured by the comparison of census regions.

Briefly, a review of the data based on the size of the local community shows the following major points of interest.

Urban-Rural Comparisons

There is a definite urban-rural difference to be seen in the different types of funerals conducted. The more urban and metropolitan the area, the lower the percentage of traditional funerals reported. When firms requested to conduct only traditional funerals are compared, the differences become even more pronounced: 51.8 percent of the rural area funeral directors reported they conduct only traditional funerals compared to only 8.2 percent of the large urban area funeral directors. The proportion of funeral directors who have public funeral services but no public committal service also increases with city size. A funeral service with no public viewing also appears to be an urban phenomenon. Approximately 40 percent of the funeral directors living in areas over 100,000 population reported this type of service. Funerals in which there is private viewing, or no viewing, or a graveside service only, all correlate with the size of city, that is, the larger the area served, the greater the percentage of funeral directors who reported this type of funeral. The practice of privately disposing of the body followed by a memorial service is more prevalent in the areas of 100,000 to 1,000,000 population than in any other area including population areas of over one million. In the 100,000–1,000,000 population area, 40 percent of the funeral directors conduct some (albeit few) memorial services compared to 30 percent for the very large cities and 4 percent for the very small towns. The donation of the body to medical science with or without a memorial service shows a direct relation to size of area served. Nearly 50 percent of the very large urban funeral directors have donations and service calls compared to 2 percent in the small rural area. Mostly, large city funeral directors (that is, over 1,000,000 population) have donations without a service.

Funeral directors living in large urban areas report the most change in funeral services. In areas under 25,000 population, one out of two respondents reported no change in funeral services over the past decade compared to the large urban area funeral directors of whom four out of five noted changes. What was reported to be increasing were private committals, private viewings, or services in which there was no viewing and immediate disposal of the body with or without a memorial service. An increase in immediate disposal without a memorial service was particularly noted.

Removal from hospital and/or nursing home, even in the rural areas, is now the norm even though, of course, the percentage of funeral directors who conduct such removals is greater in the large metropolitan areas.

Prearrangement of funerals is related to urban size. Twice as many funeral directors from large urban areas as from the rural centers report that they prearrange funerals. Very few funeral directors in any area, however, reported that more than 25 percent of their funerals in 1966 had been prearranged. Of funeral directors who do prearrange, fewer than 5 percent of all their funerals were of this type.

Generally speaking, it can be said that the larger the area the greater the proportion of prearranged funerals which had to be changed. Moreover, the main reason for change is selection of a more expensive funeral by the family. While the selection of another funeral director seems to be related to urban size (where the opportunity to do so is greater and where mobility is also a greater factor) price change or change in details as reasons do not seem to be related to the size of the area served. Prefinanced funerals now on file, as would be expected, vary directly with the size of the community.

The viewing of the body also appears to be associated with size of area. While half of the respondents from all areas saw no change in viewing patterns, the remainder if from smaller cities cite an increase in viewing and if from larger urban centers a decrease.

The largest percentage of respondents from each population area agreed that funeral attendance in general is decreasing. The proportion of respondents who report this increases as the size of the community increases.

The report on children's attendance at funerals by urban size is fundamentally divided with as many funeral directors reporting an increase in attendance as a decrease.

It is generally agreed that the practice of prearranging a cemetery plot or crypt is on the increase.

The time spent by family members for a funeral seems to be inversely proportional to the size of the community, that is, the larger the community the less time spent by the family.

There is consensus from a considerable proportion of funeral directors in all census regions that there is a decrease in the effort spent by family members for a funeral.

While funeral directors from the larger areas seem to notice a decrease in the amount of money spent on a funeral, the general consensus is that the money spent today for a funeral is increasing.

The larger the area served, the study shows, the more frequently funeral directors commented on having noticed changes of a critical nature in clergy and family attitudes both toward themselves and toward the contemporary funeral.

Finally, the majority of all funeral directors advertise, with the proportion who do generally increasing as the size of the city increases. There does not appear to be a relationship, however, between size of community and the kind of advertisement employed.

Discussion

The results of this latest study complement, in important respects, certain of the findings of the two previous studies reviewed here. The present study goes beyond mere confirmation of the previous two however. The present analysis shows that the funeral in contemporary America is a different thing to different people. It has shown that while the traditional funeral is almost totally characteristic of the great central portion of the United States and the predominant mode of behavior everywhere else, it is subject to modification and change. New rites and practices for coping with death and for disposing of the dead are emerging. Emergent variability is a fact in funeral service as it is throughout all of society. Change is at work not only in the mode of disposal of the dead, but in every sphere of funeral service as well—from the type of establishment constructed, to the emotional climate in which the funeral is conducted, as well as to the "meaning" given to death itself.

In order to grasp the significance and implications of the findings of this study as well as the two that preceded it, these studies must be placed within the larger context of American life. A funeral does not take place in a vacuum. What has been reported here can be understood to mirror, albeit in a small way, what society as a whole is evidencing by way of its values and goals, both with respect to its larger abstract self and to its smallest unit—the individual.

First, it must be remembered that we are, according to religious tradition, made in the image of God. According to the Christian doctrine, however, man is born in sin and the image therefore is flawed. Man's death, it is believed, is the consequence of that sin and is a necessary experience of every man before he may be restored to his perfect form. The funeral, traditionally, has been an instrument of such belief and its ritual has served in the liturgy for the dead.

The image of man in this traditional, theological sense is changing in America. Today, the idea is being entertained that death no longer is as certain as taxes. And no longer, too, can it be said with assurance that life is the gift of God.

The papal encyclical on birth control in 1968 created a storm of continuing debate in this country that has had almost no precedent. Protests, petitions, and pronouncements by clergy and laity of all religious faiths strongly opposed to the papal edict. The same year saw the first successful heart transplant in the United States, the continued progress toward kidney and other organ transplants, and increased speculation regarding the unlimited possibilities being opened by medical science technology. The religious, moral, and legal arguments surrounding such operations and their future implications are only now beginning to take definite form. One thing, however, appears increasingly clear as never before—modern man refuses to accept the inevitability of death. With death, as well as with birth, man seeks to be the final judge.

A case in point is that of the great Russian physicist Landau, who, after a serious automobile accident several years ago, "died" four times on the operating table. His value to Russian science was of such magnitude, however, that his death was not "permitted" and he was restored to life by brilliant medical ministrations. The converse of this story is equally dramatic and significant of the times in which we live. It has been reported that prison inmates in the United States have been used as "human guinea pigs" for new experimental drugs and medicines without, according to the allegation, being properly informed of the possible consequences to their health and welfare.[4] In another instance, it was reported that live cancer cells were injected into hospital patients, apparently without their consent.[5]

These are isolated instances to be sure, and there is no wish to convey an undue sense of alarm. However, the beginnings of the Nazi crimes were equally small.[6] At first there was only the subtle shift in the perspective of physicians that there was such a thing as a life not worthy of living, or that one person had a greater claim to life than another.

The invention of the kidney machine in Seattle, Washington several years ago brings the issue of life and death into distressingly sharp focus for American citizens today. The non-medical criteria that were initially established conjointly with the medical

[4]Alan J. Davis, "Sexual Assaults in the Philadelphia Prison System and Sheriff's Vans," *Trans Action*, (December, 1968), pp. 8–16.

[5]E. Langer, "Human Experimentation: New York Verdict Affirms Patients' Rights," *Science*, 151: 663, 1966.

[6]In 1931, Bavarian scientists were publicly discussing sterilization and the euthanasia of persons with chronic mental illness. In 1936 Hitler ordered euthanasia for these persons. All state hospitals were to report on those persons who had been ill for five years or more and who were unable to work. Reports were made to boards of leading psychiatrists who passed judgment. A "Charitable Transport Company for the Sick" carried patients to "Charitable Foundations for Institutional Care," where they were put to death. The victims were all those unable to work and considered nonrehabilitable. Within a few years about 275,000 Germans were put to death. From that established base, it was merely a matter of logic to include the Gypsy, the Jew, and all other "enemies" of the state.

criteria to select the first kidney patients contradicted our traditional democratic philosophy and said, in effect, that some men have a greater claim to life than others. Of course, it has always been true that wealthy persons could afford better medical care than the poor, but it has never been an official medical proposition that a person of wealth had a greater claim to life than any other person. It was, however, established by an anonymous committee of seven, known portentously as the "Life and Death Committee," that one's right to a life-sustaining machine was in part a function of his potential or actual contribution to society. The doctor, the lawyer, the executive on his way up, it was implied, have a greater claim to life than the unskilled, the unemployed, or the unwanted. While these past few years have seen the production of large numbers of kidney machines, as well as the development of kidney transplant techniques, the moral and ethical issues raised by the Seattle kidney machine still remain to be resolved.

There are other factors more immediate and direct that we must consider if we are to understand fully the information provided us by the survey.

The first point to consider is the fact that in the United States the population over the age of 65 now totals 19,000,000 persons. Death in contemporary society is increasingly an experience of the aged. In 1967 of the approximately two million persons who died, over 64% were persons aged 65 years or older. In excess of 60% of these deaths, moreover, took place outside of the family home, that is, either in hospitals or nursing homes. In contrast, 61 million, or 30% of the population, are children under 15 years of age. They account for less than 7.5% of all deaths. This is a dramatic reversal in our mortality statistics compared to the 1920's. These new social facts present us with what could be called the first "death-free" generation in the history of the world. That is, it is now one generation or twenty years that a family can normally expect, statistically, not to experience a death among its members. The implications of this development for our discussion cannot be overlooked, for they color our view of death and our notion as to what constitutes an appropriate response to it.

A second factor to be considered is the seemingly relentless inflationary character of the American economy. Coupled with typically low, fixed incomes of this burgeoning population of aged citizens, the inflationary spiral seriously threatens the private household economies of literally millions of American families. Death expenses, regardless of the provisions made beforehand, cannot help but be a source of anxiety and concern to them. Such concern is enhanced, moreover, by the changing character of the American family itself.

The American family has been transformed from a large, extended family into a small, nuclear group. It is more mobile today, socially as well as geographically, than ever before. Today's family can be characterized as more child-oriented than adult-oriented, more democratic than communal, and more individualized than integrated. The young, contemporary family, moreover, is no longer a part of a rural community or a neighborhood-enclosed group, but rather increasingly is isolated in an urban environment. In the modern-day megalopolis, the elderly are segregated while the younger members live out lives of increasing anonymity. Death, as it has been pointed out, is increasingly an experience of the aged, most of whom are retired from work, free of parental obligations, and frequently outside of or absent from the main current of family life. Moreover, the extension of medical service and the advances in medical science research make possible not only the prolonging of life of the elderly, but often cause those hospitalized to be further separated from their families. Familial and friendship commitments are made fewer by such separations, and emotional and societal bonds are loosened by time and distance. Not the least consequence of this development is the fact that great numbers of the elderly must not only live alone but, as this survey shows, must die alone as well. The disengagement of the aged from society, therefore, prior to their deaths means that their dying will little affect the round of life.

The death of a leader such as President Kennedy or of his brother, Senator Robert Kennedy, or of Dr. Martin Luther King can seriously disrupt the functioning of modern society. The vacuum they left in the social and political life of the United States has been sorely felt. For the average family, however, it is the death of someone in the middle productive years of life, or someone young and unfulfilled, that will have a comparable effect upon them. The death of the elderly, becoming less relevant as they are to the functional ordering and working of contemporary secular society, does not compel such attention, and like the late General McArthur's "old soldier," they, too, eventually will not die, but merely fade away.

That this may well be the case for a certain segment of the population is suggested by the changing attitudes toward the funeral as a meaningful rite for the dead, and in the criticism and attacks that have been directed toward it in recent years. In a society in which only half of the population is church-affiliated, and in which the social and spacial mobility of its citizens is one of its more remarkable characteristics, the religious, emotional, and economic obligations that a funeral has traditionally imposed on a family are seen even today by many as burdensome and inappropriate. Increasingly, the funeral service is for that member of the family least functionally relevant to it. He has been, as noted, often spacially removed from the family, perhaps by a long illness or confinement. In a society with a strong trend towards a one-generational bias, as well as a strong impulse towards economy and efficiency, the expenses of the funeral strike the utility-minded citizen where he is most sensitive.

Advocacy of memorial services, with the body absent, cremation and/or the medical donation of the body or its parts, are various attempts within the context of emerging contemporary values to resolve the different problems associated with the traditional disposal of the dead.

Finally, what has been described finds both strength and motive power from a yet undiscussed but important source, namely, education. One of the most significant revolutions to have occurred in this country is the general acceptance of public education as the *summum bonum*. While we have had colleges and universities in America from our earliest beginnings (Harvard was founded in 1636), it is only since World War II that education, particularly higher education, could in any real sense be considered a public enterprise. Since that time, however, the enrollment in our colleges has more than doubled. From a population of less than 3 million students in 1945, college enrollment today has surpassed the 7 million mark. It is predicted, moreover, that by 1980, 10 to 12 million students will be enrolled in institutions of higher learning across this country.

But numbers alone can in no way convey the impact that modern education is having upon our society. Education is a cumulative phenomenon. Geometric in its growth, it is exponential in its consequences. Moreover, it is secular. It is this-world oriented. Its focus is on the manipulation and control of the growing present. While it is blind to race, color and faith, it is not democratic. Modern education, furthermore, is rational. It is a vast undertaking of the intellect, not the emotions. It is a solvent that no social form can long contain for by the very nature of free inquiry it challenges the present and questions the future.

Modern education, finally, is the inheritance of youth, who in many instances, perceive life as well as death as existentially absurd.

Conclusion

What of the funeral and the American funeral director in the face of these trends and developments? The present study shows that despite the appearance of new elements in our society the traditional funeral continues to prevail in all areas of the country. The impulse to reform, and practices departing from the traditional funeral ceremony, where they occur, appear to be associated with such specific factors as religious heterogeneity, urban size, volume, advertising, and census region. Specifically, the Pacific Region and the New England states command attention. In the case of the Pacific Region it was found that in many respects the responses of the funeral directors have their complement in the replies of those persons from that region who participated in the American public survey of 1962. Now, as then, certain distinctive characteristics of the Pacific Region residents must be acknowledged. On the other hand, the nature of funeral service in that region and the practices of the Pacific funeral director must not be overlooked if the results of the study are to be fully understood.

The findings of the study should by no means invite complacency among funeral service practitioners. What today is the concern of the Pacific Coast funeral director and the problem of funeral directors in other specific localities in this country can tomorrow be the concern of all. Modern communications technology promises in the very near future to make every community a part of the vital metropolitan life of America if, indeed, it is not so already.

With this prospect before funeral service and in view of what has been written thus far, it can be asked, "How best may the funeral director articulate his place and function in contemporary life?"

While the present study gives few direct clues for replying to this question, a partial answer can be attempted.

It would appear that a carefully developed rationale for funeral service can go far toward resolving many of the issues discussed here as well as contribute to a better understanding between the American public and the modern funeral director.

As a part of that rationale the following can be argued: the loss of a significant other by death is a crisis situation. Medical and behavioral science experts have taught in recent years that such loss evokes powerful emotions within us which need to be given proper expression. The ritual of the funeral, when it is responsive to the psychological needs of the survivor, can aid in this ventilation and facilitate the normal dissolution of grief.

The anthropologist, Geoffrey Gorer, for instance, conducted a study in England of recently bereaved individuals.[7] He found that in Britain today there is a repudiation and a denial of death that leaves the survivor grievously alone and ill-equipped to cope with the myriad personal and social difficulties that are attendant upon a loss.

Like the divorced person of several decades ago, ostracized and neglected, the bereaved individual today, Gorer reported, is to a large extent without traditional religious resources or community support and often lacks the skills necessary to deal adequately with his loss.

The personal consequence of this development, Gorer found, was the appearance of a considerable amount of maladaptive response to death ranging from "meaningless business" and "private rituals of mummification" to "the apathy of despair." It is his opinion that new secular customs and social techniques will have to be developed to reach those whom death has touched but for whom there is no longer an adequate social response.

The cumulation of psychological and sociological evidence argues for some acknowledgment of a death. For many, this will be part of a religious rite. On the other hand, if for some a death is no longer meaningfully dramatized within the framework of traditional theology, then it should be dramatized in terms of the fact that a specific life has ended and certain social relationships have been ruptured.

As pointed out, the funeral has been expected to perform several different functions. Some people today, however, look for little from a funeral. For them, the death of a relative is an occasion for the barest acknowledgment and the most expeditious disposal. In such instances, the death could be described, for lack of a better expression, as a "low grief potential" death. In such a death, loss is slight and grief is muted.

On the other hand, a death may be perceived as inappropriate and may be resented and rejected by the survivors. In such a case, the emotional needs of the survivors are infinitely greater and their problems more extensive. Such a death as this could be described as possessing a "high grief potential."

Just as the traditional funeral should not be expected of the survivors for whom it does not convey either their beliefs or sentiments, care must be taken, on the other hand, not to define too narrowly which funeral rite or what behavior is appropriate for the bereaved. To do so can lead to tension or conflict. For the Christian clergy, for instance, to define the funeral as a rite of passage only and to stress death as a victory that should be rejoiced in by the survivors is to ignore the fact that death is also the separation of a husband from a wife or a father from a daughter and, like any irrevocable separation, can be experienced as a profound loss.

The ceremonialization of death compels the recognition that a death has occurred. In a society where there is a strong tendency for many to respond to the death of another by turning away, the funeral is a vehicle through which recovery from the crisis of bereavement is initiated.

The funeral is also a ceremony that recognizes the integral worth and dignity of man. It is not only a sociological statement that a death has occurred, it is also a declaration that a life has been lived. To fail to acknowledge the death of a man is

---

[7]Geoffrey Gorer, *Death, Grief and Mourning* (New York: Doubleday and Co., 1967.)

ultimately to admit to the abandonment of a personal identity for self. In this regard then, the funeral director has an important role to play in assuring that the ceremonialization of death is a life-confirming event.

Man is a social being and his life is lived out with others of his kind. It is for funeral service as for the other care-taking professions to recognize that by their services they facilitate and preserve group life and in doing so enrich the life of the individual.

Introductory Commentary
on the Appendices

The material in the appendices could have been incorporated in the text of pertinent chapters of the book. However, it was felt that the nature of such material would make it easy to refer to and use if separated. This has been done.

The following explains each of the Appendices.

Appendix I

There are millions of people who have not had someone close to them die. Therefore, many of them have had no "real" funeral experience. Some wonder why there are funerals and funeral directors. This appendix, referred to in the Chapter on "Public Information Programs," consists of a series of ads which tell of the historical and contemporary facets of the funeral as a service to the living while their dead are being cared for in a manner that gives dignity to man.

The ads can be used in whole or in part and/or adapted by funeral director associations and individual funeral homes.

The asterisks divide the copy material public relations consultant George DeGrace planned as 12 ads—4 dealing with "Serving the Living"; 4 as to "Caring for the Dead"; and, 4 regarding "Giving Dignity to Man."

Appendix II

This is the text given many times before groups of all sorts and all sizes. The material in it is basic. Updating such as the reference to funerals for persons of renown may be necessary to make the text current. (Referred to in "Public Information Programs.")

Appendix III

Many of the people who have no death-funeral experience are young. Some of them have read or heard derogatory statements on the funeral and about the funeral director. Most of them welcome more of the facts including those on the "other side." The text of the talk, which is this appendix, has proven interesting to youth—teenagers through undergraduate college students. It is generally basic with some specifics spelled out to explain or to emphasize. The text will be "current" for a long time. (Referred to in "Public Information Programs.")

Appendix IV

The majority of Americans profess a religious belief. For them, the funeral is a religious rite.

More and more groups within religious institutions are seeking a speaker on the funeral from within funeral service. This appendix is a suggested text for such talk.

"Comforting the Sorrowing" was written by Kermit Edison, a Stoughton (Wisconsin) funeral director. It has been revised slightly since he first gave it.

There are two personal references in Mr. Edison's text—one to his years in funeral service. The other is to an experience he had. It is easy for someone using this basic text to substitute his years in the profession and a similar experience—if he had one. If not, that portion of the talk can be disregarded. (Referred to in "Public Information Programs.")

Appendix V

The interest of churched persons in the funeral is shared by clergymen and seminarians. However, the approach to be used by a representative of funeral service in appearing before them as a group must be different. It must get down to matters of more specific concern to those who minister or who will minister to grief sufferers than is the case when talking to those who will be ministered to.

This appendix is the opening or introductory portion of a presentation before a ministerial group, most of which are "local" in nature. It also can be used for a talk before seminarians.

The representative of funeral service should consider supplementing this material with a review of "local" customs and usages before a ministerial group with clergy of various denominations in the audience. This might also be feasible before some seminaries. Then too, rituals and symbols associated with the religion of the seminary—if it is a single religion seminary—might be reviewed in relation to the funeral.

In both the instance of the ministerial association presentation and the one for seminaries, time should be allotted for questions from the audience. Consideration also should be given to the distribution of literature as spelled out in "Public Information Programs" where reference is made to this appendix.

Appendix VI

This appendix is best described in its original reference in "Public Information Programs." It is a manuscript for a public-information vocational-guidance talk for career days, job fairs and other occasions when youth are present who might consider funeral service as a profession. It was prepared originally by Robert C. Slater for use with slides available from the NFDA headquarters office.

Appendix VII

This appendix is self-explanatory. It is of recommended packets of printed matter available from the NFDA headquarters office. Reference is made to this list in "Public Information Programs."

Appendices VIII and IX

These forms are the subject of "A Visit With the Clergymen With Whom You Serve" in "Clergy and Funeral Director Relations." A review of them makes clear their use.

Appendix X

General Counsel of NFDA, Thomas H. Clark, made a state by state study of the laws which govern the prearrangement and prefinancing of funerals and the control of monies paid in advance for merchandise and/or service.

This appendix is a chart which gives a brief summary of the laws of each of the states. Where there is no law it is so stipulated.

The column captioned "Amount of Income Part of Trust" is to show deviations from 100% of the income on the trust funds becoming part of the trust. As an example in California an amount sufficient to pay expenses and forfeitures can be taken from the income of the trust funds.

APPENDIX I

The Fundamental Purpose of the Funeral—
The Most Significant Function of Your Funeral Director. . .

SERVING THE LIVING

St. Augustine said it about 400 A.D.: "The laying out of the body, the burial rites. . .are more of a consolation to the living than of assistance to the dead."

Since that time many others qualified to speak from the religious, psychological, sociological or medical point of view have agreed.

A minister who is a leading authority on grief, stated: "There are eight specific purposes and values of the funeral that every person should come to know and understand:

A funeral faces the reality of death—does not avoid it;

A funeral provides a setting wherein the religious needs of the bereaved may be satisfied;

A funeral provides faith to sustain spirit;

A funeral helps free one from guilt or self-condemnation;

A funeral helps one express feelings;

A funeral directs one beyond the death of a loved one to the responsibilities of life;

A funeral, in a personal way, helps one face a crisis with dignity and courage;

A funeral, above all, provides an environment where loving friends and relatives can give the help needed to face the future with strength and courage."

* * *

Your funeral director, through his training and experience, is well aware that his most significant function and the fundamental purpose of the funeral is to Serve the Living.

The contemporary American funeral is usually a religious service, supported by the practices and customs of the community and the personal desires of the bereaved. The clergyman relates the experience of death and bereavement "to a dimension beyond the human to proclaim a strength greater than human strength, to offer comfort more sensitive than human comfort, to present an understanding more profound than human understanding."

The funeral director is responsible for all other aspects of the funeral, and together with the clergyman provides a united service for those who suffer the loss which a death creates.

* * *

Modern funeral service today performs, by design, many of the functions that primitive man performed by instinct.

The funeral with the body present impresses the reality of the situation upon the minds and emotions of the bereaved. Constant and continuing experience indicates that the vast majority of people want and need this confirmation.

Among all men and in all time, custom has devised a meeting place between the living and the dead. This is more than a show of sympathy for the bereaved family. It is more than a parting from someone well regarded. It is a way of saying that the sorrows of one are the sorrows of all. Today this meeting place is usually the funeral home—where none are formally invited, but all are welcome to come.

* * *

The funeral is truly an experience of great value, when in its aftermath, the survivor—his grief adequately expressed and his emotions properly channeled—can think and talk of his deceased loved one without pain. That is when he will begin to carry with him all the happy recollections of their life together—and these will remain with him always in the world of the living.

Yes, for all people everywhere, funerals and funeral ceremonies satisfy basic needs, allay suffering and help to rescue death from the horror of meaninglessness.

Your funeral director stands ready to serve you in the manner in which you wish to be served, in accordance with your own beliefs and personal desires.

*   *   *

The Funeral Director Is Your Personal Representative in...

CARING FOR THE DEAD

Man has always buried his dead with respect and ceremony—beginning with the early Egyptians, about 3,000 B.C., right up to the familiar American funeral of today.

The roots of American funeral customs and practices extend back through western civilization into early Judaeo-Christian beliefs concerning the nature of God, man, and the hereafter. Most people believe that the sacred quality of man exists in the soul or spirit and that the body which housed the soul during life deserves dignified treatment after death.

Regarded only as a physical fact, a dead body is a worthless thing. But nothing can deny or obscure the knowledge that just a brief moment ago it was someone dearly loved who loved in return. And so, for what it was, rather than what it is, the body is almost universally treated with reverence and dignity.

*   *   *

In Colonial times, everyone in the community was somewhat involved in each death. Today, almost the entire responsibility to care for the dead rests with the immediate family of the deceased. Then, practically everyone died at home. Neighbors, friends, relatives and fellow churchmen prepared the body for burial, made a coffin, dug the grave and did whatever else was necessary for the funeral.

However, as significant changes took place in the American mode of living it was no longer feasible for all these various tasks to be handled by volunteers. Gradually there emerged specific persons in each community who performed one or more of these services. They were originally called "layers out of the dead." Then the term "undertaker"—one who undertook to bury the dead—came into popular use. Now such a person is known as a funeral director because—in addition to caring for the dead—he, as his title implies, directs the funeral, and in so doing, serves the living, too.

The vast changes in American life had other widespread effects on the care of the body and the funeral. The general movement to the cities and the shift from single dwellings to flats and apartments made the development of the funeral home a necessity.

*   *   *

Today, less than half of all deaths occur at home. And due to the increasing mobility of the population, many persons die elsewhere than the community in which they live or will be buried. This mobility has also made it essential to gain time between death and the funeral so that a brother might return from across the country or a daughter might come home from another state to pay their last respects. Unless the body is embalmed, this time cannot be gained.

When death is difficult to realize because it was sudden and violent or occurred after a devastating illness, embalming takes on added significance. The skilled practitioner can usually restore the body to an earlier, more familiar appearance. This greatly aids the bereaved in accepting the reality of death—an all-important step in a healthy grieving process.

Then, too, a funeral service with the body present is an integral part of most religions. Therefore, custom, religion and properly channeled grief have put a greater emphasis on the necessity for embalming and care of the body in our American funeral.

*   *   *

When there is a death, the funeral director is your personal representative in caring for the remains. He comes to you with knowledge, experience and understanding at a time when you are faced with duties often strange to you. He is thoroughly familiar with all the burial laws and regulations, as well as the community customs and religious ceremonies pertinent to each situation. Quietly and efficiently he performs the many professional services required to lighten your burden and fulfill your needs and desires.

Today's funeral director exists because you want him to exist. The services he renders are those which you want him to render. He is motivated by a desire for personal service, and acts with a deep appreciation of the trust and confidence you place in him when you ask him to care for your dead.

*   *   *

The Philosophy of Funeral Service—
The Primary Concern of Your Funeral Director. . .

GIVING DIGNITY TO MAN

Every funeral is really a testimonial to the dignity of man and the goodness and justice of a Supreme Being. To show reverence for the dead and compassion for the living arises out of the deepest needs and highest motives of human nature. Thus, each funeral gives dignity not only to the departed, but at the same time, to all mankind.

The English poet John Donne expressed it this way some three and one-half centuries ago: "No man is an island, entire of himself. Every man is a piece of the continent, a part of the main;. . .any man's death diminishes me, because I am involved in mankind; and therefore never send to know for whom the bell tolls; it tolls for thee."

The funeral is an ageless custom which sees man as an individual of worth. Knowing the great value of human life, we honor that value when we commemorate the death of one who has lived amongst us.

*   *   *

Nowhere in the world is there a lack of concern regarding death, care of the dead or the readjustment of the bereaved. The conception of body, soul and afterlife varies greatly in different societies, in different religious beliefs and on different continents. Yet, the crisis of death is universally recognized.

There is no group, however primitive at one extreme or civilized at the other, which does not dispose of the bodies of its members with ceremony. From within man alone, as an aspect of his human nature, comes the desire to care for his dead.

Funerals lie at the very innermost core of life's experiences. They represent grand and not trifling moments. The funeral tends to reflect the whole viewpoint, the basic philosophy of life of the culture in which it is found.

*   *   *

What has been said and written about man and funerals in every era is just as true now, for actually man has changed but little since the beginning of time. He has altered his environment, and he may know or think he knows more about himself and the world around him, but his drives, emotions, his wants and needs remain basically the same.

Americans recognize today what men in all ages have perceived, that even though in death the personality has left the body, the body remains as the only medium through which that person was known to other men. And as St. Augustine said: "Since the body is the organ and instrument used by the soul in the performance of good works, it is a natural duty that we pay respect to the body."

*   *   *

The funeral of every person, no matter how humble was his state in life, is just as meaningful and necessary to his survivors as the funeral of a well-known personage is to his bereaved. Every man is equally important in the eyes of God. And who, but God, is to say which ones loved Him more or served Him better? The clergyman reminds us in the funeral ceremony of this equality of man as he offers spiritual comfort, hope and encouragement to the living.

The professional services rendered today by your funeral director are in direct response to the innate desire in all of us to care for and honor our beloved dead as individuals of worth. Thus, it follows that the philosophy of funeral service and the primary concern of our funeral director must be—Giving Dignity to Man.

APPENDIX II

The Funeral: What It Has Been—What It Is—What It Does

A featured article in the *Miami News* some time ago told about eight-year-old Eugene Lemire. Eugene had run away from his home and was found at the Seaquarium. He apparently is emotionally disturbed because some time ago his pilot father was lost at sea and someone told him that the sharks may have eaten his dad's body. He went to the Seaquarium to see the sharks.

Those who know say that Eugene Lemire is a deeply troubled youngster because the reality and finality of his father's death has never been confirmed for him.

A somewhat similar situation is partially responsible for the intense interest in death and funeral ceremonies of the British anthropologist, Geoffrey Gorer, who recently wrote a book which was published both in England and in the United States.

Mr. Gorer's father was drowned in the "Lusitania." In the autobiographical introduction of his study of contemporary society called *Death, Grief and Mourning* he writes that following the death of his father, as rational hope diminished, he constructed elaborate fantasies that his father was surviving on some desert island in the Atlantic. And, for at least some months he put off the acceptance of his final disappearance by these dreams.

The June 1968 issue of *Psychiatric Opinion* includes a case report on grief written by Dr. Henry Grunebaum who is a senior psychiatrist at the Massachusetts Health Center. The case involves a young married woman who lost a baby during the delivery. Her grief was prolonged and unresolved. But over a brief series of interviews she was able to grieve.

The last of Dr. Grunebaum's comments is:

". . . perhaps [the] most vital issue is the influence of the hospital and its ways of dealing with stillbirths and the patient's inability to grieve. She was helpless during the delivery, not allowed to see the baby, and encouraged to sign an autopsy and burial permit for a mass grave. We may wonder whether her grieving would not have proceeded more normally had she seen her baby and been able to give it an appropriate funeral service. . ."

Sometime after the mine disaster in Mannington, West Virginia an Associated Press wire story told of the widows who came to a church not far from the mine where the bodies of their husbands are sealed off. They came to the church to pray. And, the release says, "Their prayer is always the same: They want their husbands' bodies back so that they can bury them properly."

I relate these instances to you because never before in the history of mankind have there been so many individuals studying death and the problems associated with it as there are presently. Paradoxically, while this is going on there are some working hard to discount or disregard the findings of objective studies by questioning the place of the funeral in modern American society.

What has the funeral been?

The funeral goes back into the history of mankind. For example:

– About 5,000 years ago Egyptians were burying their dead with ceremony.

–The historical roots of the funeral dig deep also into the soil of ancient Greece where before the birth of Christ tombs and other architectural memorials were built in honor of those who died.

–The Romans had distinctive burial customs.

–The customs of the Orientals today are similar to ancient practices which have survived.

The early Hebrews washed the dead body, anointed it and wrapped it in linen with spices. Interment was always made—in shallow trenches for the poor and in natural caves or artificial sepulchers for the wealthy.

The early Christians also prepared the body for burial. They closed the eyes, washed the body and placed it in linen sprinkled liberally with spices. During those days hundreds of years ago there were wakes. In fact, canon law decreed that the body should be laid out with lights beside it and that holy water be placed with it and a cross be put in folded hands on the breast of the deceased.

After the persecution of the Christian church ended, the requiem Mass began. The dead were brought into the church. Burial became a function of the church predicated on the doctrine that the dead body is not worthless.

Much of that which we do in the funeral today is predcated on Judaeo-Christian practices. The most convincing proof of this is the funerals that have been conducted over the years and are still being conducted for many of the hierarchy of many churches of all denominations.

What is the funeral now?

Dr. William M. Lamers, Jr., a West Coast psychiatrist, defined the funeral as "an organized, purposeful, time limited, flexible, group-centered response to death."

This definition is self-explanatory. A few years ago the concluding words—"a group-centered response to death" would have been looked upon as too fundamental to be emphasized. But, because the funeral is a response to death and because it is group-centered and because we are living in a death denying—death defying—culture it is important to review this problem of magnitude facing Americans in the same way as Gorer says the problem confronts the English.

We are living in a youth culture. There are just as many Americans twenty-seven years of age or younger as there are those over that age. The so-called youth market is the largest single segment of most markets.

The expression "youth culture" embraces more than young people. It also takes in those who would like to stay young forever. All of us have seen "girls" of questionable age wearing clothing that would not become even the shapeliest of those who are two generations younger. Men are dying their hair. The merry Oldsmobile of the song was advertised for a while as the Youngmobile. Some people are even reticent to admit their age when a financial benefit is available to them because of it. In this regard there is the news that went around the country about the woman who wrote to the Social Security office that was sending her checks requesting that the checks be sent in a blank envelope instead of one of the Social Security Administration. The reason given the Social Security Regional Director was that she did not want to make her age known.

When those caught up in the youth culture do get old, many times they are sent to segregated communities for the elderly. Or, they are told that they cannot live in certain areas because they are over forty-five years of age.

It could well be that our culture is changing from a family to a generation culture.

The knowledge explosion has made the youth of today the most informed of all times. Many of them have most, if not all, of the things they want. Often they have their own apartment in the same city in which their parents live, before they are married. When they marry, many times their job takes them to a city miles away. And, as science prolongs the lives of their parents, their family is separated by age, by distance between homes and by knowledge.

Additionally, many people today of all ages are less religious than they once were or than their predecessors were. They don't want to die because to them advanced age and death are the end of a pleasurable and useful life.

The efforts of those in the wonderful world of science give hope for an even more prolonged youth and life. The present age of anatomical transplants recently led a biologist to ask—Are we being mentally immunized against death?

Up to now at least every person who lives must die. And, when death does occur there is a meaning and purpose and value in the rites of passage.

There are an increasing number of men and women of learning who maintain that a healthy philosophy of death is essential to a healthy philosophy of life. They are among the experts who say that those who deny expression of grief reduce their lives to triviality. They concur that unless grief is expressed it is usually repressed which repression often shows up in mental or physical illness or both.

So much for what the funeral has been and what it is. Now let us look at what the funeral should be because of what it does.

Death is no longer commonplace as it once was. In America over 60 percent of the deaths now occur in hospitals or on highways or on battlefields. In the cities the percentage is much higher. Many times the place of death is a distance from where the funeral service and/or burial are going to be conducted. As a result most Americans do not have an opportunity to view a dead body immediately after death. Furthermore, most Americans prefer to view a body after it has been prepared for burial with the ravages of a devastating illness or the mutilation of a violent death having been removed by the art of the individual or individuals associated with the funeral home which is called.

For most people, for the funeral to be complete, it should be held with the body present. When the body is being "waked" or is "lying in state" the body should be viewed if at all possible to view. Let me give you an example:

A funeral director was called to take care of the body and service of a woman who died of cancer of the face. Her husband did not want the body to be viewed under any circumstances. The funeral director talked to him about his responsibility to his teenage daughters and to the other members of the family who really hadn't seen the face of the deceased for some time. He also spoke with him about relatives and friends who would be traveling some distance to the funeral service. The husband permitted the restorative work to be done. After he saw the body of his wife his daughters did likewise. Then one of them expressed her thanks for being able to do so as she said, "I forgot how pretty Mommy was."

Unless the family insists otherwise, when the religious service begins, the casket should be closed. When the casket is closed the emphasis is to be on the religious aspect of the funeral. When once the reality of physical death has been confirmed thoughts should shift beyond the temporal to the spiritual.

There should be a procession to the cemetery or crematory and the family and relatives and friends should go to the cemetery or crematory and there is where the committal should be held. Reverend Irion writes:

"The committal service provides, as nothing else. . .does so graphically, a symbolic demonstration that the kind of relationship which has existed between the mourner and the deceased is now at an end."

The so-called total funeral is best for survivors as part of the grief cycle.

The funeral for President J.F. Kennedy and later the services for his Senator brother did much for the members of the Kennedy families and for the nation.

As an example, in the September 1968 issue of *McCalls*, Harvard psychiatrist Gerald Caplan writes much about grief and the funeral in his "Lesson In Bravery." He deals mainly with the Robert Kennedy children. Here are two of the points he makes:

"If the three older children had by Saturday experienced over and over again the reality of their loss, it was at the funeral Mass itself that the younger children were to feel the impact of that reality. . . .

"By inclusion in the funeral, the children were made to feel the comfort and support and steadfastness of adults. They were rewarded for doing their public duty by being made to feel concretely part of a vast throng of people who stood by them, sharing their sorrow, mourning their dead father. This merging with the multitude has an enormous supportive effect for any child. Thus it is the recognition of reality and the strength to bear it that accrue to a child at the funeral of a parent."

During the period of the funeral for former President of the United States, General Dwight D.

Eisenhower, Bernard D. Mossiter of the *Washington Post* wrote an article which one midwest newspaper headlined "Funeral Pageantry Offers Relief After Past Events." In his piece the writer said there "might be a sense of release in this prolonged funeral." He referred to the ceremonial ritual and added that the "long pause for this elaborate funeral may even have some therapeutic value for a people numbed with speed, sensation and instant gratification."

We can affirm death by the funeral and the affirmation is therapeutic. But the question is asked—do the same meanings and values of the ceremonies, the rituals and the symbols in the funerals of individuals of great renown such as General Eisenhower, President and Senator Kennedy, and Cardinal Spellman carry over to the so-called common man?

They do!

The funeral of every person, no matter how humble was his state in life, can be just as meaningful and necessary to his survivors as the funeral of a well-known personage is to his bereaved. Every man is equally important in the eyes of God and who but God is to say which one loved Him more or served Him better.

A funeral with the body present does important things for most people.

—The funeral helps to confirm the reality of death. Such reality is important and that is why much time and effort is often spent to recover the body of a drowned person or search a mountain peak for weeks or months after someone has been lost thereon who couldn't possibly be alive. Seeing is believing.

—A funeral service with the body present is evidence that a life has been lived and that a death has occurred.

—The funeral provides a climate for mourning and the expression of grief. After a death, without the funeral, would people be of the same mind and mood and disposition? Without the funeral would the sorrows of one become the sorrows of all? Remember, joy shared is joy increased. Grief expressed is grief diminished.

—The funeral is a vehicle for the community to pay its respects. Without it what other sort of an arrangement would be devised? Or would honor and dignity disappear?

—Finally, the funeral encourages the affirmation of religious faith. It channels religious thought as to the soul of the person who has died. In relationship thereto it allows for evangelism for those who have survived the death and are attending the funeral service.

As a well-known cleric said over a decade ago, "The funeral can be an experience of value as it meets the needs of those who mourn."

Toward that goal the funeral directors of the United States have invested much in staff, in facilities and in equipment. Toward that humanitarian purpose they have dedicated their lives.

Young People and the Funeral

I appreciate the opportunity to talk to you. I can remember the time when I was young, and also, because as Reverend John E. Naus has written:

"Never, perhaps, and surely never against greater odds, has a young generation refused to be controlled by its environment, and formed for itself truly human values which reflect a newborn concern for the dignity and beauty and destiny of every human being. Soon it will be their world. May we be happy to be a part of it."

But there are some who don't agree with Father Naus. They say they are not happy with the youth of today because they are acting up like they have never acted up before.

Those who maintain this do not know all of the facts.

Hundreds of years ago the Greek philosopher Socrates complained about the unrest and actions of the students of his day.

There also were student uprisings in ancient Rome. And as history moved on there were the "town and gown" riots involving those with the "gowns" at Oxford in England and the townspeople living nearby.

Thereafter there were student hostilities expressed in our country at Harvard, Yale, Princeton and other colleges and universities.

What is happening today not only has an historical background, it also cuts across economic and ideological lines. Student demonstrations are not limited to the capitalistic western world. They are found in Russia, China, Japan, India, France and other places too numerous to list.

A lot of what is going on is rightfully attributed to change. But while modes, methods, beliefs and philosophies may change, some things remain constant.

Babies continue to be born, most of whom become children and then young adults. At the same time the young of yesteryear become old. Life at all times is a phasing in and phasing out of people. As it is now, there always has been and always will be a generation gap.

While there may be this pulling in opposite directions, there is a holding together of our society by the strength of our social institutions as they help us meet our fundamental needs and assist us during our personal crises.

The baby is yet to be born who will live and die without confronting the major crises of entrance into the world, of growing up and perhaps marrying, of living, and of dying.

While all this is taking place the person as an individual relates to his family, to his fellow man, and perhaps to a supreme being—to his God. As he does this there are rituals and ceremonies that give meaning to these relations. There are symbolic acts which at first might seem to be without reason but which do have meaning.

John Donne said many years ago that no man is an island. Certainly this has never been more evident than it is today after the "moon walk." Yet there are some who momentarily disregard the truism that society is made up of individuals and that for man to find meaning in a world he must be a member of a group. In the process persons can be themselves and they can have their way as long as the society in which they are a part continues to function. I repeat: society is made up of individuals; social institutions are the collective expressions of the individual's needs, desires and experiences. The individual and society, it can be said, are twin-born.

Sometimes rituals and ceremonies which are a part of social institutions seem to have little meaning or value to an individual. When this is the case, the individual may want nothing to do with that ritual or ceremony. Take a wedding, for instance. Maybe a young man and woman would like to run off and get married with the barest of ceremony—only that which would make the union legal.

But if this is done there may be the elimination of something, or somethings, very important to persons other than the "bride and groom." What may seem undesirable to the young couple may be very important to others—to the grandparents who want to see their first grandchild married, to the maiden lady school teacher who through a favorite student enjoys a ceremony she never had, to the "buddy" of the groom who wanted so badly to be his "best man."

True these people are not the most important. But they are important. And if turn about is "fair play" they may later, in turn, do certain things which disappoint or emotionally injure the young couple. Then things can become very confused. Shared values, expectations and meanings lose their currency or their credibility. When this happens the "fly wheel" which keeps the machine called society running spins off and the machine disintegrates and chaos rules.

When a death occurs, for example, regardless of how, there will be some who will be affected by it; some more than others. Therefore, certain things must be done.

The death must be confirmed. And seeing the dead body is the best way to do it. University of Michigan psychiatrist Andrew Watson commenting on the death of assassinated President John F. Kennedy said: "I knew that he died, but I could not feel his death unless I could see his body. This is not rational, of course, but neither is it abnormal. We must be allowed somehow to feel."

A feature article in the *Miami News* some time ago told about eight-year-old Eugene Lemire. Eugene had run away from his home and was found at the Seaquarium. He apparently is emotionally disturbed because some time ago his pilot father was lost at sea and someone told him that the sharks may have eaten his Dad's body. He went to the Seaquarium to see the sharks.

Those who know say that Eugene Lemire is a deeply troubled youngster because the reality and finality of his father's death has never been confirmed for him.

A somewhat similar situation is partially responsible for the intense interest in death and funeral ceremonies of the British anthropologist, Geoffrey Gorer, who recently wrote a book which was published both in England and in the United States.

Mr. Gorer's father was drowned in the "Lusitania." In the autobiographical introduction of his study of contemporary society called *Death, Grief and Mourning* he writes that following the death of his father, as hope diminished, he constructed elaborate fantasies that his father was surviving on some desert island in the Atlantic. And, for at least some months, he put off the acceptance of his final disappearance by these dreams.

The June, 1968 issue of *Psychiatric Opinion* includes a case report on grief written by Dr. Henry Grunebaum, who is a Senior Psychiatrist at the Massachusetts Health Center. The case involves a young married woman who lost a baby during the delivery. Her grief was prolonged and unresolved. But over a brief series of interviews she was able to grieve and finally accept her baby's death.

The last of Dr. Grunebaum's comments is:". . .perhaps (the) most vital issue is the influence of the hospital and its ways of dealing with stillbirths and the patient's inability to grieve. She was helpless during the delivery, not allowed to see the baby, and encouraged to sign an autopsy and burial permit for a mass grave. . . ."

Grief must be expressed. If it is repressed and unresolved it could lead to physical and mental illness, or both. There are case studies of persons with ulcerative colitis and other illnesses because of unresolved grief. There are records of juvenile delinquency caused by a child being "protected" from or against a death of someone close to him.

It is axiomatic that just as joy shared is joy increased, so grief expressed is grief diminished.

When grief is being felt, group support is very important. When death occurs there is therapy in doing, in talking, and in sharing. All of these involve more than a mourner. They involve the group.

A death does not signal the end of life. Before that *death* occurred a *life* had been *lived.* Someone loved, worked with, benefitted by, helped, or depended on the deceased. It is wrong for such a person or persons to feel that the dead person is still alive. It is just as wrong to feel that his death closes the door to anything more than his physical life on earth. The life that the dead person lived no matter how humble or how great can be of help to those who survived it.

Finally, a death for a religious person—especially an untimely one—strains the belief of the survivors often to a breaking point. At this time an affirmation of religious faith is one of the answers.

Confirmation, expression, group support, testimony and affirmation are all good following a death.

How are each and all of them realized? Through the funeral, through the rites of passage which are part of our social institutions and processes and which permit man to express desires and satisfy needs in approved patterns of behavior. As he does he allays the deepest of hurts and suffering and rescues death from meaninglessness.

The statement I just made is paraphrased from the conclusion of *Funeral Customs The World Over* by Habenstein and Lamers. Never before in the history of mankind have there been so many individuals studying death and the problems associated with it as there are presently. Paradoxically, while this is going on there are some working hard to discount or disregard the findings of objective studies by questioning the place of the funeral in modern American society.

But there is a definite place for the funeral with the body present.

The funeral helps to confirm the reality of physical death. Death is no longer commonplace as it once was. In America about 65 percent of the deaths now occur in hospitals or on highways or battlefields. Many times the place of death is a distance from where the funeral service and/or burial are going to be conducted. As a result most Americans do not have an opportunity to view a dead body immediately after death. Furthermore, most Americans prefer to view a body after it has been prepared for burial with the ravages of a devastating illness or the mutilation of a violent death having been removed by the art of the individual or individuals associated with a funeral home.

For most people, for the funeral to be complete, it should be held with the body present. When the body is being "waked" or is "lying in state" the body should be viewed if at all possible to view. Seeing *is* believing!

The funeral provides a climate for mourning, for the expression of grief, and for group support. After a death, without the funeral, would people be of the same mind and mood and disposition? Without the funeral would the sorrows of one become the sorrows of all? And, when else is love given and not expected in return?

The funeral is a vehicle for the community to pay its respects. Without it what other sort of an arrangement would be devised? Or would honor and dignity disappear?

Finally, the funeral encourages the affirmation of religious faith. It channels religious thought as to the soul of the person who has died. In relationship thereto it allows for evangelism for those who have survived the death and are attending the funeral service.

Dr. William M. Lamers, Jr., a West Coast psychiatrist, defined the funeral as "an organized, purposeful, time limited, flexible, group-centered response to death."

Dr. Robert Fulton, Associate Chairman of the Department of Sociology at the University of Minnesota, says that death is too personal to be private and that the funeral is a *rite* for the dead as well as a *right* for the living.

I hope it will be many years before any of you will have to make funeral arrangements. But when you do, remember that the funeral is a ceremony of proven worth and value for those who mourn. It provides an opportunity for the survivors and others who share in the loss to express their love, respect, and grief. It permits facing openly and realistically the crisis that death presents. Through the funeral the bereaved take that firm first step toward emotional adjustment to their loss.

Because a death touches and affects a world, be it large or small, of relatives, friends and associates in a direct and forceful way, in arranging a funeral it is well to consider the feelings of others who shared in or benefited by the life of the deceased.

The funeral does nothing "for" the dead person that he or she is aware of. But those left behind in various ways and walks of life are affected.

There is just one funeral per person and no opportunity to do it over. Doing something wrong could hurt someone. Not doing something could deprive people of their sensory capacity or cause them to avoid a confrontation which is necessary and healthy.

Before coming here to talk to you I was well aware that youth "tell it as it is" and that they want others to do the same thing. I have done that.

I knew also that most young people won't be victimized. I have presented what pertinent facts I could in the time alloted me. You may accept or reject in whole or in part what I have said.

Above all, I realize that most youth are honest in their feelings. So was I as I spoke and am as I conclude by saying that we are living in a period when people need people; when facing life and death realistically is essential; when only a few of your number have had the experience of a death in the family; and when you want truly human values expressed with dignity when there is a death.

It is as Pastoral Psychologist Paul E. Irion says, "the funeral can be an experience of value as it meets the needs of those who mourn."

Thank you for listening.

APPENDIX IV

Comforting the Sorrowing

When we are concerned about our fellowman, then comforting the sorrowing is natural. It is an expression of our feelings and of our concern—it is human. It applies to the churched as well as to the unchurched.

Yet, many fail to do that which their conscience dictates when a friend or relative has experienced a loss of a loved one. If I should ask you, "How many have baked something special for a family in sorrow?", I am sure many of you would raise your hand. Then, too, I am sure some of you would say, "I often thought about it but did not do it." Others might say, "I wanted to go and see them, but I was afraid I might not say the *right thing.*" This is a common thought, but I want to tell you that you need not be concerned about saying the right thing. Your friends are not necessarily looking for words; instead they simply want your presence. They only want *you* as they *KNOW* you. If you try to be anything but yourself, you will fail in your mission.

Comforting the sorrowing may take on many forms: first, your presence, concern and kindness; secondly, encouraging your husband and your brothers to be casket bearers when asked so to serve. Also, you can participate in the prayer service of the church at the visitation prior to the church or chapel service. You may attend the funeral; you can offer your own prayers for the bereaved and for the deceased if this is the practice of your church.

Edward R. Martin in his book, *Psychology of Funeral Service,* says, "Communicate with your friends; don't isolate them." This is very important. People in sorrow need to talk; they need you to listen. Don't monopolize the conversation, and don't limit your communication and concern to the days that precede and the day of the funeral. Let us say that you do all these things, but what about the day after the funeral, the week after, or the months that follow. This is an area in which most of us fail; we fail to *follow through.* These are lonely days for the bereaved person. They are trying days. Your visits or phone calls will be strengthening and a great consolation to those who are left alone.

Just recently a church in Minneapolis, Minnesota, initiated a program within the church called "HEALING FELLOWSHIP." They recognized the need to surround the bereaved person with a "special interest" during those days that follow the funeral. A leader of theirs said, "One of the finest healing agents for the sorrowful heart is the healing fellowship of Christian friends." Some have the mistaken idea that people in sorrow want to be alone. *This is far from the truth.*

In your communication with the bereaved, don't be afraid to talk about the deceased and don't be afraid of causing tears. If you have ever been disappointed with yourself for saying something that caused a tear to fall, just remember that tears are a *GOD-GIVEN* release valve for built-up emotions and anxiety. Hiding tears is like taking sedation for grief. It only makes matters much worse because you have not allowed yourself to react normally to your grief. When the effect of sedation is gone, you have two problems—one, the original problem, and two, a depressed feeling caused by the sedation regardless of its form. In our communication we should not hesitate to talk about the deceased—his life, his accomplishments, his hopes, and his family.

There is the incident about the lady whose husband had died, and six months later some friends asked her to join them one evening to go out to eat. During the course of the meal, one of them accidentally mentioned her husband's name and quickly apologized for it. The lady replied, "Don't apologize. You know it has been six months since the funeral and no one has mentioned his name since. Let's talk about him." They did, and this is the right thing to do. Talk about the person who has died as you knew him in the fullness of life.

251

Readers' Digest published an article entitled "In Time of Sorrow: The Gift of Your Presence." The author tells that he never bothered to go to funerals. He had the idea that "they will never miss me"; and when he saw his friends or relatives on other occasions, he would make up some excuse to cover up his absence. But when his father died, he, too, was touched by the kindness of others. He said that a man came up to him and shook his hand and said, "You wouldn't know me, but I worked for your father when he first started in business." Just that, and he was gone. Another couple who did not know his father took off the time from work, got a babysitter, and attended the funeral. Acts of kindness by others caused him to say, *"NEVER IS THE SOLACE OF FRIEND-SHIP MORE NEEDED—MORE CHERISHED."*

Learned men who have made a study of grief and funeral practices have concluded that the traditional American funeral is *"an experience of value."* At first this seems incredible, and you might ask, "HOW can it be an experience of value and when and where did it start?" We do know that the roots of American funeral customs and procedures extend back through Western civilization into early Judaeo-Christian beliefs concerning the nature of God, man, and the hereafter. Man has continued to bury his dead with ceremony down through the ages. It is only the manner and the conduct of the people that are different in the various cultures of the world. Ceremony in connection with funerals has withstood the *test of time* because of what it accomplishes.

A funeral provides a setting wherein the religious needs of the bereaved may be satisfied

For many it is a time of renewal of one's faith in God, in one's self, and in his fellowman. In my 22 years of funeral service I have seen all these things become a reality. I know of many people who have fallen away from the church, have fallen away from the fellowship of their families until there was a death in the family circle. Then they needed something to support them. *Through the funeral* and the ministry of the church, together with families and friends, they found support.

A funeral faces the reality of death—does not avoid it

Sometimes people feel it is easier to avoid reality than to face it. *This is not true.* Several years ago a woman called from the hospital to say that the doctor had told her that her mother would very likely live only a few hours. The purpose of her call to me was to say that she did not want a funeral, no embalming, no casket, and no flowers and that, when the time came, we should make arrangements for immediate cremation. I told her that I should appreciate an opportunity to discuss the matter with her before finalizing arrangements. She said, "I will think it over." An hour later the hospital called to say the lady had died. I inquired if the daughter was still there. She was; so we made an appointment to discuss the matter. I told her that we could not proceed with immediate cremation, that the law was specific that there must be a 48 hour interval between death and cremation. Besides the regular certification of death and burial permit, a separate authorization had to be secured from the coroner. The law is specific here because cremation would destroy any evidence of foul play if such should exist. During our conversation, I learned that her mother did have a church affiliation. So I suggested that she have an elder of that church conduct a private funeral, thinking that she might be opposed to having others in attendance. This was not the case, however. The fact was that her father had died when she was too young to remember and that she had never attended a funeral. She was totally unaware that others might be interested in her and her mother. She said, "You may contact the elder, but don't list the funeral as private. *Nobody will come anyway."* The reason she was reluctant to have a funeral was that "her mother looked so terrible at the hospital." She had lost a lot of weight, her hair was disheveled, her dentures had been removed, decomposition was present, and muscles had relaxed. By embalming and restorative work, there came about a transformation in her appearance. Her hair was set and combed out and she was dressed and placed in a casket. The horror picture of death was removed, and she no longer displayed the agony of death itself. This procedure is part of our training and experience. We know that this service is very consoling to families. Some of you know what I am talking about. It was consoling to this lady, too, because when she saw her mother in the casket, she changed her mind about cremation and now wanted her buried next to her father in a cemetery in northern Wisconsin. Incidentally, the funeral home was filled to capacity that afternoon, filled with friends who had put aside their work that day just to share with the daughter a moment of respect and dignity for a human life now ended. The lady was very appreciative of this and later told me that she never thought a funeral could be beautiful.

A funeral, in a personal way, helps one to face a crisis with
dignity and courage

While one function of the funeral is caring for the dead, an even more important function is that it *serves the living.* There are a few people in our country that propose a revision of the entire funeral procedure. The proponents of this movement are mostly nonreligious people.

They say that when you are dead that is the end and that the funeral serves no useful purpose. They disregard the work done in the field of grief by psychiatrists, psychologists, clergymen, and sociologists. The reasoning upon which some of them base their thoughts is an attempt to *deny* death and to dispose of the body as quickly and cheaply as possible. This contributes nothing to dignity. It avoids the reality of death and certainly does not give members of a bereaved family the opportunity to express feelings and face a crisis with dignity and courage.

A funeral helps one express feelings, and, above all, it provides an environment where loving friends and relatives can give help needed to face the future with strength and courage.

We are creatures of ceremony; our inner selves dictate this. Consider baptisms, weddings, festivals in the church and in the community. Much of the ceremony during and following these occasions could be eliminated, and some do just that. Others again look at the occasion differently because of what it means to them. This is also true about funerals.

Some funerals cost more than others because the family of the deceased wants it this way. We could not exist if some families did not select an above-the-average funeral. The operation of the funeral home can be compared with the operation of the church. Like the church, we provide a service for the rich and poor alike. As to the latter, it is a dignified service. They are treated just as though they were paying their own way. Like the church, we serve the unconcerned—those who take us for granted. They say, "You are there anyway, and now when I need you, I want you to pay particular attention to me." Just like the church, we are happy for those who pay their way, and again like the church, we have those who pay more than their way. This is why we, too, can serve the poor and the unconcerned in the manner we do.

I have already talked about some of the things you can do to help others face the future with strength and courage. But there is another group of people that are frequently overlooked in these times of crisis. *They are the children.* In this connection I want to share some thoughts of Dr. Edgar Jackson, one of the nation's foremost pastoral psychologists. The adults become so taken up with self-concern and planning that the children are disregarded. They are frequently pushed aside with the thought that *they don't understand anyway.* Doctor Jackson says, "This is a serious mistake. Besides being pushed aside, they are lied to about death, and a child senses a lie quickly. Then he is troubled even more. Death is very much a part of a child's world—he sees it on television, he reads about it in books, and, when it happens in his own family, he is often denied the right to attend the funeral." Just recently a boy of 11, when his father died, asked immediately if he could go to the funeral and recalled that last year when Grandma died Dad would not let him go to the funeral. Doctor Jackson has this to say: "A child should never be forced to go to a funeral; but if he wants to go, he should not be denied that experience."

The funeral gives dignity to man

In order to evaluate the present practice of funeral ceremony, we can consider the opposite. A prominent rabbi has something to say about the opposite. He says, "We (the Jews) know what it is to have funerals without dignity, without ceremony, without flowers, without prayers, without caskets, and without processions. We had six million of them, and we did not like it." Today there is a memorial to those six million Jews in Jerusalem. The names of six concentration camps are engraved in the floor, and an eternal flame glows to the memory of those who perished. I stated previously that people who have religious convictions can understand and can talk about death, funerals, and comforting the sorrowing. This is because they have hope and faith. They recognize that the God who has given life has the authority to set the time and place to take it from us.

In closing, I would like to use the words of a poet unknown who seems to express in a very real way the concerns of those who COMFORT THE SORROWING:

The poem, "The Weaver," answers the question, "Why?" "Why my family?"

> My Life is but a weaving
>   Between my Lord and me;
> I cannot choose the colors,
>   He worketh steadily.
>
> Oft times He weaveth sorrow
>   And I in foolish pride
> Forget He sees the upper
>   And I the underside.
>
> Not 'til the loom is silent
>   And the shuttles cease to fly
> Shall God unroll the canvas
>   And explain the reason why.
>
> The dark clouds are as needful
>   In the weaver's skillful hands
> As the threads of gold and silver
>   In the pattern He has planned.
>
> He knows, He loves, He cares,
>   Nothing this truth can dim;
> He gives the very best to those
>   Who leave the choice with Him.

APPENDIX V

Suggested Text of a Statement to Be
Adapted for Use by a Funeral Director
Before a Ministerial Association Or a Seminary
In His Community Preceding Questions and Answers

If I were to talk to a group of funeral directors today instead of to you clergymen (or seminarians), I would begin in about the same manner as I am going to approach my subject this morning.

There are changes going on in just about everything of interest or concern to those of us in the United States—to people in all walks of life.

The knowledge explosion has resulted in many individuals being curious about many things in which their counterparts a generation or even a decade ago were never curious.

Certainly the quest for knowledge is admirable. But many of those who seek it believe that they have to become non-conformists in the process. At the same time there is a depreciation of values if not an actual crisis in them where tradition is involved. I need not tell you that some traditions, as well as some funeral customs, are being ridiculed and often by people who are totally disregarding the worth of such traditions and customs.

They tell us that soon about one-half of the people in our land are going to be twenty-seven years of age or younger. Additionally some of the ideas of these young people will be adopted by some who range in age from fifteen to seventy-five. There probably will be an increase in the segregation of old people which will lead to a further disintegration of the family. More and more grandparents and grandchildren, and parents and children are going to be separated by age, by distance, by knowledge, and by philosophy of life and death.

As a basic human custom—with distinct American overtones—the funeral is often affected and thereby limited by people who are trying to intellectualize or rationalize their emotions.

Dr. William M. Lamers, Jr., a San Francisco psychiatrist, had defined the funeral as an essential "organized, purposeful, time limited, flexible, group-centered response to death."

In his book, *The Christian Funeral* the Reverend Dr. Edgar N. Jackson spends much time on the significance of the funeral during which he refers to the Lamers definition. He writes about the modern dilemma which he describes as objective research regarding death and the funeral going in one direction with recommendations in regard to reform in funeral practices going the opposite way. Dr. Jackson lists four of the reasons for "this apparent failure." They are:

1. We are witnessing the subtle and pervasive intrusion of secular values into individual and group behavior of our American culture. In this area, costs seem to be all-important, with the leaders of the movements for reform maintaining that the good funeral is the inexpensive one and the bad funeral is the one which costs a lot.

2. There is the contrasting judgment of those who provide services to families at the time of death. Dr. Jackson feels that the facilities and furnishings that a funeral director has available put him in a vulnerable spot in objectively judging the criticisms directed toward him.

3. There also is the prevalent "antimortal philosophy by which man looks at himself." The dependence of the individuals upon technology and their faith in science and the fact that a large segment of the population are "scared to death of death" looms large in many discussions of death and the funeral.

4. The author refers to the "remoteness" of objective scientific inquiry from the prevalent

emotions. He mentions that the strong emotions of a death denying, death defying culture have in practice prevented the findings of the careful researcher from being considered generally.

Reverend Paul E. Irion has said that the funeral is an experience of value insofar as it meets the needs of the mourners. Dr. Jackson is of the same mind as he sets forth these things that the Christian funeral should do for those who share in it:

First, it should recognize that what is done is to meet the social, psychological and spiritual needs of those who are able to participate in it. It is not a service for the dead but a service about the dead and their experience of death. It is a recognition of the religious community that no man is an island and that, when anyone dies, we all die a little. It is a time for the living to face the fact of their mortality, that they for a time live a life measured by space and time. Yet in the midst of the measurable they are never unaware of the timeless and the eternal. This living need is the base upon which the service is built.

Second, the service is aware of the powerful emotions that are at work and tries to fulfill the feelings rather than deny them. The person who is trained as an intellectual tends to meet life crises at the intellectual level. This may mean that feelings are denied. But grief is essentially a feeling, and it is not satisfied by intellectualizations. Faith is made up of belief that is intellectualized, emotion that is expressed through conviction, and action which puts belief and conviction to work. The funeral gives people a chance to do certain ritualized acts that make it possible to work through the convictions that cannot easily be put into words. Then, when this has been fulfilled rather than denied, the sustaining power of spiritual truth can become more valid for the distressed mourners.

Third, the funeral is a time for facing reality rather than for denying it. Death is a part of man's experience. It cannot be ignored or avoided without disrupting moral practice and social responsibility. Even though it is a natural inclination for man to seek the comfortable and avoid the unpleasant, it is not a good enough basis from which to meet life. The Christian faith is geared to even the most distressing aspects of reality, and its message can become triumphantly relevant only when all of life is accepted without illusion or limitation. The viewing of the body prior to the religious service and the presence of the closed casket at the service are the quiet evidence of death and man's willingness to stand in the presence of it in faith, not in fear, in fact, not in fancy. It gives to the service its quality of uniqueness, for there has never been a service quite like it before, and there will never be another quite like it again. It is an affirmation of the uniqueness of personality. It would be unfortunate to deny this expression of faith by a retreat into a generalized, superficial and impersonal moment of embarrassed defiance to the ultimate fact of man's mortal nature.

Fourth, while it would not deny the fact of the event, neither would it deny the validity of the emotions that attend it. Grief is an honorable emotion. It is the expression of the feeling we have about the value of life. It recognized the relationships that are now broken in loneliness. It recognizes the love now moved beyond the physical object to its spiritual meaning. These feelings have their important place in life. While the Christian funeral would not play upon these feelings mercilessly, neither would it fail to recognize that the feelings exist and need to find a healthful expression. For we do not decide whether or not we will have the feelings. We have only the choice as to how wisely and well we will manage them. We know from sad experience that denial, repression, and suppression are poor substitutes for the honest recognition and valid expression of our feelings. The funeral should give the climate where it is possible to do this wisely and well.

Fifth, the funeral should give the members of the religious community a chance to give evidence of their emotional and spiritual support of the bereaved. In the time of great emotional need it is important to be able to respond. It is also well to remember that, when the need is greatest, it is often the time when it is the most difficult, and we are inclined to run away. It is the homely child that stands most in need of love. So, also, those who are most sorely distressed and difficult to reach are apt to be the most needful of understanding and support.

Sixth, the Christian funeral should be a time of great affirmation. Our whole tradition states that it is not a time of defeat and despair. It is a time to affirm the faith, and, by affirming it in the most distressing circumstances, to strengthen it for all other times of life. It is not a time to stand dumb before the ruthless events so attendant upon our physical natures. Rather it is the time to state and restate in most effective form the faith that undergirds and gives meaning to all of life. Like any other service of worship it invites man to stand before the ultimates of existence and face them, not with anxiety and fear, but with fortitude and faith.

I need not tell you what your funeral director does to meet his civic, church, service club, veterans' organization and fraternal group responsibilities. The funeral directors in your community are their own best examples of this. My purpose today was to tell you something about new insights into the funeral—insights which are responsible for sociologist Dr. Robert Fulton saying the funeral is a *rite* (spell out) for the dead and a *right* (spell out) of the living. Toward this end those of us in the funeral profession will continue to serve.

Funeral Service is a Heritage, a Challenge and a Future . . . .

Funeral Service is *my* profession. It has been and is the profession of many persons. We are proud of the heritage which has been passed on to us. We will do what we can to maintain and further it for the good of those we will be called upon to serve.

I am pleased to have this opportunity to share the insight, purpose and function of my profession with you.

In the history of mankind, to all people in all ages and cultures the disposition of the dead has seemed an act of such solemnity as to require group concern for its fitting ceremonial observation. Out of a sense of loss, grief, mystery, or terror men of all times have slowly developed patterns of conduct to provide for their behavior during the death cycle. Chief among the many factors setting such patterns have been religious beliefs. Thus funeral and burial customs have been created and developed.

Today, funeral service has accomplished a shift in emphasis from preoccupation with death and the dead to a genuine concern for life and the living, from safeguarding the physical health of the survivors to safeguarding their mental and emotional health.

The young men and women of today who select funeral service as their profession will find it necessary to be adequately trained and socially sensitive to the professional responsibility required for licensure and social service.

Yesterday, today and tomorrow, young men and women have confronted, confront or will confront the choice of a lifetime career. Approximately 1,800 each year choose funeral service to fulfill their desire to profess a lifetime of sound service. Affirmative answers to these questions would indicate an interest in an aptitude for a funeral service career:

Do you believe in and recognize the inherent dignity of man?

Do you recognize the importance of ceremony as a means of expressing the feelings and needs of people?

Do you have a sincere desire to serve people, especially when they are unable to meet their own needs for service?

Do you realize the need for each individual to express his personal feelings as best fits his emotional reactions?

Do you possess tolerance and understanding as each person expresses and uses his religious faith and practice?

Do you desire, in return for deep personal satisfaction, to dedicate your life to a service profession which demands your sensitivity to the needs and desires of persons in bereavement?

Do you desire to learn and become adept in those skills which enable persons in bereavement to face the reality of death?

Funeral service needs young men and women so motivated. At the present time the number entering the profession does not quite approximate the vacancies that occur each year. Qualified graduate licensees find little difficulty in securing satisfactory placement and projected trends indicate little if any change in this respect. Funeral service personnel, like pharmacists, doctors, lawyers and nurses, must meet certain requirements to get a license from the state in which they want to practice. Each state sets up its own requirements, which you can learn by writing the licensing agency in that state or any college offering training in funeral service.

These requirements generally include: (1) The minimum of a high school graduation; (2) in one state one year of college, in 19 states 2 years of college; (3) in every state at least a year in a professional curriculum; (4) passing a state board licensing examination; and (5) in every state a period of "internship" or apprenticeship ranging from six months to three years with the norm being one year.

Proficiency in professional practice is evaluated by graduation from an accredited curriculum and by either national or state board examinations or both. State board examinations may consist of written, oral and practical examining techniques.

Throughout recorded time men everywhere have sought by funeral ceremonies to honor their dead, and to aid the bereaved to return to normal activity. The rites they have used to accomplish these ends were as various as the cultures and religious beliefs in which they found root. Today, funerals in the United States are implanted in a fairly stable culture, and manifest a rather uniform pattern. But, whatever their forms, funerals can never be casual matters. The solemnity of the fact of death itself militates against mere fashion and whim; and the desire to show reverence for the dead, and respect and sympathy for the living, arises out of the deepest needs and the highest motives of human nature.

A funeral is the only ceremony to which none is formally invited but all may come. When the remains are present and viewable, at least while in state, the reality and finality of death are confirmed for the survivors.

The period of the funeral provides a proper climate for the natural and therapeutic expression of grief by those who have suffered loss. The bereaved may lessen their sorrow by sharing it, and confirm the love and sympathy of friends and relatives at a time when no love is asked in return. In addition, where a religious service is held, the profound consolations of the supernatural are added to these natural benefits.

Graduates today join approximately 65,000 men and women who serve the public in approximately 23,000 funeral homes in the United States. These men and women licensed by their respective states have chosen funeral service as their profession. For them funeral service fulfills a personal desire to serve their fellowmen in return for a deep satisfaction of accomplishment.

The typical licensee, serving in his community, is a stable, home-loving, community-minded citizen, recruited largely from stable segments of the population. He has better than average education which, as a result of his occupational demands, he would probably have even if state licensing laws did not require this higher level of formal training. Similarly, he has mental ability and cultural interests that set him apart from the average.

The direction and conduct of funerals brings the funeral director into close working association with practitioners in other service professions, and with a variety of businessmen. He has frequent contacts with physicians, health officers, medical examiners and coroners in the legal and medical aspects of postmortem examinations. In co-operating with these officials, he is alert to conditions surrounding death, and to any other evidence which may create suspicion of criminal action.

In addition to membership in professional groups, the majority of funeral directors hold memberships in one, several, or many service clubs such as Rotary, Lions, Kiwanis, or fraternal lodges, religious societies, or trade or business organizations. Many funeral directors are leaders and workers in community service events, campaigns, or governing bodies. One of the most satisfying compensations their profession brings is the opportunity of serving with the best elements of the community in such worthwhile community services.

There is a definite place for women in funeral service. As a secretary or stenographer she does office work and usually receives the telephone calls. As a receptionist or lady assistant, she meets with families to discuss clothing for women and children, hair dressing, cosmetics, and other details of preparation and funeral service. Her other duties may include responsibility for floral arrangements and bookkeeping.

Training for a receptionist or lady attendant usually involves a secretarial course, including typing, shorthand, and accounting. Additional training or experience in hair dressing and cosmetology is recommended. Most of the women now employed have learned their duties through practical experience. Perhaps the important item for selecting a person to act as a lady attendant is her personality and ability to converse freely with people under severe emotional strain.

Women do hold positions as embalmers and funeral directors. Although as yet the number is small (approximately 1 percent of all licensees), they may qualify as employees or owners of funeral homes. Their duties parallel those of the male funeral-director–embalmer, but might well include all or part of the duties of the lady attendant.

Much knowledge and information relative to a profession can be gained by reading its literature. Your funeral director or the National Funeral Directors Association, 135 West Wells Street, Milwaukee, Wisconsin, can tell you where and how any or all of the printed matter and films relating to the profession can be obtained. Today, training in Funeral Service Education is offered in seven colleges or universities and thirteen private proprietary schools. An individual desiring to train himself for this profession may select any one of these schools on the basis of its excellence in curriculum or for other reasons that make it personally desirable to him. The American Board of Funeral Service Education is charged with the accrediting of funeral service education curriculums. As in all other professions the rigorous curriculum required is subject to constant upgrading and change. The student, the profession, and the public is insured of the finest in academic preparation.

Funeral Service Is My Heritage, My Challenge, and My Professional Future Because—

" . . . a true profession must perform some special, clearly marked and socially significant function that is not and cannot be performed by any other group or by the generosity of mankind. This function is one requiring preparation consisting of training of a specialized character which in turn is based upon a general education and is often interrelated with a period of apprenticeship. . . .

Therefore, I believe:

Funeral Service is a heritage passed on to all peoples of all cultures to meet the basic emotional and ceremonial needs as they bury their dead with dignity.

Funeral Service is a challenge to its professional members to continue to provide in the communities where they are located, care for the dead and service to the living.

Funeral Service is a future both for the professional practitioner and the peoples of the culture that will preserve the American Way.

Thank you for your consideration and kindness.

APPENDIX VII

Recommended Packets of Printed Matter

FOR A HIGH SCHOOL LIBRARY

BOOKLET OR PAMPHLET

*The American Funeral–Caring for the Dead–Serving the Living–
    Giving Dignity to Man* (NFDA Publication) . . . .
What About Funeral Costs (NFDA Publication) . . . .
Some Thoughts to Consider When Arranging a Funeral (NFDA Publications) . . . .

BOOKLET OR REPRINT

The Significance of the Christian Funeral (Channel Press) . . . .
The Funeral–An Experience of Value, Paul E. Irion . . . .
"Funerals Are Good for People–M.D.'s Included" William M. Lamers, Jr. . . . .
    (Reprinted from *Medical Economics*)
"The Widow-to-Widow Program" Phyllis Rolfe Silverman . . . .
    (Reprinted from *Mental Hygiene*)

BOOK

Funeral Customs the World Over, Habenstein and Lamers
    (Bulfin Printers, Inc.) . . . .
The History of American Funeral Directing, Habenstein and Lamers
    (Bulfin Printers, Inc.) . . . .
You and Your Grief, Edgar N. Jackson (Meredith Press) . . . .
For the Living, Edgar N. Jackson (Channel Press) . . . .
The View from a Hearse, Joseph Bayly
    (David C. Cook Publishing Company) . . . .

BOOK OR STUDY

Funeral Service Facts and Figures, Eugene F. Foran (NFDA Publication) . . . .

FOR A JUNIOR COLLEGE LIBRARY

BOOKLET OR PAMPHLET

*The American Funeral–Caring for the Dead–Serving the Living–
    Giving Dignity to Man* (NFDA Publication) . . . .
What About Funeral Costs? (NFDA Publication) . . . .
Some Thoughts to Consider When Arranging a Funeral (NFDA Publication) . . . .

BOOKLET OR REPRINT

"The Significance of the Christian Funeral" Edgar N. Jackson . . . .
    (Part of *The Christian Funeral*)
The Funeral–An Experience of Value, Paul E. Irion . . . .
"Funerals Are Good for People–M.D.'s Included" William M. Lamers, Jr. . . . .
    (Reprinted from *Medical Economics*)

261

"The Widow-to-Widow Program" Phyllis Rolfe Silverman
(Reprinted from *Mental Hygiene*)   . . . .

BOOK
The Christian Funeral, Edgar N. Jackson (Meredith Press)   . . . .
Funeral Customs the World Over, Habenstein and Lamers
 (Bulfin Printers, Inc.)   . . . .
The History of American Funeral Directing, Habenstein and Lamers   . . . .
 (Bulfin Printers, Inc.)
You and Your Grief, Edgar N. Jackson (Meredith Press)   . . . .
Funeral—Vestige or Value, Paul E. Irion (Abingdon Press)   . . . .
Telling a Child About Death, Edgar N. Jackson (Channel Press)   . . . .
For the Living, Edgar N. Jackson (Channel Press)   . . . .
The View from a Hearse, Joseph Bayly (David C. Cook Publishing)   . . . .

BOOK OR STUDY
A Compilation of Studies of Attitudes Toward Death, Funerals and
 Funeral Directors—Participated in by the Clergy, the Public
 (Including Critical Segments Thereof) and Funeral Directors
 Robert Fulton   . . . .
Death, Grief, Mourning, The Funeral and the Child, William M. Lamers, Jr.   . . . .
Funeral Service Facts and Figures, Eugene F. Foran (NFDA Publication)   . . . .

FOR COLLEGE, UNIVERSITY AND COMMUNITY LIBRARIES

BOOKLET OR PAMPHLET
The American Funeral—Caring for the Dead—Serving the Living—
 Giving Dignity to Man (NFDA Publication)   . . . .
What About Funeral Costs? (NFDA Publication)   . . . .
Some Thoughts to Consider When Arranging a Funeral (NFDA Publication)   . . . .

BOOKLET OR REPRINT
The Significance of the Christian Funeral (Channel Press)   . . . .
The Funeral—An Experience of Value, Paul E. Irion   . . . .
"Funerals Are Good for People—M.D.'s Included" William M. Lamers, Jr.   . . . .
 (Reprinted from *Medical Economics*)
"The Widow-to-Widow Program" Phyllis Rolfe Silverman   . . . .
 (Reprinted from *Mental Hygiene*)

BOOK
The Christian Funeral, Edgar N. Jackson (Meredith Press)   . . . .
Funeral Customs the World Over, Habenstein and Lamers
 (Bulfin Printers, Inc.)   . . . .
The History of American Funeral Directing, Habenstein and Lamers
 (Bulfin Printers, Inc.)   . . . .
You and Your Grief, Edgar N. Jackson (Meredith Press)   . . . .
Funeral—Vestige Or Value, Paul E. Irion (Abingdon Press)   . . . .
Telling a Child about Death, Edgar N. Jackson (Channel Press)   . . . .
Explaining Death to Children, Earl A. Grollman (Beacon Press)   . . . .
For the Living, Edgar N. Jackson (Channel Press)   . . . .
The View from a Hearse, Joseph Bayly (David C. Cook Publishing Co.)   . . . .

BOOK OR STUDY

A Compilation of Studies of Attitudes Toward Death, Funerals and
   Funeral Directors—Participated in by the Clergy, the Public
   (Including Critical Segments Thereof) and Funeral Directors
   Robert Fulton . . . .

Death, Grief, Mourning, The Funeral and the Child, William M. Lamers, Jr. . . . .

Understanding Grief, Edgar N. Jackson (Abingdon Press) . . . .

Cremation, Paul E. Irion (Fortress Press) . . . .

Funeral Service Facts and Figures Eugene F. Foran (NFDA Publication) . . . .

Appendix VIII

NFDA Form 5-P

CLERGYMAN PREFERENCE FORM
(Protestant)

Name of Church........................
Name of Pastor........................
Date of Interview........................

CLERGYMAN

1. Full name ....
2. Street address ....
3. Mailing address (if different) ....
4. Telephone numbers — Church ....
   Parsonage ....
5. Name of clergyman as it is to be used on memorial folders, calendars, etc.: ....

CHURCH

1. Full name ....
2. List of other churches served, if any ....

NOTIFICATION OF A DEATH

1. Should the clergyman be notified of death as soon as possible, regardless of the hour?
   YES ( ) NO ( )
   A. Any qualifications to above answer ....
2. When the clergyman is not available, who should be contacted?
   Name ....
   Telephone number ....

THE FUNERAL SERVICE AT THE CHURCH

1. What hour is preferred, if available? ....
2. When the family is brought into the church, where does the clergyman wish to be?
   ( ) In the pulpit.
   ( ) Preceding the family walking in.
   ( ) Coming from the sacristy.
   ( ) Other, explain:
3. If the clergyman wishes to walk in preceding the family does he wish to:
   ( ) Walk with the funeral director.
   ( ) Walk alone.
4. How does the clergyman wish the family to be seated?
   ( ) On the side of the pulpit.
   ( ) On the side opposite the pulpit.
   ( ) Other, explain:
5. How does the clergyman end the church service? With a prayer ( ), benediction ( ), obituary ( ), announcement ( ).
   A. If obituary is used at any time during the church service should the funeral director prepare it? YES ( ) NO ( )

6. Does the clergyman wish to precede the casket out of the church after the services?
   YES ( ) NO ( )
   If yes, will he change his vestments first? YES ( ) NO ( )
7. What about music?
   ( ) The clergyman wishes to arrange this with the family.
   ( ) The clergyman wishes the funeral director to make the arrangements.
   A. If the funeral director is to make the arrangements:
      1. How many selections should be sung or played? ....
      2. Are there any "songs" that are prohibited? ....
   3. Should the organist start playing before the services begin? YES ( ) NO ( )
      If yes, for how long a period? ....
   B. Other data
      1. Name, address and telephone number of organist: ....
      2. Name, address and telephone number of choir director: ....
      3. Other individuals to be contacted: ....
      4. What about honorariums for any or all above named: ....
8. Miscellaneous information as to church funerals —
   A. When there is a military funeral:
      1. Shall colors be posted in the church? YES ( ) NO ( )
      2. Shall military personnel be seated as a group in the church? YES ( ) NO ( )
      3. Other comments: ....
   B. What about lodges or other organizations; what are the clergyman's preferences? ....
   C. What about flower placement (as to church, chancel, altar)? ....
      1. Does the clergyman wish any flowers delivered to the church after the funeral?
         YES ( ) NO ( )
         If yes, where ....
   D. If church ushers are to be used, give name, address and telephone number of head usher: ....

E. Name, address and telephone number of caretaker of the church:

....

9. Use of the church by non-members —

A. Is church available for funerals of non-members? YES ( ) NO ( )

B. If yes, is there a charge? YES ( ) NO ( ). If yes, what amount. ....

THE FUNERAL SERVICE AT THE FUNERAL HOME

(It is understood that when the funeral service is for a member of a clergyman's congregation, many of the same preferences will prevail as if the service were in the church. These are additional matters to be considered both as to services for members and non-members conducted at the funeral home.)

1. Does the clergyman wish to speak with the family immediately before and/or after the service at the funeral home?

....

2. Where a family room is available, does the clergyman wish the immediate survivors in such room for the service or would he prefer them not in a room by themselves? ....

3. Will the clergyman conduct services at a funeral home:

(a) For a non-member of his church? YES ( ) NO ( )
(b) For a person of a different denomination? YES ( ) NO ( )
(c) For a person who has no church affiliation? YES ( ) NO ( )

4. Other comments as to funerals where the service is held in the funeral home:

....

THE SERVICE AT THE CEMETERY

1. The name of the church cemetery, if there is one. ....

2. Who should be contacted for the following data at such cemetery? (Give names and telephone numbers.)

A. Administration matters ....
B. Opening of grave ....
C. Sale of lots ....

Procedures to be followed at all cemeteries:
(It is customary the clergyman lead the funeral party to the grave. The funeral director will walk along to show the way.)

A. Does the clergyman prefer flowers, earth or nothing for the committal rite?

B. If he wishes earth or flowers, does he want to place these on the casket or have the funeral director do it? ....

C. When organizations are involved, what order of committal will be followed?

D. Who is to make the announcements at the conclusion of the ceremony, if any are to be made? The funeral director will await this before proceeding to excuse the family.)

(It is assumed the clergyman will talk with the family immediately after the service.

HONORARIUM

1. What is the clergyman's policy as to an honorarium for the service of a member of his church:

A. Will he accept one? YES ( ) NO ( )

B. If yes,

1. Would he prefer it be given personally by the family or through the funeral director?

....

2. If a family asks the funeral director to suggest an amount, what does the clergyman suggest the funeral director say in reply? ....

2. What is the clergyman's policy as to an honorarium for the service of a non-member?

....

OTHER MATTERS

1. What is the clergyman's attitude toward a funeral service for a stillborn?

....

2. What is the clergyman's opinion on how to handle the request of a family for a private service?

....

3. Does the clergyman wish memorial envelopes to be used? YES ( ) NO ( )

If yes, does he have any special ones for this purpose?

....

OTHER COMMENTS BY THE CLERGYMAN

....

Notes to be made by the funeral director following the interview.

....

265

CLERGYMAN PREFERENCE FORM
(Catholic)

Name of Church ....

Name of Pastor ....

Date of Interview ....

CLERGYMAN

1. Full name ....

2. Street address ....

3. Mailing address (if different) ....

4. Telephone numbers — Church ....

           Rectory ....

5. Name of clergyman as it is to be used in memorial folders, or calendars, etc.: ....

CHURCH

1. Full name ....

2. List of other parishes (missions) served, if any ....

NOTIFICATION OF A DEATH

(It is assumed that most times a close relative of the deceased will notify the pastor of a death soon thereafter and make tentative plans for the funeral. The answers to some of the following questions will prove helpful, however, if this is not done.)

1. Does the priest wish to be notified of death as soon as possible, regardless of the hour?
YES ( ) NO ( )
    A. Any qualifications to the above answer ....

2. When the priest is not immediately available, is there someone else to call to try to locate him?
.... telephone number.
Who ....

3. When he is not available, what other priest should be called? ....
.... What is his telephone number? ....

INFORMATION DEALING WITH THE WAKE AND FUNERAL

1. Will the priest get information as to the organizations to which the deceased belonged so that the time for vigil and rosaries can be set and publicized? YES ( ) NO ( )
Comments: ....

2. Will the priest come to the home or funeral home for prayers before leaving for church?
YES ( ) NO ( )

3. Will the funeral party be met at the entrance of the church? YES ( ) NO ( )

4. Does the priest wish the casket to be covered with a pall in his church? YES ( ) NO ( )

5. Does the priest wish the pallbearers to be seated? YES ( ) NO ( )
If yes, what arrangement:
    ( ) 3 on each side of the aisle.
    ( ) All 6 on one side (which side) ....

6. At what distance does the priest wish the candles to be positioned from the casket? ....

7. Does the priest usually have a sermon? YES ( ) NO ( ). If yes, where will it come in the order of worship? ....

8. When leaving the church after the Mass, will the priest change his vestments and lead the recessional? YES ( ) NO ( )

9. When and how does the priest wish the casket removed? ....

10. When organizations are involved what are the priest's desires?
    A. Military groups
       1. Shall colors be posted in church? YES ( ) NO ( )
       2. Shall military personnel be seated in church as a group? YES ( ) NO ( )
       3. Other comments: ....

    B. What are the priest's wishes as to Knights of Columbus, Altar Societies and other church organizations?
       1. Processional ....
       2. Seating ....
       3. Entrance ....
       4. Recessional ....

11. Cemetery arrangements:
    A. When military organizations are involved does the priest desire that their part of the ceremony will follow the blessing and prayers at the cemetery? YES ( ) NO ( )
    B. After the committal, is it the policy of the priest to extend further condolences to the family?
YES ( ) NO ( )
    C. If there is no Catholic cemetery in the area, is there another cemetery in which ground has been, or graves can be consecrated? YES ( ) NO ( ). If yes, who should be contacted to make these arrangements?

Name ....

Telephone number ....

MASS CARDS

1. What are the priest's desires regarding the handling of Mass cards?
    ( ) The family should collect them.
    ( ) They should be given to the priest.
       (Unless otherwise instructed, blank Mass envelopes will be provided to all who come to the wake.)

OTHER MATTERS

1. Does the priest wish some funeral flowers delivered to the church after the funeral?
YES ( ) NO ( )
If yes, where should they be delivered at the church? ....

2. If a person is not entitled to be brought into the church for the funeral service, would the priest conduct a service at the funeral home? YES ( ) NO ( )
Comments: ....

3. At what age does the priest think it proper for a child's body to be brought to church for the funeral? ....

OTHER COMMENTS BY THE PRIEST

....

....

Notes to be made by the funeral director following the interview.

....

....

APPENDIX X
Basic Data on State Pre-Need Trust Laws

STATE	PRE-NEED STATUTE	STATE CONTROL AGENCY	PERMIT REQUIRED	AMOUNT OF PAYMENTS PUT IN TRUST	AMOUNT OF INCOME PART OF TRUST	AMOUNT BUYER CAN WITHDRAW
1. ALABAMA	no law					
2. ALASKA	no law					
3. ARIZONA	yes	yes	no	100%	100%	100%
4. ARKANSAS	yes	yes	yes	100%	100%	none
5. CALIFORNIA	Funeral directors only	yes	no	100%	Used to pay expenses and forfeitures	100% of payments
6. COLORADO	yes	yes	yes	85%	Up to 15% of contract	Amount of payments & interest accrued.
7. CONNECTICUT	Insurance law governs	yes	yes			
8. DELAWARE	Participation in such activities considered grounds for suspension of revocation of license.					
9. DISTRICT OF COLUMBIA	no law					
10. FLORIDA	yes	yes	yes (only licensees can arrange)	100%	100%	100%
11. GEORGIA	yes	yes	yes	100%	100%	100%
12. HAWAII	no law					
13. IDAHO	yes	no	no	100%	100%	100% less cost of operating trust
14. ILLINOIS	yes	yes	yes	95%	95%	Amount in trust account less 25% or $35.00 whichever is greater.
15. INDIANA	yes	yes	yes	100% less trustee's expense	100% less trustee's expense	Amount in trust account less 10% or $35.00 whichever is greater
16. IOWA	yes	no	no	80%	100%	Amount in trust account on mutual consent

STATE	PRE-NEED STATUTE	STATE CONTROL AGENCY	PERMIT REQUIRED	AMOUNT OF PAYMENTS PUT IN TRUST	AMOUNT OF INCOME PART OF TRUST	AMOUNT BUYER CAN WITHDRAW
17. KANSAS	yes	no	no	100%	100%	100%
18. KENTUCKY	yes	yes	yes	100%	100%	100%
19. LOUISIANA	Participation in such activities possible grounds for revocation of license.					
20. MAINE	yes	no	no	100%	100%	100%
21. MARYLAND	yes	no	Licensed funeral director and embalmer only	100%	100%	100%
22. MASSACHUSETTS	no law					
23. MICHIGAN	yes	no	no	100%	100%	100%
24. MINNESOTA	yes	no	no	100%	100%	100%
25. MISSISSIPPI	Pre-need contracts limited severely and controlled by Insurance Commissioner					
26. MISSOURI	yes	yes	no	80%	none	73%
27. MONTANA	yes	yes	no	100%	100%	100% on mutual consent
28. NEBRASKA	yes	yes	no	100%	100%	100%
29. NEVADA	Life insurance law governs					
30. NEW HAMPSHIRE	no law	Burial associations prohibited				
31. NEW JERSEY	yes	no	no	100%	100%	100%
32. NEW MEXICO	Life insurance law governs					
33. NEW YORK	yes	yes	no	100%	100%	100%
34. NORTH CAROLINA	yes	yes	yes	100%	100%	100%

STATE	PRE-NEED STATUTE	STATE CONTROL AGENCY	PERMIT REQUIRED	AMOUNT OF PAYMENTS PUT IN TRUST	AMOUNT OF INCOME PART OF TRUST	AMOUNT BUYER CAN WITHDRAW
35. NORTH DAKOTA	yes	yes	Can be engaged in only by operators of licensed funeral establishments	100%	100%	100%
36. OHIO	yes	no	no	100%	100%	100%
37. OKLAHOMA	yes	yes	yes	90%	100%	100% of amount paid into trust fund
38. OREGON	yes	no	no	100%	100%	100%
39. PENNSYLVANIA	yes	yes	no	last 70%	100% on deposit	last 70% of payments.
40. RHODE ISLAND	no law -- Pre-need arrangements may be grounds for suspension or revocation of license					
41. SOUTH CAROLINA	no law -- funeral directors may not collaborate with life insurance companies in this area					
42. SOUTH DAKOTA	yes	no	no	100%	100%	100%
43. TENNESSEE	yes	yes	no	100%	100%	100%
44. TEXAS	yes	yes	yes	90%	100% less trust expenses	All of payments held in trust -- no interest
45. UTAH	yes	yes	yes	at least 75%	100% of trust	90% of the amount placed in trust
46. VERMONT	no law					
47. VIRGINIA	yes	no	no	100%	100%	Mutual consent
48. WASHINGTON	Insurance law governs					
49. WEST VIRGINIA	yes	yes	no	95%	95%	Amount in trust less 25% or $35.00 whichever is greater

STATE	PRE-NEED STATUTE	STATE CONTROL AGENCY	PERMIT REQUIRED	AMOUNT OF PAYMENTS PUT IN TRUST	AMOUNT OF INCOME PART OF TRUST	AMOUNT BUYER CAN WITHDRAW
50. WISCONSIN	yes	no	no	100%	100%	100%
51. WYOMING	Commissioner of Insurance sets out rules and regulations					

INDEX

G